Understanding Contemporary Wa.

This book is published by The University of Wales Press in association with The Open University.

This book forms part of the Open University course D172 *Contemporary Wales*. Details of this and other Open University courses can be obtained from the Student Registration and Enquiry Service, The Open University, PO Box 197, Milton Keynes MK7 6BJ, United Kingdom (tel. +44 (0) 845 300 60 90; email general-enquiries@open.ac.uk).

To purchase Open University materials visit www.ouw.co.uk or contact Open University Worldwide, Michael Young Building, Walton Hall, Milton Keynes, MK7 6AA, United Kingdom for a brochure (tel. +44 (0) 1908 858793; fax +44 (0) 1908 858787; email ouw-customer-service@open.ac.uk).

Understanding Contemporary Wales

Edited by Hugh Mackay

GWASG PRIFYSGOL CYMRU
UNIVERSITY OF WALES PRESS

Published by

The University of Wales Press
10 Columbus Walk, Brigantine Place
Cardiff CF10 4UP
www.uwp.co.uk

in association with

The Open University
Walton Hall, Milton Keynes
MK7 6AA
United Kingdom

First published 2010

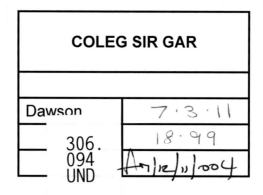

The publisher has no responsibility for the persistence or accuracy of URLs for any external or
third-party internet websites referred to in this book, and does not guarantee that any content on
such websites is, or will remain, accurate or appropriate.

Edited and designed by The Open University.

Typeset in India by Alden Prepress Services, Chennai.

Printed in the United Kingdom by Bell & Bain Ltd, Glasgow.

The paper used in this publication is procured from forests independently certified to the level of Forest
Stewardship Council (FSC) principles and criteria. Chain of custody certification allows the tracing of this
paper back to specific forest-management units (see www.fsc.org).

Library of Congress Cataloguing in Publication data: applied for

British Library Cataloguing in Publication data: applied for

ISBN 978-0-7083-23052

1.1

Mixed Sources
Product group from well-managed
forests and other controlled sources
www.fsc.org Cert no. TT-COC-002769
© 1996 Forest Stewardship Council

FSC

Contents

Notes on Contributors

Dave Adamson OBE is the Chief Executive of the Centre for Regeneration Excellence in Wales. Until recently he was Professor of Community and Social Policy at the University of Glamorgan. He has written extensively on community regeneration in Wales, and has also completed a study of regeneration in the UK: *The Impact of Devolution: Area-Based Regeneration Policies in the UK* (2010).

Charlotte Aull Davies is an Honorary Research Fellow (formerly a Senior Lecturer) in Anthropology and Sociology, Swansea University. She is author of *Welsh Nationalism in the Twentieth Century* (1989), and *Reflexive Ethnography* (2008), co-author of *Families in Transition* (2008), and co-editor of *Welsh Communities: New Ethnographic Perspectives* (2003) and *Gender and Social Justice in Wales* (2010).

Sandra Betts is an Associate Lecturer in Social Sciences at The Open University and Honorary Teaching Fellow at Bangor University. Her research interests include civil society in Wales, inclusive and participatory governance in Wales, and women and devolution. She is co-author of *The Family in Wales: Change and Transformation* (2008).

Steve Blandford is Professor of Theatre, Film and Television at the University of Glamorgan. His research interests include theatre and television writing, and representation in the construction of national identity. He edited *Wales on Screen* (2000), co-authored *The Film Studies Dictionary* (2000) and authored *Film, Drama and the Break-Up of Britain* (2007). He is a founding board-member of National Theatre Wales.

Graham Day is a Senior Research Fellow in the School of Social Sciences, Bangor University, where he was previously Head of School and a Reader in Sociology. He is the author of *Making Sense of Wales* (2002) and *Community and Everyday Life* (2006), and co-author of *Theorizing Nationalism* (2004). He co-edited *Civil Society in Wales* (2006) and has published on aspects of economic and social change in Wales.

Andrew Edwards is a Lecturer in Modern Welsh and British History at Bangor University. He has published widely on political change in Wales after 1945, specialising in the history of Welsh nationalism and devolution. He is co-editor of *Debating Nationhood and Governance in Britain, 1885–1939* (2006) and is completing *Labour's Crisis: Plaid Cymru, the Conservative Party and the challenge to Labour dominance in north-west Wales, 1960–79* (2011).

Anwen Elias is a Lecturer in European and Welsh Politics at Aberystwyth University. She has conducted research on the attitudes of political parties towards European integration, and is the author of *Minority Nationalist Parties and European Integration: a Comparative Study* (Routledge, 2008). Her other areas of interest include territorial politics in Western Europe, and party competition in regional elections.

Neil Evans taught History and Welsh Studies at Coleg Harlech and is now an Honorary Research Fellow at both the School of History and Archaeology at Cardiff University and the Welsh Institute of Social and Cultural Affairs at Bangor University. He is co-editor of *Networking Europe: Essays on Regionalism and Social Democracy* (2000) and *A Tolerant Nation? Exploring Ethnic Diversity in Wales* (2003).

Hugh Mackay is a Senior Lecturer in Sociology at The Open University and his research focuses on new media. He is co-author of *Doing Cultural Studies: the Story of the Sony Walkman* (1997) and co-editor of *The Media Reader: Continuity and Transformation* (1999).

Charlotte Williams OBE is Professor of Social Justice and Head of the School of Public Policy and Professional Practice at Keele University. She edited *Social Policy for Social Welfare Practice in a Devolved Wales* (2007) and *A Tolerant Nation? Exploring Ethnic Diversity in Wales* (2002). She is also co-author of *Race in a Welfare Society* (2010).

Preface

This book provides an accessible introduction to the broad contours and distinctive roots of contemporary Welsh society. It has been developed as the core text for the Open University course D172 *Contemporary Wales*. While designed with the needs of this course and its assessment in mind, the book will also appeal to students on other courses and also to general readers interested in learning more about Wales and where it stands today.

The book has three distinct features. First, it focuses on post-devolution contemporary Wales. Over halfway through its second term, the National Assembly has bedded down and has become an accepted and supported institution with growing powers. This political situation is accompanied by a national culture that seems more cosmopolitan and confident than ever before. Evidence of the nation's constructive momentum is wide ranging, including the set of political and cultural institutions that drive modern Wales, and the set of iconic buildings that distinguishes Cardiff as a capital city (notably the Wales Millennium Centre, the Millennium Stadium and the Senedd).

The second distinguishing feature of this book is that it will appeal to a very wide range of readers. Those who are new to studying social sciences and who are looking for an introduction to key concepts and debates in relation to contemporary Wales will find plenty of appropriate material here. They will find the reflective activities, case studies, and further reading especially useful. But the book also provides an authoritative and up-to-the-minute account of what is distinctive about Wales for readers with a general interest in making sense of contemporary Wales: its politics, culture, society and economy; what Wales's core features are, what it means to be Welsh, and what opportunities and challenges have been afforded by globalisation.

Finally, the book is organised so that it tells a coherent and compelling story about the Wales we see today. It opens with a case study on rugby that demonstrates the tensions and relationships between the twin themes of *differences* and *connections*. These themes are explored through a series of topical chapters. The first half of the book examines the differences that can be found in Wales relative to place, work, gender and 'race', and class, and how these differences can reflect both continuity and change. The second half focuses on the connections that are forged across these differences. Through a consideration of nationalism and the Welsh language, the Labour tradition, political representation and cultural representation, we examine the connections that have been forged and that structure society – they are evident in the identities, movements and practices that arise from the diversity that is Wales.

Hugh Mackay

Chapter 1
Rugby – an introduction to contemporary Wales

Hugh Mackay

Contents

1 Introduction

In recent years the distinctiveness of Wales, in terms of its institutions and culture, has grown considerably. In 1982 *Sianel Pedwar Cymru* (S4C), the Welsh fourth television channel, came into existence, the Millennium Stadium opened in 1999 and the Wales Millennium Centre (where the Welsh National Opera is based) in 2004, and the *Encyclopaedia of Wales* was published in 2007. Crucially, the first members of the National Assembly for Wales (NAW) were elected in 1999 – since when we have seen the development of a swathe of Welsh policies and bodies, in both the government and civil society. These developments are both cause and effect of how people in Wales see themselves, of how they identify with the nation – and these contemporary features of Welsh culture also shape how others see Wales and its people. Traditionally, stereotypes of Wales held by those in England have been largely pejorative (Taffy as a thief, etc.) and people in Wales have commonly referred to themselves as lacking in confidence about their nation. Today, conceptions of Wales and its people are changing.

In many ways the old icons and stereotypes live on – miners and chapels are in decline, but sheep, choirs, leeks, daffodils and druids remain prominent. Representing more of a break with the past are Stereophonics, Manic Street Preachers, Dafydd Thomas (the only gay in the village of Llanddewi Brefi in *Little Britain*), Catherine Zeta-Jones, Rhys Ifans, Ioan Gruffudd, Julien Macdonald, Stacey Shipman (from *Gavin and Stacey*), Russell T. Davies and *Dr Who*, who all provide a more modern image of Wales. Alongside the new, old icons, celebrities and institutions endure, but they take on new forms and meanings; they become accented in new ways. Shirley Bassey appeared at Glastonbury in 2007 and Tom Jones continues to reinvent himself. Rugby is another example of this; it takes place around the globe but has a very particular significance in Wales, where it has been the national game since before the start of the twentieth century.

With this in mind, the aims of this chapter are to:

■ introduce you to the subjects addressed in each of the following chapters

■ use the sport of rugby as a prism, or lens, to introduce these subjects.

Like Wales, and Cardiff especially, rugby has changed enormously in recent years. One journalist attributes to Gavin Henson, the charismatic player who made his international debut in 2001 and was the star of the team that beat England in 2005, a key role in transforming dominant images of rugby in Wales:

> He has almost single-handedly ushered the Welsh game out of the age of scrubbed-scalp, gap-toothed boyos into the new one of Cool Cymru peopled by those such as pop group Super Furry Animals and divas Katherine Jenkins and Charlotte Church.
>
> (Henderson, 2005)

Far from the consequence of one player, of course, there is much more to how rugby in Wales has changed in recent years. It has taken a new and distinctive form in becoming professional, regional and based at the Millennium Stadium. The stadium, in the centre of Cardiff, the capital city, has become an icon of the cityscape and a symbol of the nation. By examining rugby, we can make sense of much about contemporary Wales.

Citizens commonly identify with their nation in the context of major sporting events: imagining the nation is easier when there is a national team playing another nation (Hobsbawm, 1990). Rugby in Wales is a particularly strong example of this phenomenon, being perhaps the main thing that unites people in Wales. In many ways rugby in Wales defines what Wales is and what people in Wales share. From outside Wales, too, it is the rugby that commonly defines the nation – with the sport providing both widespread interest and a positive association of outsiders' perceptions of Wales. Particularly for people in Wales, rugby is, and its star players are, seen as embodying the essential characteristics and values of the nation – egalitarianism, meritocracy, patriarchy and classlessness (Evans et al., 1999). It is often said that the mood or confidence of the people of Wales, and Wales as a nation, rises and falls with the fortunes of the national rugby team.

Perhaps remarkably, it is not the case that large numbers of people play, or even watch, rugby in Wales – except when the national squad is playing (especially in **the Six Nations championship**). Figure 1.1 shows the most popular sports activities in Wales – with no reference to rugby because the rugby figure is so low that it is off the bottom of the table. Rugby is played by 2.4 per cent of men in Wales, which means about 1.2 per cent of the population. Soccer and cycling are more than four times more popular, and about ten times as many people swim.

In a sense, though, these figures are misleading, in that we might distinguish between recreation or leisure activity (such as walking) and competitive sport, but to an extent the boundary is blurred. We can also

The Six Nations Championship (or RBS 6 Nations for sponsorship reasons) is an annual international rugby union competition between England, France, Ireland, Italy, Scotland and Wales.

Figure 1.1
Most popular sports
activities in Wales
(Source: Sports Council
Wales, 2009, p. 13)

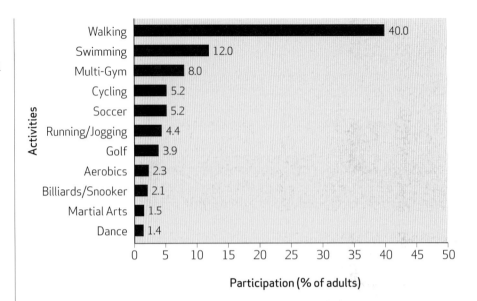

consider spectating: about three times as many people watch Cardiff City play football as go to watch one of the four professional regional rugby teams (the Newport Gwent Dragons, Cardiff Blues, Ospreys and Scarlets). However, if we add the television audience to this (explored in Section 3.4 of this chapter) we find more mass involvement in the game. (Undoubtedly, more opportunities to watch rugby on television have reduced the number of spectators at matches). But, notwithstanding the low levels of participation (and even spectating below the international level) it is through supporting the national rugby team that many people across Wales express their belonging to the nation and their pride in it. This does not happen to the same extent in relation to other cultural events and phenomena, such as the language or the music.

Activity 1.1

Examine Figure 1.2, photographs taken at the Millennium Stadium on rugby international days. Note what these images tell us about the nature and role of rugby in Welsh society and culture.

■ What do they tell us about identities and differences?

■ What are other common images or representations of such occasions?

(i)

(ii)

(iii)

Figure 1.2:
i) The First Minister of Wales and other dignitaries at an international rugby match; ii) Women at an international rugby match with daffodil hats *and* emblematic face paint iii) Charlotte Church, Max Boyce and Katherine Jenkins singing at the Millennium Stadium at the start of an international rugby match

I make no claims to be providing a definitive social science account of the phenomenon of rugby in Wales, but in this chapter I am using this sport as a way of introducing core aspects of difference and connection in contemporary Wales.

2   Difference

Communities are constructed by notions of insiders and outsiders; they both bind people together and also exclude them. Wales has always had to define itself in relation to England, its more powerful neighbour. This is one reason why (and certainly on match days) Wales might be seen as homogeneous, as made up of people sharing a core set of characteristics and values. Perhaps more significant than what people in Wales have in common, however, is the fragmentation, diversity or differences that are found in Wales. When we examine such differences we are left with a rather different, and certainly less cohesive, image of Wales. As Nicky Wire of the Manic Street Preachers explains:

> You have to be wary of romanticism. Wales is a much more complex and divided place than some people think. It isn't this glowing ember of close-knit communities. There's animosity there too. Some North and West Walians resent us talking about Welshness because we can't speak Welsh.
>
> (Wire, 1998)

This section addresses particular aspects of difference in contemporary Wales: place, work, gender and 'race', and class. Each is examined in depth in one of the chapters in Section 1 of this book.

2.1   Place

In the industrial era, communities in Wales grew up with and around their chapels, the union, the pit or quarry and, especially in south Wales, the rugby club. These institutions allowed forms of collective participation through which communities and even some sort of civic identity or citizenship have been constructed. And through local rugby clubs, players and supporters continue to express their commitment, loyalty and pride to their town or locality. This commitment to locality remains powerful. It involves processes of exclusion (defining those who are outsiders) as well as inclusion – as Gavin Henson illustrates:

> People in Swansea view Llanelli folk as foreigners, even though they're only 15 miles away. It was certainly like that when I was at Swansea. Neath people were considered almost normal, but people from Llanelli were weird. They spoke funny and had a different

outlook. As a Swansea player there was a rivalry with Neath. With Llanelli it was more of a hatred.

(Henson, 2005a, p. 130)

A commitment to locality, in rugby as generally in Wales, remains very strong. The biography of Shane Williams (who made his international debut in 1999), for example, makes frequent reference to his strong attachment to the Aman Valley (Williams and Parfitt, 2008). Such feeling of belonging is a process of imagination.

Considering the differences in Wales, imagining the nation is not straightforward, especially given the differences between north and south. In north Wales there has been less engagement with rugby; soccer is more prevalent. Like so many things in Wales – the population distribution, economic activity and the location of national organisations and institutions – rugby is more concentrated in the south. Nonetheless, there have been a few key players from north Wales in the national squad, notably Dewi Bebb from Bangor in the 1960s and more recently Robin McBryde and Eifion Lewis-Roberts. The north–south divide was exacerbated with the move to the regional structure in Welsh rugby in 2003, since all of the regions are in south Wales. Yet there are an estimated 700 debenture holders in north Wales, the Welsh Rugby Union (WRU) distributes nearly 3,000 tickets to clubs in north Wales and, of course, many travel down with tickets that have been sold privately or as part of hospitality or sponsorship packages (personal communication, WRU, 16 October 2009). So, despite the constraints of geography and the different histories of north and south Wales, there is a significant level of support in the north for the national team, albeit less than in the south.

The shift to professionalism in 1995 and to the regional structure in 2003 has meant that players are increasingly dislocated from traditional notions of a place to which they belong – they are contracted by any club, regardless of birthplace or residence. Subsequently there has been a clear increase in the number of non-Welsh players and coaches in Wales. Though the game has strong continuities with its historical roots, rugby clubs and players no longer represent communities in the way that they used to. Interestingly, while reducing local identification, the move to regionalism has coincided with enhanced identification by rugby supporters with the national team (Roderique-Davies et al., 2008).

Regionalism and professionalisation arrived at around the same time as the other great change in Welsh rugby in recent years: the opening of the Millennium Stadium. This structure in the city centre, with its dome and massive legs, 74,500 seats and an opening roof, is visible from all the arterial roads into the city. It quickly became a symbolic, indeed iconic, image of not just the city but the nation, displacing images of castles, sheep, landscapes and beaches as the dominant iconography of Wales (Pritchard and Morgan, 2003). Holding the FA Cup final at the Millennium Stadium for the six years when Wembley was being rebuilt (2001–06) added to the visibility of the city and nation, as does its use for pop concerts and similar events – contributing significantly to perceptions of Cardiff as a modern, cosmopolitan and capital city. The new stadium connects Wales more closely with England and with global culture. It not only makes Wales more visible, but also provides a *different* (and new) representation of the country.

The capital city plays a particularly prominent role in defining the national culture, so perceptions of Cardiff as the core of Wales marginalise alternative understandings of Wales. Although not far away, in cultural and economic terms Cardiff seems a world apart from some Valleys communities, let alone elsewhere in Wales.

2.2 Work

The ebbs and flows of Welsh rugby can be seen as reflecting the state of the Welsh economy. Rugby arrived with the rapid industrialisation and immigration that took place in south Wales in the second half of the nineteenth century. The rules and controlled competitiveness of rugby were consonant with the needs and interests of industrial society: rugby was seen as an improving sort of activity and an alternative to the beer hall and gin palace, a way of protecting members of the working class from the excesses of their own culture (Smith and Williams, 1980). Welsh rugby enjoyed its first golden era around the first decade of the twentieth century, the time of the peak of the economy of south Wales. It declined dramatically in the inter-war years, when Wales lost about half a million of its population. Many rugby teams dissolved in the economic depression of the 1930s and many players, including almost the entire Pontypool pack, went to work for rugby league clubs in the north of England (Morgan, 1980, p. 230). The second golden era for Welsh rugby, the 1970s, coincided with the modernisation of the Welsh economy and the arrival of newer industries. Players around this time were teachers (especially in the London Welsh team), business executives, finance advisers, industrial consultants, sports-shop owners and sales representatives (Smith and Williams, 1980). No longer miners or steelworkers themselves, many, including Barry John and Gareth Edwards, were the sons of miners. It is commonly said that the decline of Welsh rugby in the 1980s was because it had lost its roots, lying as these did in an economy characterised by heavy manual work. With heavy industry in decline, more traditional notions of masculinity held less sway.

As well as drawing on and reflecting transformations in the economy, rugby is itself an area of work. Although an ostensibly amateur game until 1995, from before the dawn of the twentieth century it was characterised by forms of **shamateurism** – starting before 1897 when the legendary Arthur J. Gould, controversially, was bought a detached house in Newport. After that the game was supported by 'boot money' and other forms of shamateurism to keep players involved and also to discourage their defection to English rugby league clubs, after playing for which players became ineligible to play amateur rugby in or for Wales. With a blind eye apparently turned by the Inland Revenue, for 100 years cash 'from the car park' and sinecures (paid jobs that involve little work) in the public and private sectors supported the players.

This was accompanied by the growing commercialisation of the game, drawing in more money. This involved the increase in merchandising (magazines, memorabilia, media coverage) and sponsorship (as brands sought to associate themselves with the game and the faces), culminating in professionalisation in 1995. Shane Williams describes his amazement (though it is commonplace) at being offered a Toyota convertible sports car, to be updated every six months (Williams and Parfitt, 2008). Professionalism and commercialisation alter some of the meanings of the game and also the lifestyle of its players.

A part of this transformation is that rugby has become *work* for the stars, not simply something undertaken for local or national pride. Clearly, the pride in representing Wales remains absolutely central, but the rewards and lifestyle that are associated with the game at this level have changed beyond recognition. Shane Williams, for example, refers to owning plots of land and ten properties (Williams and Parfitt, 2008). The work, of course, is rather different from what it was: it is gruelling, six days a week during the season, with an enhanced focus on fitness and nutrition, and negotiated agreements about the number of matches a player plays per season and having a block of time off in the summer. Discipline is tight and players are expected by their employers to present themselves in particular ways and to speak in public and to the press. So professionalisation has changed not only the organisation of the game and the remuneration of the players, but also the experience of the job of player, which is both more disciplined and no longer confined to behaviour on the pitch.

2.3 Gender and 'race'

Popular images of Wales and Welshness have been profoundly male (with the exception of the Welsh 'Mam', a representation of motherhood and nurturing) (Beddoe, 2000) – reflecting patriarchy generally but, more specifically for Wales, the nature of employment

Shamateurism refers to the sham of financial rewards being offered to players by clubs in the era (before 1995) when rugby was ostensibly amateur.

(men in coal and steel), the politics and the rugby. Since its construction in the later Victorian era, Welsh national identity has been very male, and sport generally in many ways remains the 'last bastion' of traditional masculine values (Messner, 1987). In Wales rugby constitutes something of an extreme version of such values, given the nature of the masculinity that lies at the heart of rugby (the strength and aggression that it involves) and the sport's centrality to the nation.

Excluded from the national sport until fairly recently, women have also been largely absent from sporting representations of the nation – which are so important in defining the nature of the nation (Andrews, 1996). Rugby is quite an extreme case of this, rooted as it is in a very distinctive form of masculinity, in which toughness is central and highly prized. With it goes a deep-rooted masculine drinking culture. Autobiographies by Welsh internationals, even in the era of professionalism, paint a picture of a culture of drinking games, drinking through the night, being sick on buses, being carried home legless and getting wrecked (Henson, 2005a; Williams and Parfitt, 2008).

To some extent the masculinity of rugby (as more generally) has changed and is changing. As late as the mid 1990s, the players' bar at the Arms Park, the old national stadium, was for men only, with the only woman present the barmaid; there was a separate bar for wives and girlfriends (personal communication, Eric Bowers, 22 October 2009). In the 1970s women supported rugby in the sense of providing the tea after a game, but didn't go to watch matches much. Broader changes in society – such as more women going to work and enjoying greater independence – have led to a stronger presence of women at rugby matches. This coincides with the rise of celebrity culture.

As well as becoming more prominent as supporters, women are now more involved as players. Women's rugby has been played in Wales since the 1970s, though the Welsh Women's Rugby Union affiliated to the WRU only in 1994 and women's rugby was fully integrated into the WRU only in 2007. The hyper-masculinity of rugby makes feminine play problematic; hence its remarkably low profile and the very limited media coverage of women's rugby. Thus women remain marginalised here as in other areas of life in Wales.

At the same time, new masculinities and femininities are emerging. The 'ladette culture' (smoking, drinking, swearing and fighting, with which Henson's partner Charlotte Church has been associated) is one aspect of this. And Henson represents another strand of these changes. As he says, 'It takes two hours to get ready – hot bath, shave my legs and face, moisturise, put fake tan on and do my hair – which takes a bit of time' (Henson, 2005b). Although an exception, Henson challenges hyper-masculinised images of players. Gareth Thomas, Wales's most-capped player (100 times) and former Wales and Lions captain, came out as gay in December 2009, which is quite remarkable given the masculinity of rugby culture. As Thomas said, 'It is the toughest, most macho of male sports … In many ways, it's barbaric … It's pretty tough for me being the only international rugby player prepared to break the taboo … I'm not aware of any other gay player in the game' (BBC, 2009).

As we shall see in Chapter 4, black and ethnic minorities are to be found in low numbers throughout Wales, with the exception of Cardiff and particularly Butetown, the area otherwise known as the docks, the bay or Tiger Bay. It is from this area that one of Wales's best-known black rugby players emerged. Billy Boston started his career playing for Cardiff International Athletic Club (the CIACs), and went on to play rugby league in Wigan in the 1950s and 1960s. More recently there have been a few other prominent black Welsh players, notably Glen Webbe, Nigel Walker and Colin Charvis.

The CIACs has been a truly multicultural team. The club was formed in 1946 by returning black servicemen on the basis of an explicit belief in a multicultural society and religious tolerance, embracing all 'races' and religions and reflecting the diversity of the local population. The CIAC badge incorporates clasping black and white hands and the club motto *Unus et idem*, 'One and the same'. 'The name Cardiff Internationals came up because there were so many different nationalities. But sometimes the opposition thought we were actually international players from the Cardiff City team' (CIACs, 2009). The CIACs were among the residents of Butetown who were active in the anti-apartheid movement in Cardiff from the late 1960s. They joined one of the earliest anti-apartheid demonstrations, carrying a banner depicting a black hand on a rugby ball on the try line and the slogan 'Don't deny their right to try'.

The CIACs were almost the only rugby players who actively opposed apartheid prior to the few years before the end of apartheid when almost everyone was against it. (The London Welsh player John Taylor was another of the extremely few players to take a stand.) Throughout the 1970s and 1980s, the WRU was quite happy to repeatedly play South African teams, despite the protests of students, churches and trade unions and even though South Africa was banned from the Olympic movement and was subject to a Commonwealth ban on sporting and cultural contact. In the belief that politics should be kept out of sport, the WRU and its players were among the more influential bodies to add credibility to the increasingly isolated apartheid regime, in stark contrast with the politics of the CIACs.

More recently there have been occasional allegations of racism in Welsh rugby, for example by the crowd in relation to Colin Charvis and Aled Brew at an away game against Ulster in 2007, and by a Munster player in the European Rugby Cup in 2005 who was alleged to have called the Ospreys' centre, the Samoan Elvis Seveali, a 'f*cking black c*nt'. Although the allegation was not confirmed, as Henson reports: 'racist remarks do fly around, it does go on. You hear it in some games. You even get it during training sessions' (Henson, 2005a, p. 160). This exposes the myth, examined in Chapter 4, that racism isn't an issue in Wales.

2.4 Class

In Wales rugby is often discussed, promoted and understood as a classless game, in contrast with England where it is associated with public schools. The reality is perhaps slightly less clear-cut: in Wales rugby grew out of an alliance between the working classes and the elite classes.

The origins of rugby in Wales lie in the English public schools, from where it was introduced in the 1850s to Llandovery College, Christ College Brecon and Monmouth School (Smith and Williams, 1980). Rugby clubs in south Wales were founded mostly by old boys of these schools, those in the growing class of solicitors, doctors, clerks and engineers. The sport's leadership, especially in the early years, was dominated by people from public schools. The first president of the WRU was the Earl of Jersey, educated at Eton and Balliol, a Glamorgan landowner and later a member of Lord Salisbury's Conservative government. And many famous players have come from public schools. In 1935 the entire Welsh back division against the New Zealand All Blacks was university-trained, many via the public schools of Llandovery or Rydal (Morgan, 1980).

Although it has an English and elite background, rugby in Wales has been one way in which social classes have connected. David Smith and Gareth Williams report how the gentlemanly fiction that any breach of rules was unintentional, and that it was impolite to assume otherwise, became replaced by referees; how penalties and free kicks had to be introduced for foul play, obstruction and being offside; and how the public-school vocabulary of collaring, sneaking, rouges and squashes became replaced by the terms tackling, offside, touch-downs and scrums (Smith and Williams, 1980). And historically Wales has been a major force in opposing the amateur status of the game, arguing that it had to be open to all, not just to those who had no need to worry about earning a living.

So the game has been transformed and reaccented as it has become Welsh and a symbol of the Welsh nation and its classlessness. The myth, in which there is some truth, is that rugby in Wales is something of a democracy, where the doctor scrums alongside the miner. And, indeed, precisely this has happened on numerous occasions, for example with the doctors Teddy Morgan in the team that defeated the All Blacks in 1905 and J. P. R. Williams among the stars of the 1970s.

There has, however, been some change in who goes to international matches. Cardiff on match days is more for the affluent, the **crachach**, the 'Taffia', or the establishment, than it used to be. Ordinary working-class people are less in evidence than they were. This fits with broader ways in which Cardiff and its image are being constructed and promoted as more middle-class. The higher price of seats for international matches means less involvement on the part of poorer sections of the community, and the growth of corporate hospitality has worked against participation by ordinary people. Like debenture tickets, sponsorship and corporate hospitality have replaced much of the distribution of tickets via clubs. Because they are more expensive, fewer tickets go to the grassroots. Most rugby club tickets are sold on the open market or used to generate sponsorship, with relatively few being distributed to club members at cost price. One typical club in north Wales is allocated 120 tickets by the WRU. It puts twenty tickets into a draw for members, with the remainder sold as sponsorship (personal communication, WRU, 16 October 2009). Thus the nature of the crowd has changed, with the working classes somewhat marginalised.

Crachach is the word used to describe those with airs and graces, those with power in civic life, and the elite in Wales generally.

However, the meaning of 'working class' (discussed in Chapter 5) has changed considerably, with the decline of the culture and economy of coal and steel and the rise of a consumer society. Gavin Henson's Audi sports car and celebrity lifestyle are a far cry from the game in its amateur days, when class in Wales was somehow much more straightforward.

Summary

- A strong sense of belonging to a particular town or locality in Wales is reflected in attachments to local rugby teams.

- As the employment profile in Wales has changed, so too has the way that rugby is organised, especially with the advent of professionalisation and increasing commercialisation.

- The involvement of women and people from black and ethnic minorities in rugby reflects their position in Welsh society as a whole, and also how this has changed.

- Although rugby in Wales is seen as rooted in the industrial working class, the reality is more complex – it bridges classes, and in any case notions of class have become less straightforward.

3 Connection

Having explored how differences in Wales are manifest in Welsh rugby, we turn to how, across these differences – of place, work, gender, 'race' and class – people in Wales have forged connections, ways of working together to shape the world.

People have different senses of their Welshness, but come together in various ways – around nationalism and the language, labour traditions, representation at the NAW, and representations of a variety of cultural forms. These are the topics that are dealt with in each of the chapters in Section 2 of this book. A key way in which people are brought together, of course, is through rugby, the main focus for identification with the nation.

3.1 Nationalism and the Welsh language

You have seen how rugby is one of the few (perhaps the only) forms of unified Welsh expression and how, more than anything else, it unites people in Wales – across the language divide, between north and south, and across gender, 'race' and class. The national team, especially when playing in Cardiff and against England, evokes a sense of identification, a passion and a commitment to the nation that for many is stronger than politics or religion. As Gavin Henson expresses it: 'Everyone who plays for Wales is aware of the symbolism the game represents for a small nation fighting against the odds. I'm no different' (Henson, 2005a, opposite p. 120, caption to Plate A). Success on the field raises national morale, as illustrated by Rhodri Morgan, the then Welsh First Minister: 'The Welsh rugby team against France put up the best defensive rearguard action since Rorke's Drift [in the Zulu War of 1879], it's done a tremendous amount for self-confidence. People are beginning to feel taller, prouder, more confident' (Moss and Smith, 2005).

Activity 1.2

Clearly rugby is connecting people across differences in Wales. Pause and consider, however, who is marginalised or excluded in the process.

Comment

We have seen how identification with rugby is patterned by geography (with less support in the north) and very profoundly by gender, and also that many people in Wales prefer other sports. Crucially, of course, it is other nations that are excluded in processes of identification with the national team. Passion about Welsh rugby runs highest when Wales is playing England – reflecting the fact that difference from England lies at the heart of identification with the Welsh nation. From early Welsh victories over England – the first victory at Dewsbury in Yorkshire in 1891; the first Welsh victory on Welsh soil in 1893; the first win at Twickenham 1933 – to more recent victories (Wembley in 1999, and Twickenham in 2008), Welsh rugby history highlights the national team's performance in relation to the English team. For example, in 1999 Stereophonics recorded the controversial song 'As Long As We Beat The English'.

It is, of course, not only in relation to England that Wales comes together as a nation around rugby. Given their status as rugby champions of the world, it is the beating of the New Zealand All Blacks in 1905 that, argue David Smith and Gareth Williams (1980), not only cemented the place of rugby in Welsh culture but was the day on which the modern Welsh nation came into existence.

Fervent support for the nation's rugby team has not, however, been accompanied by widespread affiliation to political nationalism, or votes for Plaid Cymru (the Party of Wales), let alone calls for independence. The historian Kenneth Morgan is among those who have suggested that 'Arms Park nationalism' (in other words, nationalism for the 80-minute duration of international rugby matches) has been a substitute for more widespread political nationalism in Wales (Morgan, 1980). This is not uncommon in the world of sport, as Grant Jarvie explains: 'patriots could show an affinity for the nation on various sporting occasions without necessarily voting for nationalist parties' (Jarvie, 2003, p. 539).

One reason for the disjuncture between political nationalism and the patriotism that surrounds the national rugby team is that conceptions of Wales and Welshness in the nationalist discourse have been largely rooted in the rural, Welsh-speaking heartland, **Y Fro Gymraeg**, and have focused on the Welsh language. For many Welsh speakers and nationalists in Wales, the language is to be equated with the culture and is seen as the defining feature of Welshness. Thus the factory worker in the Gwent Valleys is seen as 'less Welsh' than a Welsh speaker from *Y Fro Gymraeg*, leading some in the Valleys to oppose the language and the nationalist movement. More people are able to join together around the national rugby team.

Y Fro Gymraeg (literally, 'The Welsh Language Region') is the term used to refer to the Welsh-speaking heartland of Wales, focused around Ceredigion and Gwynedd.

This is not to suggest that Welsh rugby is an English-language affair, Far from it: the sport includes players and supporters from Welsh-speaking areas (notably the Gwendraeth Valley and Llanelli) and the WRU and the national squad have always operated in a bilingual culture. Like the other national institutions, the WRU has played a positive role in giving the language a prominent public face. Not unusually, at the time of writing (2009) the proportion of televised rugby players who speak

Welsh considerably exceeds 20 per cent (which is the percentage of the population of Wales recorded in the 2001 census as able to speak, read or write Welsh).

The singing with which Welsh rugby is associated says something about the standing of the language. Routinely at rugby internationals, as well as the Max Boyce and Tom Jones numbers, we hear 'Cwm Rhondda' and the national anthem ('Hen Wlad fy Nhadau', or 'Land of My Fathers') sung in Welsh. This singing shows how the language, though not spoken widely, is accepted, and to a degree understood, as central to Welsh national culture and identity. Thus rugby international crowds provide a powerful instance not of two divided language communities (those who speak the language and those who do not) but of how elements of the language permeate Welsh culture in mundane ways, and with widespread popular support.

3.2 Labour traditions

There is a long history of radical or progressive politics in Wales, in the liberal tradition of the late nineteenth and early twentieth centuries, in the labour tradition which eclipsed this early in the twentieth century and which has been the dominant strand of politics from then until today, and in the nationalist narrative. The labour tradition (examined in Chapter 7), dominant until the arrival of the Welsh Assembly with its element of proportional representation (see Chapter 8), is rooted in the industrial working class, trade unions, the Labour Party, the cooperative movement, friendly and building societies and working men's institutes. Rugby, as we have seen, has its roots in the same culture and economy. Like the chapel, rugby has been a core feature of the society that gave rise to the labour tradition.

There are various strands to the labour tradition in Wales. Some have seen its ideals as better achieved through working with and through the British state, whereas others have focused more on Welsh issues. Whatever the varieties, the labour tradition, by dint of its association with the industrial working class, has always been closely connected with Welsh rugby, which has been strongest in strong Labour-voting areas.

One consequence of most areas in south Wales returning massive Labour majorities for so long was that some local councils became sites of corruption, perhaps most notably in Glamorgan. The popular understanding is that this sometimes worked in favour of the local rugby team, with teachers being offered posts on the basis of their sporting prowess rather than their teaching qualifications or experience.

Labour politicians (more prominently than others because of their greater numbers) have consistently associated themselves with the game, and especially the national squad. They are commonly seen attending internationals – usually because of their love of the game (even if they are beneficiaries of corporate hospitality) but also because it is the place to be seen, a way of being in the public eye in the right sort of way.

Rhodri Morgan, the First Minister for the ten years until 2009, is perhaps the strongest case in point, though no one could suggest that there is anything contrived or strategic about his attendance. Morgan has written the foreword to an edited collection on sport in Wales (Williams, 2007). He would make one of the most informed and entertaining commentators on Welsh rugby, and represents an extreme case of a wider phenomenon: the support from all strands of the labour tradition for Welsh rugby.

3.3 Political representation

The reorganisation of rugby has coincided with the arrival of the NAW, which has profoundly changed the political system in Wales. In the process, some individuals, groups and interests have enjoyed better access to the new decision-making processes. So the NAW does not simply produce its own, new, policies; it has reconfigured the system of representation (as discussed in Chapter 8). Notions of representation and how it works can be applied to rugby as well as to political systems.

From the outset, rugby was seen as contributing to public life and the development of good citizens (Smith and Williams, 1980). As the paternalism of the Victorian era gave way to the labourism of the twentieth century, rugby became one of the institutions that provided training in democratic procedures and processes, allowing participation and self-organisation.

As we have seen, participation and control by local people have been replaced, to a degree, by the market. This represents the triumph, to an extent, of global consumer capitalism over community clubs. Welsh rugby has become a big business. The turnover of the WRU in 1999 was under £5 million; by 2008 it was over £50 million (largely due to the completion of the Millennium Stadium, which is owned by the WRU). Of this £50 million, only £15 million was passed down to clubs, of which over £11 million was for the professional regional teams (WRU, 2008). So who controls the WRU, and how it is organised, its constitution and its relationship with clubs and players, are important issues.

We have seen how the reorganisation of the game, its commercialisation and professionalisation, has restricted the possibilities for ordinary people to support the national team at the Millennium Stadium.

At the same time, of course, there has been increased participation by supporters in the form of those watching matches on television – both at home and in pubs, where the atmosphere, the big screen and (for some matches) Sky television are major attractions. This is significant not only for the pubs, but also as a means of popular engagement with international matches. It is notable how many of those who have been excluded now participate: a form of participation that is enabled by the same mass medium that plays such a pivotal role in the commercialisation of the game and the promotion of celebrity culture.

3.4 Cultural representations

Rugby, as a core defining characteristic of the nation, is prominent in representations of Wales. It is also a major part of the content of the Welsh mass media. The success of the *Wales on Sunday* newspaper is commonly attributed to its sports coverage, especially rugby; and rugby is a major part of the content of *The Western Mail* newspaper, particularly its Monday edition. And rugby generates substantial television audiences, with Magners League games (for which S4C has exclusive rights) sometimes generating audiences in excess of 150,000 – for whom the commentary is in Welsh (with English sub-titles available). This is among the highest audiences that S4C attracts. An average of about 640,000 people watched Six Nations matches on BBC in 2009, representing about two thirds of television viewers at those times in south and west Wales. So rugby and the mass media feed off one another.

The mass media, however, do not just report or broadcast the game, reflecting its importance: they play a major role in constructing its prominence in national life. And their coverage shapes its very nature. The mass media lie at the heart of the commercialisation of rugby, with matches played to suit the television schedules, including kick-offs at 5.30.

More than this, it is through the mass media that celebrities are produced. Without the media we would have no celebrity culture. There have always been heroes and stars, but today they are a more significant part of culture and they are more mediated and commodified than in the past. Not only are the talent of players and the nation's passion for the game promoted by the media, but players have come to lead their lives very much in the eye of the media, which takes more interest in their private lives.

Figure 1.3
Gavin Henson and
Charlotte Church: the
Welsh Beckhams?

The rugby hero of the 1950s, Cliff Morgan, travelled to his international debut by public transport, sitting with many who would soon be on the terraces watching him. Today's players, by contrast, lead a very different celebrity lifestyle. They stay in five-star hotels and arrive at matches in air-conditioned luxury coaches with tinted windows. Henson's concern about appearance and liking for gold boots (the latter influenced by Premiership football) can be seen as an aspect of this transformation of the player into a celebrity:

> I thought they looked great. Football has always been a big influence on me. I love the way some of the players look and move. ... There's nothing better than watching Cristiano Ronaldo run down the wing, boots flashing as he goes around defenders. Eric Cantona was a real hero of mine. I loved the way he played, but more than that I loved the way he strutted around as if he owned the place.
>
> (Henson, 2005a, p. 213)

Henson has been described by *The Western Mail* as 'the David Beckham of Welsh rugby' and by *Wales on Sunday* as 'the Beckham of Wales' (quoted in Harris and Clayton, 2007, p. 156).

Activity 1.3

Pause and consider: Henson is a recent and unusual rugby player. Could he exist as he has without the mass media and its priories? How does this sort of representation of rugby transform the meaning of the game and of being a player?

Comment

Playing in the era of mediated celebrity, Henson appears almost as a fashion model in lifestyle magazines, and in advertisements for Gillette razors, Brains beer and Nike Pro trainers; he has also appeared as a guest on the BBC television programme 'Friday Night with Jonathan Ross'. Obviously his relationship with Charlotte Church, a celebrity in her own right, adds considerably to media interest in Henson. 'As a rugby player', says Henson, 'I love all the attention that comes my way. I want rugby to be an exciting sport with big name personalities and I want to be one of them' (Henson, 2005a, p. 311).

Thus we can see how broader cultural processes impinge on rugby and transform the game and what it means.

Summary

- Rugby acts as a unifying force in Wales, bridging all sorts of divides as the nation comes together to support the national team.

- The Welsh language is strongly represented in Welsh rugby.

- The sport is closely connected to the industrial working class in Wales and hence the labour tradition.

- While the new political system in Wales provides new forms and channels of representation, some changes to Welsh national rugby have taken the game away from local control.

- Rugby is prominent in cultural representations of Wales, heavily covered but also shaped by the mass media.

4   Conclusion

Wales isn't just a place but a nation characterised by a particular set of political and moral values. Whatever the differences between groups and individuals, these values provide connections that, together, make Welsh society what it is. The nation engenders feelings of belonging and solidarity, with rugby continuing to bind people together as does no other cultural activity or phenomenon. Contested and transforming over time, core attributes of the nation are embodied in the national game, in its players, institutions and supporters. Despite its transformation from an amateur game to one that is more marketised and mediated, rugby continues to be prominent in representations of Wales and as a focus for identification with the nation.

References

Andrews, D. (1996) 'Sport and the masculine hegemony of the modern nation: Welsh rugby, culture and society, 1890–1914' in Nauright, J. and Chandler, M. (eds) *Making Men: Rugby and Masculine Identity*, London, Frank Cass.

BBC (2009) 'Ex-Lion Gareth Thomas reveals he is gay' [online], available from http://news.bbc.co.uk/sport1/hi/rugby_union/welsh/8421956.stm (accessed 21 December 2009).

Beddoe, D. (2000) *Out of the Shadows: a History of Women in Twentieth Century Wales,* Cardiff, University of Wales Press.

CIACs (2009) 'Cardiff International Athletics Club: CIACs RFC' [online], available from www.ciacs.co.uk/ (accessed 23 October 2009).

Evans, J., Davies, B. and Bass, D. (1999) 'More than a game: physical culture, identity and citizenship in Wales' in Jarvie, G. (ed.) *Sport in the Making of Celtic Cultures*, Leicester, Leicester University Press, pp. 131–48.

Harris, J. and Clayton, B. (2007) 'The first metrosexual rugby star: rugby union, masculinity, and celebrity in contemporary Wales', *Sociology of Sport Journal*, vol. 24, pp. 145–64.

Henderson, J. (2005) 'Big interview: Gavin's fruity passion', *The Observer*, 13 March.

Henson, G. (2005a) *My Grand Slam Years,* London, HarperCollins.

Henson, G. (2005b) 'Saidwhat' [online] available from www.saidwhat.co.uk/quotes/sport/gavin_henson (accessed 14 October 2009).

Hobsbawm, E. (1990) *Nations and Nationalism since 1780*, Cambridge, Cambridge University Press.

Jarvie, G. (2003) 'Internationalism and sport in the making of nations', *Identities: Global Studies in Culture and Power*, vol. 10, pp. 537–51.

Messner, M. (1987) 'The life of a man's seasons: male identity in the life course of the Jock' in Kimmel, M. (ed.) *Changing Men: New Directions in Research on Men and Masculinity*. Beverly Hills, CA, Sage.

Morgan, K. O. (1980) *Rebirth of a Nation: Wales 1880–1980*, Cardiff/New York, University of Wales Press/Oxford University Press.

Moss, S. and Smith, D. (2005) 'From chapel to church', *The Observer*, 13 March [online], available from http://observer.guardian.co.uk/print/0,,5146892–102274,00.html (accessed 13 October 2009).

Pritchard, A. and Morgan, N. (2003) 'Mythic geographies of representation and identity: contemporary postcards of Wales', *Tourism and Cultural Change*, vol. 1, no. 2, pp. 111–30.

Roderique-Davies, G., Mayer, P., Hall, R., Shearer, D., Thomson, R. and Hall, G. (2008) 'New teams, old enemies? A study of social identification in Welsh rugby supporters', *Contemporary Wales*, vol. 21, no. 1, pp. 187–206.

Smith, D. and Williams, G. (1980) *Fields of Praise*, Cardiff, University of Wales Press.

Sports Council Wales (2009) 'Adult participation in sport', *Sports Update No. 61*, August, Cardiff, Sports Council Wales, available from www.sports-council-wales.org.uk/23347.file.dld (accessed 22 October 2009).

Welsh Rugby Union (2008) *Annual Report*, Cardiff, WRU.

Williams, G. (ed.) (2007) *Sport: an Anthology*, Aberteifi, Parthian/Library of Wales.

Williams, G. A. (1985) *When Was Wales? A History of the Welsh*, Harmondsworth, Penguin.

Williams, S. and Parfitt, D. (2008) *Shane: My Story*, Edinburgh, Mainstream.

Wire, N. (1998) 'Everything must grow up', interview with Q *Magazine*, [online], available from www.thisisyesterday.com/ints/qfeature.html (accessed 13 October 2009).

Further reading

The definitive social history of Welsh rugby is Smith, D. and Williams, G. (1980) *Fields of Praise*, Cardiff, University of Wales Press. This is updated in the same authors' chapter 'Beyond the Fields of Praise: Welsh Rugby 1980–1999' in Richards, H., Stead, P. and Williams, G. (1999) *More Heart and Soul*, Cardiff, University of Wales Press.

There is remarkably little in the way of cultural studies or sociology on Welsh rugby. The exception is the work of John Harris, including:
Harris, J. (2009) 'Outside the fields of praise: women's rugby in Wales', *International Journal of Sport Management and Marketing*. vol. 6, no. 2, pp. 167–182.

Harris, J. (2007) 'Cool Cymru, rugby union and an imagined community', *International Journal of Sociology and Social Policy*, vol. 27, no. 3/4, pp. 151–162.

Harris, J. and Clayton, B. (2007) 'The first metrosexual rugby star: rugby union, masculinity, and celebrity in contemporary Wales', *Sociology of Sport Journal*, vol. 24, pp. 145–164.

Harris, J. (2006) '(Re)Presenting Wales: national identity and celebrity in the postmodern rugby world', *North American Journal of Welsh Studies*, vol. 6, no. 2, pp. 1–12.

Harris, J. (1996) 'Match day in Cardiff: (re)imaging and (re)imagining the nation', *Journal of Sport & Tourism*, vol. 13, no. 4, pp. 297–313.

Chapter 2
Place and belonging

Graham Day

Contents

1   Introduction

Writing this chapter led me to make several train journeys from Bangor in north Wales to the capital city, Cardiff. The trip takes a few hours, travelling to begin with along the north Wales coast within touching distance of the very different seaside resorts of Llandudno, Rhyl and Prestatyn. Much of the rest of the time the route follows the Welsh/English border, via a string of historic English and Welsh market towns, through splendid country scenery and landscapes. Eventually you arrive in the large south Wales cities of Newport and then Cardiff. Almost invariably when I talk to people in Cardiff about the journey I have just made, they comment that they themselves have rarely or never actually been to the north of the country. Crossing Wales like this, a comparatively short distance of around 230 miles, means encountering some major variations in the histories, conditions and experiences of different places and people. Depending on where it is viewed from, Wales can look a very different place.

Although a small country, Wales is diverse, and at times divided by its social, cultural and political, as well as geographical, differences. The aims of this chapter are to:

■ consider some of these differences, particularly as they relate to different spaces and places in Wales

■ explain what produces them, and the significance they have for people who live in Wales.

The chapter has three sections. The first examines some of the main regional variations in Wales; the second explores their connection to different kinds of Welsh communities; and the third looks at how Welsh communities today are undergoing change and transformation.

Activity 2.1

Think about what you already know about Wales, and how it is divided up into different kinds of places and communities.

■ What key differences come to mind?

■ How far does your own familiarity with Wales stretch – are there parts of Wales you know and understand very well?

■ Are there other parts you don't know much about, which fall outside your 'mental map'?

■ Why is this?

Comment

My own answer would include the fact that some parts of Wales are strongly Welsh-speaking, while elsewhere the English language is far more dominant. There are also some noticeable regional variations in speech and accent. Much of Wales is rural and thinly populated, with areas of near wilderness and great natural beauty. But there are also places with a remarkable history of industrial development, as well as decline. There are pockets of considerable prosperity, with investment in some exciting new architectural and environmental developments, along with well-known black spots of deprivation, poverty and neglect. There are historic town centres, and places well-known for aspects of Welsh heritage, but also many new housing and industrial estates, shopping centres, and places apparently without much character at all. Having spent most of my life living in rural north and west Wales, personally I am less familiar with industrial south Wales and the Valleys, which may influence the way I see the country as a whole.

Summary

Although a small country, Wales displays considerable diversity, in terms of:

- geographical and physical variation
- social and historical development
- differences of relative prosperity and deprivation.

2 The regions of Wales

In this section you will consider how the sense of 'being Welsh' may differ across the various regions of Wales.

2.1 One Wales or many?

Attachment to place and a strong sense of local belonging are said to be among the distinctive characteristics of Welsh people. This is because although Wales has the qualities of smallness and intimacy, it has developed in ways that foster variety and uniqueness. It has a population of almost 3 million people, a large proportion of whom continue to live in small towns and villages. It is divided and separated both geographically, by hills and mountains which even today hinder ready communication between all parts of the country, and by historical developments which created marked divisions between rural and industrial Wales, and between those parts of Wales that were

Globalisation refers to the increasing extent to which the world is becoming integrated, so that many places are felt to be losing their distinctive qualities and growing more alike.

Welsh-speaking, or more anglicised. Although with **globalisation** and integration these differences are fading, they leave a legacy of ideas and thought that help us to understand contemporary life, and provide an influential backdrop to a good deal of recent policy and decision making.

Eminent writers as different in their attitudes towards Wales and Welshness as the novelist and critic Raymond Williams and the poet R. S. Thomas agree in giving importance to people rooted in their local landscape, and its history, and in the social relationships they have with the others who live around them. Williams has written of the neighbourly environment in which he was formed as a child, which gave him his lifelong concern with the possibilities of human warmth and association in the small community, where people are familiar with and grow to really know one another. Thomas has captured the closeness of Welsh country people to the land and its natural environment, and to the culture and way of life with which it is identified. Social scientists writing about Wales have shared this fascination with the exceptional importance of locality and community, and the sense of belonging to a particular place.

2.2 Regional differentiation in Wales

Despite the country's compact size, scholars of modern Wales have frequently stressed the depth of its internal divisions and differences, which mean that people living in different parts of the country face a range of contrasting conditions and experiences. Consequently it has been suggested that there are some fundamental differences of perception and interest which tend to divide rather than connect the people of Wales. An influential attempt to capture these variations in recent times is Denis Balsom's three-Wales model (1985), which distinguishes between Welsh Wales, British Wales and *Y Fro Gymraeg* (see Figure 2.1).

Basing his analysis on answers to survey questions, Balsom focused on two key measures: whether or not a person spoke Welsh, and whether or not he or she identified as 'Welsh', 'British', or something else. By combining these indicators he was able to divide Wales into three distinct types of area, which had different cultural and political characteristics associated with distinct social groupings. According to Balsom:

> The Welsh-speaking, Welsh-identifying group is perhaps most distinctive and largely centred upon the north and west of Wales. This area is designated Y Fro Gymraeg. The Welsh-identifying,

non-Welsh-speaking group is most prevalent in the traditional south Wales area and labelled Welsh Wales. The British-identifying non-Welsh-speaking group dominates the remainder of Wales, described therefore as British Wales.

(Balsom, 1985, p. 6)

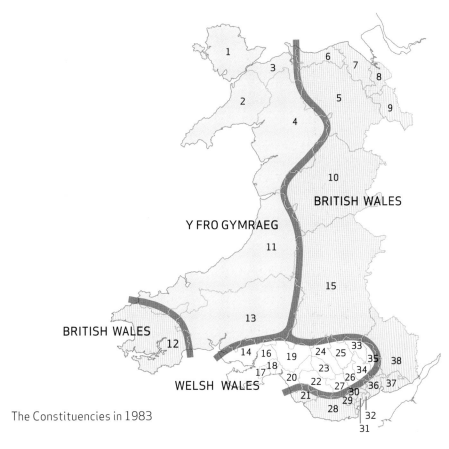

The Constituencies in 1983

1 Ynys Mon	14 Llanelli	27 Pontypridd
2 Caernarfon	15 Brecon and Radnor	28 Vale of Glamorgan
3 Conway	16 Gower	29 Cardiff West
4 Meironnydd Nant Conwy	17 Swansea West	30 Cardiff North
5 Clwyd South-West	18 Swansea East	31 Cardiff Central
6 Clwyd North-West	19 Neath	32 Cardiff South and Penarth
7 Delyn	20 Aberavon	33 Blaenau Gwent
8 Alyn and Deeside	21 Bridgend	34 Islwyn
9 Wrexham	22 Ogmore	35 Torfaen
10 Montgomery	23 Rhondda	36 Newport West
11 Ceredigion and Pembroke North	24 Cynon Valley	37 Newport East
12 Pembroke	25 Merthyr Tydfil and Rhymney	38 Monmouth
13 Carmarthen	26 Caerphilly	

Figure 2.1
Balsom's 'three-Wales' model (Source: Balsom, 1985, p. 5)

Balsom's main purpose in devising these categories was to predict and explain variations in patterns of party-political voting. He suggested that these regions were already undergoing significant change at the time he was writing. New patterns of work and industry and changing population profiles were undermining old images of a 'Celtic Fringe' based on rural, agricultural Wales, and a Labour stronghold rooted in the coal industry. Balsom was especially concerned that changes affecting what he called the 'traditional south Wales area' (his 'Welsh Wales') would throw into question a form of Welsh identity developed and expressed in the English language. He said this made it hard to imagine a future sense of Welshness that was not anchored in the Welsh language. In other words, he was predicting the likely disappearance of Welsh Wales as it merged more and more into British Wales. On the other hand, he acknowledged that Wales was still held together by a widely shared sense of being Welsh, and indeed there was evidence that this was being strengthened by the development of Welsh political institutions. From our perspective now, a quarter of a century later, we can judge the accuracy of these predictions.

Activity 2.2

Looking back over your own lifetime:

■ How far do you feel that Balsom's prediction of the weakening of any sense of Welshness that is not linked to the Welsh language was correct?

■ Do fewer people now feel Welsh than did around twenty-five years ago?

■ On what grounds other than language might people consider themselves to be Welsh?

Comment

Although speaking Welsh is an extremely important aspect of Welshness, there are many other grounds on which people can feel themselves to be Welsh. These can include loyalty to their place of birth and origin, a sense of family and community connection to Wales, enthusiasm for Welsh artistic and sporting achievements, or engagement with political processes and voluntary activities in Wales. Each of these can produce a sense of Welsh identity. Bearing this in mind, there is little evidence that people are becoming less inclined to think of themselves as 'Welsh' than they did in the past. Possibly the reverse is true: Chapters 6 and 8 discuss recent political developments which may have increased people's awareness of Welsh identity.

It can be questioned whether the areas Balsom defined were ever really so neatly self-contained and distinctive as Figure 2.1 might suggest; in reality, the boundaries between them were probably much less clear-cut. For instance, many of those who peopled the area known as 'Welsh Wales' were drawn from the more rural parts of *Y Fro Gymraeg*, and for a long time afterwards they maintained real, or sentimental, connections to it. Nevertheless, it is not unusual for Wales to be partitioned or subdivided in this kind of way, into distinct areas such as rural Wales; *Y Fro Gymraeg*, sometimes referred to as the Welsh 'heartland'; the Valleys; the cities, or urban Wales (Cardiff, Swansea, Newport, Wrexham) and so on. Often these areas or zones are said to possess different sets of attributes, with associated meanings, or regional cultures, reflecting not only the size and distribution of their population but also differences of class, occupation and lifestyle, which present their inhabitants with contrasting problems and opportunities.

Such areas have their advocates, and political representatives, and are represented in particular kinds of policy response and direction. For instance, there have been many policies and strategies for rural Wales, and others aimed at achieving urban regeneration. For several years there was a government-led Programme for the Valleys, designed to improve economic and social opportunities in a deprived part of south Wales. Since 2000 west Wales and the Valleys have received European (Objective 1 and Convergence) funding, on the grounds that they are significantly worse off economically than most European regions. Making the case for this European support required the map of Wales to be redrawn to highlight east–west divisions, emphasising the common problems faced by rural Wales and the deindustrialising Valleys of the south rather than the differences between (rural) north and (industrial) south that figure so often in Welsh political debates.

A more recent attempt to dissect Wales into its various parts is *People, Places, Futures: the Wales Spatial Plan* (2004; updated 2008), prepared by the Welsh Assembly Government (WAG). This partitions Wales into a number of distinct 'regions' or areas with contrasting characteristics, and is intended to help in making appropriate decisions for development over the next twenty years. According to this analysis, Wales has six significant 'sub-regions': north-east Wales; north-west Wales; central Wales; south-east Wales; Swansea Bay and the Western Valleys; and Pembrokeshire and the Milford Haven waterway.

The boundaries between these areas are not intended to be hard and fast; they are 'fuzzy', because there are many cross-border connections and linkages in daily activities. However, on the basis of key statistical information and data about economic, social and environmental conditions, an impression is given of the different 'social geographies' found in present-day Wales. We learn, for example, that north-west Wales 'has a very strong sense of identity, linked to the Welsh language, an outstanding landscape and coastline' (WAG, 2004, p. 38) whereas north-east Wales is described as 'a key driver of the Welsh economy' (p. 41). The 'capital network' of south-east Wales, centred on Cardiff, is referred to as an 'interdependent but unplanned urban network' (p. 49) that contains some major economic and social disparities. Central Wales consists of a 'mosaic of relatively small settlements' (p. 45) which are proving to be very attractive for their quality of life and environment.

The Spatial Plan provides a framework enabling local planning to be brought together with national aspirations and strategies. The assumption is that the people who live in a given area typically will enjoy different rewards, or face different problems, from those experienced elsewhere, and therefore require different kinds of policies and treatments. For instance, distance from and access to services like health and education present more of a problem for those living in the Welsh countryside, where the population is scattered and transport limited, than in the city centres. It is even more of a problem for those who lack the financial and other resources to overcome distances – such as ownership of or access to a car. But it is important not to oversimplify, since there are groups and individuals living in more urban contexts who face similar issues of deprivation and marginalisation.

These distinctions are not just a matter of material provisions and inequalities – the **'life chances'** people encounter – but extend to how people think about where they live, and its positive and negative features. This can translate into different social and political attitude and concerns.

Wales is officially a bilingual country, and all public bodies (and increasingly private organisations as well) are required to give the two languages equal status. But because use of the Welsh language is not distributed evenly throughout Wales, the politics of the language and the implementation of language policies vary from area to area. The language has a more prominent role in debates and discussions in Gwynedd or Ceredigion than it does in Pembrokeshire, simply because many fewer people speak Welsh, or attach such importance to it, in Pembrokeshire. Similarly, debates about open access to the countryside, or the legitimacy of hunting, get a different reception in rural areas, especially from groups connected to farming and agriculture, from the one they get from those who live in the towns, who naturally have more 'urban' interests. Different areas contain different populations, who to some degree engage in different activities and so develop different interests.

'Life chances' is a term associated with the sociologist Max Weber. It refers to the typical expectation of rewards, opportunities and deprivations that a person may have over the course of a lifetime. Comparison of life chances provides a way of assessing inequalities between different kinds of individuals and groups.

2.3 Perceptions of regional differences in 'Welsh character'

The kinds of officially defined, large-scale or 'macro' distinctions we have been considering provide only a broad interpretation of variations within Wales, and are not likely to coincide precisely with the impressions formed by ordinary people, who often see things from a more detailed, local or 'micro' perspective, formed 'on the ground'. Rather than objective and systematic scientific research based on statistical evidence, their views are more likely to rely upon everyday commonsense knowledge of the sort that 'everybody knows'. Similarly, people do not always use sociological or academic language when talking about these topics, yet in their own way they do show great interest in and sensitivity towards them. For example, in Brian Roberts's account of his research into attitudes towards Welshness in a south Wales valley he tells us that an informant referred to differences of 'character' between those living in different places. Contrasting residents of a nearby agricultural district with the inhabitants of his own ex-mining valley, he said, 'In my opinion there's a difference in the people there and in the Valleys. A different character you know' (quoted in Roberts, 1999, p. 121). Another of those interviewed expanded on this suggestion, using similar words:

> There's a Valleys' character. If you went to West Wales, you'd find the Welshman is different, it's a land-working Welshman. Here you have the industrial, south Welshman who is totally different to the north. There is a division between north and south and mid Wales.
>
> (quoted in Roberts, 1999, p. 121)

As used here, 'character' is very like the term 'identity', which has become much used in recent social scientific work. As seen in these quotations, individuals and groups can form a sense of their own identity by comparing themselves to others, seeing who they are like and who they differ from. In making these distinctions, they draw upon their everyday experiences, in the places where they live, work, and enjoy themselves. A wealth of information and understanding is hidden behind comments like those just cited, and it is striking how important geographical differences of place seem to be in organising these perceptions of social difference. They imply that the individuals concerned possess a map of social variations, arranged according to the points of the compass, which can be summarised in the comparisons they make between different areas like 'west Wales' and 'the Valleys'.

Activity 2.3

Take stock of what you have read so far.

■ To what extent would you agree that different Welsh 'characters' can be found in different parts of Wales?

■ Why might this be the case?

■ If you could discuss the question with Brian Roberts's interviewees, how do you think your views might differ from theirs?

Comment

Both the informants cited above happen to be men aged sixty or more. They emphasise the type of work (industrial or agricultural) which they believe goes into forming the character of 'Welshmen' in particular. Would the same apply to Welsh women? Or to those younger than sixty? When you think about it, it is unlikely that (as suggested) people in south Wales will be 'totally different' from those living in the north. Indeed, they are bound to have much in common. Whether you stress the differences or the similarities depends on your frame of reference: people outside Wales might not notice differences of the kind highlighted by these comments. Yet there are some genuinely interesting and significant differences between places in north and south Wales, arising from what has occurred there in the past and from features of the contemporary situation, and it is quite possible that this has a bearing on how the people living in them think and behave.

These local variations, connected to place, have given rise to a rich tradition of local studies carried out by social scientists in Wales (for example, Alwyn Rees (1950) on Llanfihangel-yng-Ngwynfa; Ronald Frankenberg (1957) on Glynceiriog; and Isabel Emmett (1964) on Llanfrothen). These studies explore themes of identity and belonging, and the nature of Welshness, in a variety of different contexts. This tradition of social science work has ensured that Welsh social scientists, and Welsh places, have influenced how these issues have been thought about more generally. There is also a vein of important literary writing about Welsh places and communities that parallels the academic work in capturing what is special and distinctive about different places.

Summary

■ In social research, for official purposes and in ordinary speech, Wales is often divided into distinct parts or areas, which are assumed to have differing characteristics.

- These social geographic differences provide a basis on which it can be argued that there are different kinds of Welsh people, or different kinds of Welshness, made visible in attitudes and behaviour.

- However, the boundaries between these regions are not firm or fixed and the social map of Wales can be drawn in different ways, for different purposes.

3   Wales: 'a community of communities'

This section introduces the idea of community as an important link between place and social identity. People's identities and sense of belonging are often anchored in a feeling of identification with a particular community.

3.1 What is a community?

'Community' is a complicated and often hotly contested concept in social science, but difficult to avoid when considering the relationship between people and places (see Day, 2006, for a full discussion). In Wales, there has been a lengthy debate about the nature of 'community' itself, and about the strengths and weaknesses, virtues and vices of particular communities. In this section you will consider what is meant by community, and become acquainted with some examples of Welsh **community studies**.

The studies mentioned above were carried out in rural locations and may now be rather dated, yet they tell us a great deal about the influences that have shaped Wales as it is today. The field was established by a classic study by Rees (1950), described by a leading Welsh social geographer as a delicate investigation into the traditional, integrated, way of life of social groups in a specific area (Carter, 1996). Rees carried out a community study of Llanfihangel, a parish in northern Powys with a population of about 500 people. His aim was to explore the intricate web of relationships through which the community functioned, and assess the impact of economic and social change upon its longstanding social customs.

A **community study** is an investigation that provides a description and analysis of how a particular community works, identifying its distinctive features and more general characteristics.

This approach set the tone for many of the studies that followed. The impression they conveyed was that a community in Wales typically formed a closed social world, filled with the solidarity of family, kin and locality, in which relationships even with adjoining communities could be fraught with tension and sometimes downright hostility. Involvement in a set of close-knit relationships tended to generate a feeling of pride in their own place among the members of a community, combined with a sense of difference from and readiness to comment critically upon the places of others: important factors in the formation of strong local identities. An account by Stephanie Jones (2003) of an outing by supporters of a local rugby club to a match in Cardiff provides a nice example of this. As the fans from Blaengwyn arrived in the capital city, they puzzled onlookers by chanting derogatory verses about the team from their neighbouring village of Fairview.

Rees put great emphasis on 'tradition' and on the long history that lay behind patterns of belief and behaviour observed in places like Llanfihangel. These rural communities were seen as having evolved over a prolonged period of time, into a form of living tightly fitted to the needs and demands of the land and its cultivation. The authors of such studies argued that the implications went far beyond the immediate effects on rural life and farming, since there was something quintessentially Welsh about the characteristics of life in rural Wales. These included not only the routine use of the Welsh language, but also a lack of class distinctions within the population; an emphasis on the home and hearth; the centrality of Nonconformist religion; and engagement with a set of literary and cultural traditions which could be displayed and publicly evaluated in a village, or eventually national, *eisteddfod*.

These values form the backdrop to Balsom's notion of *Y Fro Gymraeg* and its social and political culture. It should be noted that while *Y Fro Gymraeg* coincided with rural Wales to a large extent, there were always parts of rural Wales, like southern Powys and Pembrokeshire, where this was not the case. Equally, there were districts in industrial and urbanised south and north Wales that remained strongly Welsh-speaking, and religiously Nonconformist, even though they might not be thought of as forming part of *Y Fro Gymraeg*. So once again there is only an approximate correspondence between significant social variations and geographical or territorial divisions.

3.2 The importance of 'traditional' Welsh communities

Although the brief description of 'community' above was derived mainly from the investigation of villages and small towns in the Welsh countryside, many of the same characteristics applied to the coal-mining and slate-quarrying communities found in the more industrialised parts of the country. These were also relatively small, self-contained, and often quite isolated from one another. Like farming communities, they too rested on the foundation of a dominant shared occupational background, which meant that the majority of people living in them, both men and women, necessarily shared a common way of life.

Writing about the quarrying town of Blaenau Ffestiniog, Emmett provides a brilliant analysis of the depth and density of personal knowledge that can come to be shared among members of such a community:

> Those who have grown up in the town have such a wealth of knowledge of each other as to make each encounter densely elaborate. Men and women are known as parents, as drinkers or non-drinkers, as singers and speakers, in some version of their work records, and in some version of their record as lovers. Over the course of their lifetime men and women ... have gone on meeting or passing in the street most of those they have ever kissed, most of those they have ever quarrelled with, and many of those they have ever worked with. Every aspect of their life is used in the picture others have of them. One woman said of another, with whom she periodically played darts, 'Whenever I play darts with her, I remember that she pinched my bag when we were in the infants'.
>
> (Emmett, 1982, pp. 207–8)

Activity 2.4

In the quote above Emmett describes a level of knowledge about others living nearby that it is probably hard to reproduce today.

- Where might this happen, if at all, in contemporary Wales?

- If it can't be found, what factors have made this impossible?

- What do you think the consequences of this are for the way people relate to one another socially?

Comment

Although you might think nothing comparable to this degree of mutual understanding exists in the larger settlements of Wales, its cities and large towns, it is worth noting that one of the few major community studies carried out in such a context, Colin Rosser and Christopher Harris's study of Swansea (1965), begins with a description of 'Mr Hughes of Morriston', who shows exactly the same detailed familiarity with a set of relatives and neighbours living nearby. This was possible, the authors argued, because Swansea was divided into a number of distinct 'urban villages' which, although joined physically on the ground, socially were rather like the villages of rural Wales. In this respect, 'urbanisation' in Wales was deceptive, since it did not necessarily eliminate the key features of place and belonging.

A major difference between studies of rural communities and this urban example was that, as well as being spatially divided, Swansea was divided by class, so that different classes, working and middle, occupied different parts of the city. There were patterns of movement such that social mobility between classes, for instance as a result of educational success, led to geographical mobility between neighbourhoods, or sometimes away from the city altogether. It is generally understood that mobility has major implications for community, weakening the stability of social relations that is assumed to be necessary for strong ties of community and identity to develop. Alternatively, people must find ways of rebuilding their social bonds as and when they move, in order to recreate forms of community. A follow-up study suggested that by the 1960s middle-class residents had developed ways of dealing with mobility, by learning new 'suburban' habits in residential estates, which tied them less firmly to particular places (Bell, 1968).

3.3 Coal and the decline of traditional community

Mining communities like those of south Wales are widely considered to be exceptional in the extent to which they could create powerful feelings of belonging and solidarity. The depth of common knowledge and experience among their inhabitants is captured in the distinctive visual imagery of crowded and monotonously similar housing, demonstrating how closely people living in very similar circumstances were packed together (see Figure 2.2).

Figure 2.2
Streets of mining
housing

A classic sociological statement of the nature of such communities is provided by Martin Bulmer, who draws out both the high degree of local social integration and also their separateness from the wider world. While he is not referring specifically to the Welsh case, his description certainly fits the Welsh experience:

> The traditional mining community is characterised by the prevalence of communal social relationships among miners and their families. ... The social ties of work, leisure, family, neighbourhood and friendship overlap to form close-knit and interlocking locally based collectivities of actors. From this pattern derives the mutual aid characteristic in adversity and the inward-looking focus ... derived from occupational homogeneity and social and geographical isolation from the rest of society. Meaningful social interaction is confined almost exclusively to the locality.
>
> (Bulmer, 1975, pp. 87–8)

Following the decline of the British mining industry, such conditions now lie very largely in the past, but it can take generations for their effects to die away, as some of the reflections in the following chapters reveal.

Writing about one such community, Ynysybwl in the Taff Valley, Phillip Jones (2004) provides a snapshot of the break-up of the traditional community structure as early as the 1960s. Using evidence from a small survey of local households, he notes that although mining still accounted for nearly half the male jobs, the industry no longer attracted younger men, while there were also signs that women, especially married women, were beginning to find new and more varied opportunities for employment. These economic changes were drawing people out of the locality, either as regular commuters or through longer-term changes of residence. Jones identifies several types of change coming together to affect the stability of places like Ynysybwl.

Activity 2.5

Read the quote below from Phillip Jones's study and consider the following questions:

■ How many sorts of change can you identify in this passage?

■ How do you think they were likely to alter social relationships within a community like Ynysybwl?

> By the mid-1960s it was evident that in some geographical situations coal mining had to take its place within a rather more diversified

employment structure. ... The majority of other types of employment were not necessarily new, but were clearly expanding ... Local authority manual workers, nurses within the growing health service, a variety of secretarial posts, shop assistants, lorry and van drivers of various descriptions are among the many examples. Few individuals were employed in the more obvious middle-class occupations, such as the civil service. This paucity was in marked contrast to the considerable numbers of school teachers, doctors and similar professions which feature in the occupations of non-resident children. Out-migration – whether to coastal Wales, to England (mainly the London area and the Midlands) or to the Commonwealth – was evidently still exacting a severe toll on the better-educated members of the younger generation raised in Ynysybwl. Other economic and social trends were also gathering pace – which some ten years later were identified as having deeply detrimental impacts on the fabric of life in the south Wales valleys. The most pervasive and damaging was the increasing geographical concentration of employment opportunities, in both services and manufacturing industry, in the favoured stretch of the M4 corridor between the major coastal cities, especially Cardiff. ... Increasingly the Valleys faced contractions in the number and quality of the jobs located there; the demise of the coal industry was in fact symptomatic of a wider malaise.

(Jones, 2004, pp. 92–4)

Comment

Ynysybwl was being affected by a combination of generational, class and gender changes. New sorts of work, in new geographical locations, were encouraging new patterns of mobility, and as well as moving physically across space, some of the local population were experiencing social mobility, into new, more 'middle-class' positions. These developments disrupted the continuity of relationships necessary for a 'traditional' community to persist unchanged, including relationships between men and women, and parents and children – in this case, perhaps especially fathers and sons, who no longer expected to work together in the same industry. Jones sees these developments as part of the emergence of a 'post-industrial' future for the Valleys. There is no doubt that since he carried out his study these trends have continued, and in some cases accelerated, breaking down communal bonds. (The transformation of Wales from an industrial to a post-industrial economy is considered more fully in Chapter 3.)

Importantly, Jones warns us against over-generalising from a limited case, since, as he says, 'each valley's experience was different, whilst within large valleys such as the Rhondda or Taff, there were often important internal distinctions' (Jones, 2004, p. 86). This reminds us to keep in mind the local variations in conditions and experience that people will encounter and respond to, variations that can be lost when we think about the bigger picture of social and economic change. Nevertheless, Jones concludes that the results of change were generally negative for the Valleys, leading to declining populations and a diminishing sense of community. These were the forces that Denis Balsom felt would eventually destroy the idea of a 'Welsh Wales', which was virtually synonymous with the south Wales Valleys.

Examining the Valleys some thirty years after Jones, Roberts confirms the extent of change, while also spelling out more fully what might be understood as the unique 'character' or identity of Valleys culture:

> ... South Wales is often portrayed in terms of the mines, rugby, singing and chapels. However, these activities are now indicators of a declining tradition – used as a simple view of Welshness from outside, while becoming 'endangered' inside. For those in the Valleys, these activities were merely part of a more general culture; they were among its outward features, growing from the rhythms of mining life and embodying a deeper Welsh character and communality associated with the area. ... There is even a strongly felt sense that Valley life is Welsh character, due to a sharp awareness that the hardship of the mining communities produced a distinctive and vibrant culture which aided physical survival and enriched a shared experience. ... Now it is perceived that a traditional social identity, in decline for so long, is at a final turning point as its content and symbolic boundary markers are challenged. This Welsh character, usually described by local residents in terms of communal values (for example, friendliness, sharing and helping), may now be fading due to the decline of the close knit between work and communal patterns.
>
> (Roberts, 1999, pp. 120–1)

3.4 Two versions of traditional community?

When Roberts mentions a 'strongly felt sense that Valley life is Welsh character', he sets up a potential rival to the view indicated earlier, that the true home of Welshness lies in rural Wales, or *Y Fro Gymraeg*. This distinction is endorsed by one of his interviewees, who says that people from other parts of Wales, and particularly west Wales, 'don't recognize you as Welsh' if you come from the Valleys.

Ideas of community depend heavily on recognition of similarities and differences. While there were important similarities between traditional mining communities and the towns and villages of rural Wales, there were also some marked differences. In some respects the culture and politics of Welsh miners were very different from those of their farming compatriots, for example because of the impact of trade unions and the surrounding social institutions of the welfare hall, social club and library on their everyday lives. These institutions had no exact counterparts in rural Wales, where chapels were the main (and sometimes only) focus of community activity.

This suggests that two competing ideas of 'community', and associated conceptions of 'Welshness', have been passed down from Welsh history. Dave Adamson has noted the existence of these two dominant conceptions of Welsh community: 'a sense of rural community with an emphasis on kinship, neighbourhood and identifiable patterns of language, culture and religion', and 'a sense of industrial community, associated with coal and steel production, with networks of mutual aid, traditions of working-class politics and labourism' (Adamson, 1996, p. 41). In line with these distinctions, the communities of rural and industrial Wales contributed to the development of rather different political traditions, Liberalism on the one hand (discussed in Chapter 7) and Labourism on the other (discussed in Chapter 8), though, as will be seen, both were tinged with a shared radicalism.

Yet there were also unifying factors at work. In both kinds of community people were used to living among a restricted number of familiar individuals and families. Their entire lives could be played out within the narrow confines of a small village, where the same people met in a variety of different contexts and every aspect of life became connected, so that individuals worked, played and prayed together and very often had close family connections as well. Hence, as Adamson comments, farmers in the Llŷn peninsula could feel as committed to the idea of community as miners from Maerdy were, and see it as something they had in common as Welsh people despite their other differences. The convergence between these two variations around a common theme famously led Saunders Lewis, a founding figure in twentieth-century

Welsh nationalism, to refer to Wales as a 'community of communities', thereby tying together the local expression of Welshness with its national identity. The communalism some regarded as an inherent property of Valleys communities could be celebrated equally in other parts of Wales, in the countryside and wherever people spoke Welsh together.

Miners and farmers, like slate quarrymen and steelworkers, could also share a sense of the close connection between the way their social lives were organised and the requirements of working with their local environment – the farm, pit, quarry, or mill – as a productive resource, with all its consequences for the look and shape of the landscape around them. Over generations, the place itself would be shaped physically by the people inhabiting it. In rural Wales especially, family or even personal names became attached to particular pieces of land, or landscape features. In quarrying and mining areas, the local scenery could be transformed entirely by human work. These processes of physical and geographical transformation meant that places became imbued with historical memories and social meanings. The geographer Pyrs Gruffudd has discussed some of these processes in the context of rural Wales, observing how particular landscapes can achieve the status of national icons:

> Even specific physical features (mountains, rivers, forests) can become emblematic of national identity and can offer cultural relationships through which a people make a land their land. ... In many cases, rural landscapes are imagined as the 'real', 'authentic' essence of the nation.
>
> (Gruffudd, 1999, p. 50)

Wales has a number of candidates to serve as potential geographical icons of its cultural identity; they might include, for example, the mountains of Snowdonia; a typical farming scene set in a Welsh landscape; the remains of a slagheap or colliery pithead wheel; or, as in Figure 2.3, debris from one of the slate quarries of north Wales. Each image conjures up an idea of Wales, but, as we have seen, none corresponds exactly to the whole of Wales and its many communities.

Figure 2.3
Blaenau Ffestiniog

Summary

■ As a result of the historical importance of a few basic industries, Wales has been endowed with memories of strong local communities, similar in the strength of their social relationships although producing divergent political and cultural traditions.

■ These memories form an important aspect of Welsh consciousness.

■ But as traditions that grow increasingly remote from present-day reality, you might question their relevance to contemporary circumstances.

4 Change and transformation in contemporary Wales

The kinds of traditional community that have been described exert an influence over the social analysis of modern Wales even today. Arguably this is because while it takes many years, perhaps generations, to build strong communities, it also requires time for them to decay and vanish altogether in the face of change. Furthermore, their influence tends to persist in people's imaginations long after reality has grown into something different. However, to modern eyes, some of their aspects are bound to appear rather quaint and old-fashioned. What relevance do such depictions of 'traditional' community life have for us now? How far is social life today organised so directly around the requirements of the physical or material circumstances of productive labour? And to what extent can people expect to spend most or all of their lives surrounded by the same narrow circle of family, friends and acquaintances? If this is not what defines communities in contemporary Wales, then what does?

A picture of Wales based only on these kinds of places also leaves a lot out – most obviously the urban Wales of Cardiff, Newport, Wrexham and the various holiday towns strung along its coast, like Tenby, Rhyl and Llandudno, where in fact the largest concentrations of population are found. Where do they fit into an account of Wales and its places? Do they all belong together in Balsom's 'British Wales', places that are not really 'Welsh' at all, or is this an intellectual construct needing revision? Notions of Wales based on its more 'traditional' communities alone are dated and selective, and need substantial modification in the light of recent changes.

4.1 Loss of community or revitalisation?

Wales has undergone fundamental social and economic transformations since 1945. These include the dwindling of key industries and occupations that once provided the underpinning for traditional forms of community life. Once there were 280,000 miners in Wales, now there are just a few hundred. Farming is no longer the backbone of the rural economy, while the slate quarries are valued as much for their contribution to the tourist industry as for their industrial production. As their original reasons for existence have been transformed, many places in Wales have gone through extraordinarily difficult times, with inevitable consequences for the shape of Welsh communities and identities.

A symbolic moment in the 'death' of traditional community was the 1984–5 miners' strike, fought in Wales to defend 'community' as much as jobs. The return to work of the Maerdy miners, defiantly marching behind their union banners, captured both the spirit of unity that sustained them during the bitter and long-drawn-out dispute, and also the realisation that there was no future for many of the conventional aspects of life in a pit village. Loss of reliable male employment, relocation of work away from the Valleys, and the changing balance of control between the sexes and generations were among the key challenges to be faced. Features of life that gave strength to these communities in the past, such as the inward-looking nature of social relations and reliance on mutual support between neighbours and co-workers, became disadvantages as the labour market increasingly required mobility and a readiness to face new experiences and gain new skills. The collective power of community faced increasing pressure from the growing individualism of modern economic and social life. Like the rest of the developed world, Welsh communities had to meet the challenge of adapting to new conditions and new expectations. Some managed this better than others.

Change affects different places unevenly; while some are under threat or in decline, others may flourish, producing new dynamism and creativity. Unlike the slow growth and development associated (often mistakenly) with the communities of the past, today's communities and places face continual pressure to change and adapt. For this reason, policies addressing communities tend to put heavy stress on the need for 'modernisation', 'regeneration', growth and development: values which have largely ousted the earlier preference for stability and continuity as the touchstones of a 'good' community. Faced with these new conditions, there have been both winners and losers among Welsh places and communities.

4.2 Decline and deprivation

For over forty years, a persisting pattern has shown some parts of Wales, including particular districts and places, suffering prolonged economic and social disadvantage and decline. These include places that previously were among the most vibrant and celebrated centres of Welsh social and political life (see Figure 2.4).

Across Wales, economic changes have produced instances of acute social deprivation and marginalisation, with associated problems of crime and disorder. For example, port towns like Holyhead and Fishguard, along with small market towns, quarry villages and Valleys communities, figure prominently in Welsh indices of joblessness and multiple deprivation, as they struggle to find a new niche for themselves in the developing economy and society of twenty-first-century Wales. By the start of this century, parts of the south Wales Valleys had gained a reputation as home to 'socially excluded communities whose members

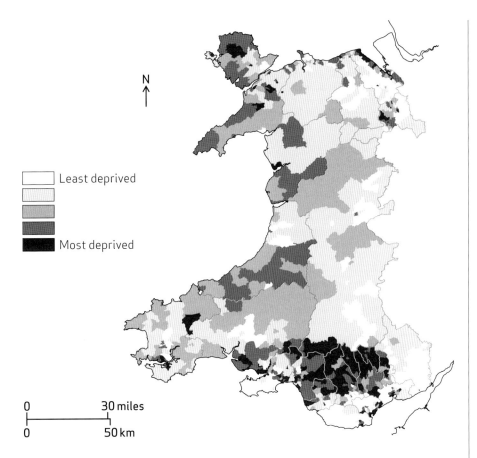

Figure 2.4
Wales Index of Multiple
Deprivation 2000
(Source: National
Assembly for Wales
(2000)/Welsh Index of
Multiple Deprivation/
London: National
Statistics.)

have little opportunity to access jobs, services, and adequate housing'
(Dicks, 2000, p. 12). They seemed stranded by the tides of history. The
result was an outward flow of those who could manage to get away,
moving towards more prosperous locations in south-east Wales, drawn
mainly towards Cardiff and its surrounding area. This resorting to
individual mobility as a solution to the problems of declining
communities accentuated a sense of the disintegration of a way of life
and a distinctive cultural identity.

Observers report that such conditions can produce a wide range of
individual and social problems. For example Bea Campbell's (1993)
account of life in the poorer parts of urban south Wales paints a very
disturbing picture, highlighting occurrences of crime, violence and
disorder, often with racial and gender overtones, involving activity by
young white males. It is a useful antidote to some more upbeat versions
of everyday life and change in modern Wales, which focus on the gains
made in other places. Such differences in fortune perpetuate variation
between places: some become known as particularly respectable or
desirable places to live; others gain a reputation, or stigma, as sources of
social problems and disorder. Labels of this sort, attaching to places and

neighbourhoods, can easily become identified with those who live in them, and there is a tendency for favourable and unfavourable images to perpetuate themselves over time, influencing people's actions in avoiding or being attracted towards different locations.

Since 2001 the WAG has addressed some of these problems through its Communities First programme, directing support and funding towards the hundred most deprived communities in Wales, as well as other smaller pockets of disadvantage located within better-off areas. So far the programme appears to have made a useful, if limited, contribution to bringing about necessary improvements (Adamson, 2008), and from 2010 the policy is being taken forward, with extended coverage of more communities, and more emphasis on achieving targets and outcomes. Experience suggests that hard and painstaking effort is required to reverse the damage done to communities and their members by hostile social and economic forces, especially those of economic decline and loss of purpose.

4.3 Growth and renewal: the rise of Cardiff and its 'city region'

The struggle to revitalise deprived districts like the older Valleys communities of south Wales can be contrasted with the massive redevelopment process centred on Cardiff Bay, and smaller but still significant developments in Swansea and other urban growth areas. Parts of Cardiff continue to show high levels of deprivation and associated social problems. But for the most part Cardiff has been presented as the outstanding economic and cultural success of recent years, sharing in the modernisation of Welsh politics and society and benefiting from the changes associated with political devolution. This makes 'greater Cardiff' a place for developing new ideas of Welshness, more cosmopolitan and multicultural in character than those that prevailed in the past.

Commentators like Huw Thomas (1999) and Kevin Morgan (2007) have noted the curiously ambiguous position the city occupies as the capital of Wales, a status achieved only in 1955. Cardiff owes its development to the industries of south Wales but is not itself an industrial city, having begun as a coal-exporting dock and evolved into a centre for the provision of services, government and opportunities for consumption. This makes it well suited to take a leading role in a 'post-industrial' Wales, but its growth has been viewed with suspicion by would-be competitors who believe they have a stronger claim to represent the true nature of Wales and Welshness. These include Swansea, Merthyr, Aberystwyth, even Machynlleth. The case against Cardiff is that it is not really Welsh, and specifically Welsh-speaking, enough, but belongs instead to a more British, imperial, or cosmopolitan ethos, making it 'hardly a city which typifies or symbolizes the cultural distinctiveness of the country' (Thomas, 1999, pp. 174–5).

Nevertheless Cardiff appears to be thriving thanks to the advent of the Welsh Assembly, the development of new government offices, the rise of media and cultural services, and the city's success is drawing people to it. Every day some 70,000 or more commute into the city to work. Longer-distance movements bring others from further away, including young people from rural north and west Wales, who helped raise the proportion of the city's population able to speak Welsh from 10 per cent in 1991 to 16 per cent in 2001. Like other capital cities, Cardiff attracts the young, thanks to 'its array of labour markets, its cultural diversity and its sense of social and sexual freedom' (Morgan, 2007, p. 133), which contrast with the limitations met in villages and small towns elsewhere in Wales. The city is sufficiently large to have its own spatial patterning, in which different areas specialise in accommodating distinct social groupings, marked by variations in age, lifestyle, family structure, and class and ethnic background. It has the largest, most varied concentration of people with ethnic minority backgrounds in Wales (as discussed in Chapter 4). Important aspects of its recent development have been the upgrading of city-centre facilities and the creation of a number of locations – the Millennium Stadium, Senedd (the building that houses the debating chamber of the Assembly) and Wales Millennium Centre – which symbolise its national, as well as regional, significance.

Cardiff is being reshaped into a place fit to be acknowledged as a European capital: an ambition which might seem grandiose, given its relatively modest position as no more than a medium-sized British city. In the process, older historical places and communities are transformed. Butetown, noted as the location of one of Europe's oldest settled black communities (as discussed in Chapter 4) and a place that has given birth to its own very distinctive version of Welshness, has been shunted to one side by new road layouts and the extensive dockland redevelopment. At the same time, there has been a deliberate attempt to reconfigure the people of Butetown, formerly one of the most stigmatised elements of the Welsh population, into a symbol of a new multicultural Wales, in which older ethnic and racial divisions can be replaced by a common identification with the emerging institutions of a civic Wales. This issue is explored more fully in Chapters 4 and 8.

The Spatial Plan sees south-east Wales developing into a networked city region, with growing connections between Cardiff and its hinterland of Valleys towns and communities. Cardiff's future role will be 'international yet distinctively Welsh' (WAG, 2008, p. 98), acting as an economic dynamo for the wider region and for the country as a whole. It is hoped that eventually this will benefit the more remote parts of the Valleys, which continue to be blighted by 'a high concentration of social deprivation and economic inactivity, allied to low levels of educational attainment and skills, poor health and declining population' (2004, p. 49). Recognising that Valleys communities have diverse characteristics and needs, the Plan suggests that:

> Opportunities exist in ... Pontypridd and Pontypool to promote wider community regeneration and provide essential links between the coastal belt and Heads of the Valleys corridor ... Merthyr Tydfil and Ebbw Vale ... provide the population size and strategic development opportunities necessary for sustained economic development, retailing, housing and service provision. These centres should act as a catalyst for the regeneration of the upper valleys, helping to retain and attract a socially mixed population and provide a counterweight to the coastal urban areas.
>
> (WAG 2004, p. 50)

Roberts (1999) presents an optimistic version of the path followed by the Valleys, noting the 'greening' taking place as relics of the old industrial economy are obliterated. He sees signs of revitalisation of the Welshness of the region, a process drawing on past symbols, including a revival in speaking Welsh, allowing people to reassert the distinctiveness of their way of life without clinging to outdated tradition. Roberts insists that this grassroots upsurge of a new kind of Welsh consciousness should be distinguished from the formation of a more commercial 'heritage Welshness', expressed in the Welsh tourist industry. An example of the latter, although with some input from local people, is described in a study of the Rhondda Heritage Park (Dicks, 2000). The real history of the mining industry, with all its complexities and contradictions, and its negative as well as positive attributes, has been transformed into a recollected 'heritage', which weaves solid facts and memories together with a considerable dose of romantic sentimentality and myth. The strength of 'community' is upheld, but made to look like something left behind somewhere in the past.

4.4 The transformation of rural Wales

Rapid and disturbing social change affecting the character of places and their occupants has not been confined to the cities of Wales, or its former industrial areas. Researchers investigating rural Wales towards the close of the last century commented on how much the countryside had altered since the classic studies of village life and community. Many districts of rural Wales 'have witnessed dramatic processes of restructuring in their local economies. The role of agriculture and other primary industries has declined considerably, while manufacturing and particularly service-sector employment have become much more dominant' (Cloke et al., 1997, pp. 3–4).

The Welsh countryside now depends as much on tourism and the leisure industry as on farming. The focus has shifted from production of food and raw materials towards the consumption of recreation and relaxation, enjoyment of a pleasant environment, and the values of 'peace and quiet' and retreat from the pressures of urban living. This puts rural Wales among the more desirable locations to live, so that large numbers of people, including many entering retirement, have opted to move there. At the same time others, including some younger, well-educated, enterprising members of the local population, are being lured away to the 'bright lights' of the cities, in Wales and further beyond.

The opening-up of the countryside, and its integration into the wider economy and society, has changed rural life forever. Modernisation and relative contraction of the agricultural sector, along with associated diversification of employment, mean that villages no longer exist as isolated, self-enclosed environments immune to external pressures – if indeed they ever really did. And ironically, although the majority of people living in rural Wales now work in service industries, access to some essential services (like transport, education, healthcare and housing) has become worse for many rural residents, imposing on them a greater need to travel over longer distances. The consequence has been a major change in the social mix among the rural population. It can no longer be assumed that most or all of those living in the countryside have a keen interest in agriculture, in rural hobbies and pursuits, or in the social and cultural traditions of village life. Only a minority will expect to spend the greater part of their lives living in the same place. Instead there is considerable mobility, generating some interesting encounters between differing styles of life, as can be seen for example from Noragh Jones's lively account (1993) of the diverse types of people living in rural Ceredigion. The cultural tensions and conflicts that can arise within individual communities have helped to fuel some wider-scale protests about the changing composition of the Welsh rural population (Cloke et al., 1997).

In some ways, like the Cardiff city region, rural Wales can be viewed as a success story. The Wales Spatial Plan picks out the advantages it offers in terms of quality of life. The pattern of declining population which once threatened to empty many communities has been reversed. The fabric of many towns and villages has been refurbished and brought up to date. Many rural residents enjoy a comfortable standard of living, even if others are marginalised and struggle to get by. However, these gains have been made at some cost to the established values and meanings associated with Welsh rural communities. Two interconnected aspects of change have attracted particular attention: inward migration and the pressures exerted on the Welsh language.

The impact of 'incomers' of various kinds relocating to rural areas during recent decades has been a major topic among rural sociologists, including those working on Wales. Arriving from elsewhere, for their own reasons and at varying stages of the family life cycle, they are unlikely to attribute the same meanings to places as those who are 'local' and perhaps born and bred there. A sizeable proportion of the total population of Wales – around a quarter – has made such a journey, having been born outside Wales. Their impact has been especially notable in rural Wales and within the 'heartland' zone of north and west Wales. For some local people, these incomers represent a disturbing element, introducing new and possibly challenging ideas and behaviour. This comes across in comments collected by Cloke et al. from their case study locations:

> 'The foreigners moving in don't have the same attitudes, so the neighbourliness has been diluted.'

> 'They just don't know how to behave. They drive the wrong cars, put up the wrong curtains, and create pretty front gardens that don't fit in.'

> 'The problem with these people is that they're working on a Sunday – you know, cleaning their cars, and mowing the lawns. They shouldn't do it on a Sunday – they should be in chapel.'
> (quoted in Cloke et al., 1997, p. 155)

These remarks hint at the 'gentrification' occurring in some Welsh villages, as people from different class backgrounds and with different tastes settle among local families with closer ties to traditional rural society. Because the great majority of these incomers are English, they add an ethnic and national dimension to local social relationships. Their presence can be especially disruptive in those areas that are Welsh-speaking, because many incomers are reluctant to learn Welsh and so cannot enter into more traditional Welsh activities and organisations (like the remaining Welsh-speaking chapels). Simply by being there, they increase the pressures towards making English the dominant language and contribute to the erosion of *Y Fro Gymraeg* as a distinctive linguistic and cultural region.

The gradual retreat and fragmentation of this part of Wales have been documented in poignant detail by social geographers (Aitchison and Carter, 2000), and unsurprisingly there has been vigorous opposition to these developments, in the name of the language and of the communities associated with it. One group, Cymuned (Community), has made its objective the defence of communities in which Welsh is held to be the 'natural' language, arguing for measures to restrict further inward migration and to encourage incomers to learn the language and adapt themselves to living in a Welsh environment. Cymuned aspires to seeing the counties of north-west Wales revert to something like the old *Y Fro Gymraeg*: a region within which daily life, including time at school, could if one wished be conducted wholly in Welsh.

The strength of feeling about these issues is a reminder that definitions of place and belonging are charged with emotion, and have political as well as social and cultural significance. Cymuned's battle on behalf of Welsh-speaking communities, and ultimately to defend a certain ideal of what it is to be Welsh, resembles the action taken by support groups during the miners' strike to defend the established way of life of their communities. In both cases, those involved were pursuing aims going well beyond merely local issues, since they implied beliefs about what make a 'good' community and a 'proper' Welsh existence. The passion behind their commitment shows how much it matters to people how the social map of Wales is drawn, and redrawn over time by forces of social and economic change.

Summary

- Wales has seen huge social and economic changes since 1945, epitomised by the loss of its mining industry.

- Parts of the country, such as the south Wales Valleys, have suffered real deprivation as a result.

- Other areas, especially Cardiff, have experienced considerable regeneration.

- Rural Wales has seen a decline in farming and an expansion in tourism and the leisure industry, with an influx of 'incomers' impacting on traditional community life.

5   Conclusion

The themes considered in this chapter come together in a comment made by two academics, reflecting on the continuing importance of community and language in Welsh political life, and therefore on the sort of response a movement like Cymuned can inspire. From our point of view, what is noteworthy is the way it unites elements of physical and social geography ('land' and 'community') with references to language, culture and identity, to present a statement about Wales in terms of its 'beating heart'. Like several of the views we have met, it also implies an argument about what it is to be truly ('authentically') Welsh:

> In Wales, 'heartland communities' ... provide a powerful focus for policy initiatives developed in their name. The phrase appeals to a

hierarchy of presumed cultural authenticity, distinguishing a set
of favoured enclaves where the 'heart' of Wales beats loudest.
These communities are rooted most deeply in the 'land' of Wales,
building on a productive association between supposed national
distinctiveness or identity and images of gwlad – 'land', as in
Hen Wlad Fy Nhadau, the 'Land of My Fathers' of the Welsh national
anthem. Phrases like 'Welsh-speaking communities' or even the
innocent-sounding 'small communities' tap into a familiar ideological
seam of meaning which predisposes us to find intense cultural value
in communities, often with the idea of the Welsh language embedded
in this idea.

(Coupland and Bishop, 2006, p. 36)

This brief survey of the social significance of some of the distinctions of
place and belonging that exist within Wales suggests that rather than a
single answer to the question 'Where can one be authentically Welsh?',
or even a neatly ordered hierarchy from 'more to less Welsh' places,
several versions of Welshness compete for space with one another. All of
them are subject to change, and this makes it hard to define fixed or
sharply drawn boundaries between them.

There are some major social processes at work, such as the ever-growing
rate of personal mobility, which tend to undermine the distinctiveness
of place and weaken the identity of communities. One way in which
people react to these forces is to insist, sometimes more strongly than
ever, on the need to protect and defend their existing communities and
social relationships, and what they stand for. In Wales, we can see many
examples of people defending ideas of community and identity that
seem to be under threat.

During the last half-century or so, Wales has witnessed some staggering
social and economic changes. Yet this should not blind us to the
existence of certain continuities as well. In a rare example of a return to
an earlier study, researchers from Swansea have repeated some of the
work done by Rosser and Harris (1965) and discovered that substantial
numbers of people (59 per cent of the sample studied) continue to live
the greater part of their lives in the town (Charles and Davies, 2005).
Among these, it was still possible to find strong family connections and
shared experiences; for example, people who had been to school
together, worked together and lived in the same neighbourhoods. This
high level of residential stability enabled the formation of some close-
knit locally based networks. Membership of this kind of network is often
felt to be a particularly Welsh characteristic, and makes people feel
especially Welsh. In other words, 'community' lives on in the experience
of many Swansea people. However, undoubtedly there are also very
many Welsh people who experience nothing like this degree of stability

and closeness, because their lives are far more mobile and changeable. Our understanding of modern Wales has to be able to take into account both of these kinds of experience, and the contrasting perceptions of Welshness they create.

Finally, it should be noted how at various points in this chapter you have come up against the gap between communities as they really are, and as they are thought to be. The respondents to Cloke et al.'s (1997) rural research, for instance, who sought to regulate the type of cars, curtains or gardens their neighbours had, to conform with an idea of what a proper Welsh community should be like, are drawing lines around what they feel is acceptable in order to belong. This tells us a great deal about how they imagine their community should be, but not always much about how it actually is. After all, it is not only 'foreign' or English incomers who don't feel it is necessary to go to chapel, or to avoid cleaning their cars on a Sunday; most of their Welsh neighbours feel exactly the same. The person who complained about the lack of proper Sunday observance seems to have in mind a form of Welshness appropriate to the time of the classic community studies, but which vanished long ago as a reflection of how most Welsh people actually live. A hard-won lesson of research on questions of place, community and belonging is the need to take care not to allow nostalgic or romanticised impressions of life in the past to hide the real character and quality of life found in places and communities today.

References

Adamson, D. (2008) 'Still living on the edge?,' *Contemporary Wales,* vol. 21, pp. 47–66.

Adamson, D. (1996) *Living on the Edge? Poverty and Deprivation in Wales,* Llandysul, Gomer.

Aitchison, J. and Carter, H. (2000) *Language, Economy and Society: The Changing Fortunes of the Welsh Language in the Twentieth Century,* Cardiff, University of Wales Press.

Balsom, D. (1985) 'The three-Wales model' in Osmond, J. (ed.) *The National Question Again,* Llandysul, Gomer.

Bell, C. (1968) *Middle Class Families: Social and Geographical Mobility,* London, Routledge, Kegan & Paul.

Bulmer, M. (1975) 'Sociological models of the mining community', *Sociological Review,* vol. 23, pp. 61–93.

Campbell, B. (1993) *Goliath: Britain's Dangerous Places,* London, Methuen.

Carter, H. (1996) 'Foreword: *Life in a Welsh Countryside*: a retrospect', to
A. D. Rees, *Life in a Welsh Countryside* (reissue), Cardiff, University of Wales Press.

Charles N. and Davies C. A. (2005) 'Studying the particular, illuminating the
general: community studies and community in Wales', *Sociological Review*,
vol. 53, no. 4, pp. 672–90.

Cloke, P., Goodwin, M. and Milbourne, P. (1997) *Rural Wales: Community and
Marginalization*, Cardiff, University of Wales Press.

Coupland, N. and Bishop, H. (2006) 'Ideologies of language and community in
post-devolution Wales' in Wilson, J. and Stapleton, K. (eds) *Devolution and
Identity*, Aldershot, Ashgate.

Day, G. (2006) *Community and Everyday Life*, London, Routledge.

Dicks, B. (2000) *Heritage, Place and Community*, Cardiff, University of Wales Press.

Emmett, I. (1982) 'Place, community and bilingualism in Blaenau Ffestiniog' in
Cohen, A. (ed.) *Belonging: Identity and Social Organisation in British Rural Cultures*,
Manchester, Manchester University Press.

Emmett, I. (1964) *A North Wales Village*, London, Routledge & Kegan Paul.

Fevre, R. and Thompson, A. (eds) (1999) *Nation, Identity and Social Theory*, Cardiff,
University of Wales Press.

Frankenberg R. (1957) *Village on the Border: a Social Study of Religion, Politics and
Football in a North Wales Community*, London, Cohen and West.

Gruffudd, P. (1999) 'Prospects of Wales: contested geographical imaginations'
in Fevre and Thompson (eds) (1999).

Jones, N. (1993) *Living in Rural Wales*, Llandysul, Gomer.

Jones, P. N. (2004) 'A valley community in transition: Ynysybwl in 1967', *Llafur*,
vol. 9, no. 1, pp. 85–94.

Jones, S. (2003) 'Supporting the team, sustaining the community: gender and
rugby in a former mining village' in Davies, C. A. and Jones, S. (eds) *Welsh
Communities: New Ethnographic Perspectives*, Cardiff, University of Wales Press.

Morgan, K. (2007) 'Cardiff and the valleys: the rise of a new city region?', *Llafur*,
vol. 9, no. 4, pp. 125–40.

Rees, A. D. (1950) *Life in a Welsh Countryside*, Cardiff, University of Wales Press.

Roberts, B. (1999) 'Welsh identity in a former mining valley' in Fevre and
Thompson (eds) (1999).

Rosser, C. and Harris, C. C. (1965) *Family and Social Change: a Study of Swansea*,
London, Routledge.

Thomas, H. (1999) 'Spatial restructuring in the capital: struggles to shape Cardiff's built environment' in Fevre and Thompson (eds) (1999).

Welsh Assembly Government (2008) *People, Places, Futures: the Wales Spatial Plan Update 2008*, Cardiff, WAG.

Welsh Assembly Government (2004) *People, Places, Futures: the Wales Spatial Plan*, Cardiff, WAG.

Further reading

There is a revealing account of how the map of Wales was redrawn so as to qualify for European assistance in Kevin Morgan's article 'How objective 1 arrived in Wales: the political origins of a coup', *Contemporary Wales*, vol. 15, 2002, pp. 20–30. This includes some discussion of how people use mental maps.

Together with Adam Price, Morgan sets out the case for west Wales in *The Other Wales*, Cardiff, Institute of Welsh Affairs, 1998.

Harold Carter's 'Foreword' to the 1996 reissue of Alwyn D. Rees, *Life in a Welsh Countryside* (listed in the References) discusses both the context for the original study and subsequent developments in community studies and how they reflect key social changes.

Michael Sullivan discusses the importance of community for people in south Wales in his chapter on 'Communities and social policy' in R. Jenkins and A. Edwards (eds), *One Step Forward? South and West Wales towards the Year 2000*, Llandysul, Gomer, 1990.

Paul Cloke et al.'s *Rural Wales: Community and Marginalization* (listed in the References) pp. 16ff deals with ideas of Welsh identity and in-migration; pp. 156ff. discuss the idea of community and how people interpret it.

Chapter 3
Work

Dave Adamson

Contents

1   Introduction

This chapter examines the world of work in Wales. Its key objective is to develop an understanding of the relationship between economic change in Wales and the patterns of work and employment that have emerged in the period since the Second World War. The Welsh economy has evolved rapidly during this period and working life has changed with it. Industries and activities that once dominated the Welsh economy have virtually disappeared and **economic globalisation** and technological innovation have brought new patterns of work and employment. Major changes have occurred in the structure of the workforce and in the working conditions that people experience.

Economic globalisation is a process in which local and national economies become integrated into a global system of exchange and trade

The aims of this chapter are to enable you to:

- map the outlines of the changing economic structure in Wales

- understand the key outcomes in regard to work experience in Wales

- gain an insight into some of the social consequences of a changing economic and work climate.

We begin by considering the shape and nature of the contemporary economy in Wales and the patterns of work that emerge from it. An understanding of the current strengths and weaknesses of the Welsh economy is essential in order to make sense of much of the social, cultural and political life in Wales. One of the primary tasks of the Welsh Assembly Government is to provide a strong economic footing for the achievement of many of its social and cultural objectives. However, there are key structural weaknesses in the Welsh economy that present major challenges to Wales achieving affluence and prosperity comparable to the wider UK experience.

We shall now outline these challenges before tracing the historical patterns that created them.

2   Economy and work in contemporary Wales

This section provides a review of the current Welsh economy and world of work.

Activity 3.1

Take a moment to reflect on what images you might already have of work in Wales.

- Think of representations of working lives in Wales in film and literature.

- Also think about how the Welsh economy is presented in the news media.

- Write down three dominant images you associate with work and employment in Wales.

Comment

I can say with almost certainty that one of your images will be of a miner with helmet and Davy lamp, or perhaps black-faced and cloth-capped. A second image might be that of a steelworker, silhouetted against the glow of a furnace and sparks of molten steel. A third might be that of a solitary sheep farmer, carving a meagre existence high in the hills of north Wales. Did you also think of a Welsh 'Mam', perhaps picturing her in sepia brown, leaning in the doorway of her 'little palace', whose work in the domestic realm underpins the more visible labour of her menfolk?

In many ways these have become stereotypical images of Wales, replicated in literature, art, film, photography and television. However, the modern Welsh economy is a diverse and complex mix of activities which range from heavy industrial production to industries characterised by innovative uses of high technology. Wales remains one of the UK regions and nations with the highest dependence on manufacturing industry and, although the significance of steel manufacturing and heavy fabrication has declined, other forms of industrial manufacturing have taken their place. Some of the high-profile modern activities include the manufacture of European Airbus aircraft wings at Broughton in north Wales and the production of car engines at Bridgend in south Wales. The policy of attracting inward investment to Wales has ensured the presence of the manufacture of textiles, electronics, automotive components and consumer goods. Consequently, for many people in Wales the experience of work centres on a factory, with over 12 per cent of the workforce employed in manufacturing processes.

However, recent trends have seen a shift in the dominance of manufacturing, as this has fallen from being the second largest sector in 2001 to the fourth largest in 2007. The largest sector of the economy has, since the late 1990s, been the distribution sector – made up of the retail, wholesale, motor trades and repairs businesses. This certainly reflects the increasing role of out-of-town shopping parks, which have become one of the most visible forms of economic change in Wales. Here the dominant work experience is part-time or casual employment, with wages close to the UK minimum wage. Finance and business activities are now the largest sources of employment in Wales, a major departure from the industrial past associated with the Welsh economy. Much of this employment is in back office and administration as well as in call centres, providing customer support for major banks and insurance companies. Here the work experience is one of routinised administration, with little personal autonomy and correspondingly low wages. The work may be defined as 'white-collar', but it shares many of the characteristics of factory work.

Economists often group sectors such as health, education, retail and finance under the general heading of 'the service sector'. Now over 77 per cent of jobs in Wales lie within this element of the economy. Table 3.1 shows the distribution (in 2007) of employment in the different industrial groups in Wales.

Table 3.1 Workforce employment in Wales by industry, 2007

Industrial sector	Numbers in thousands	% of total
Agriculture, hunting, forestry and fishing	38	2.8
Mining and quarrying	2	0.2
Manufacturing	168	12.4
Energy and water	5	0.4
Construction	100	7.4
Retail, wholesale, motor trades and repairs	215	15.9
Hotels and restaurants	92	6.8
Transport, storage and communications	61	4.6
Finance and business activities	191	14.1
Public administration	93	6.8
Education	123	9.0
Health	184	13.6
Other industries	82	6.0

Source: Welsh Assembly Government Statistical Directorate (2009, p. 4, Table 1)

Gross value added (GVA) represents the value of the goods and services produced per head before taxes and subsidies are considered. When the latter are added, the total is referred to as gross domestic product (GDP).

Three key problems facing the contemporary Welsh economy can be identified (Bryan and Roche, 2009). The first of these is Wales's consistent underperformance in comparison with the majority of other UK regions. The economic output of a region is usually measured in terms of its **gross value added (GVA)**.

Wales currently produces goods and services at only 75 per cent of the GVA for the UK, with the Isle of Anglesey and the Gwent Valleys measuring lowest at 56 per cent and 58 per cent, respectively. This gap is also gradually widening despite the major European Union (EU) investment of structural funds. The European Regional Development Fund (ERDF) and European Social Fund, together with match funding, spent some £3.2 billion on the Objective 1 programme to develop the Welsh economy between 2001 and 2006. Qualification for ERDF funds relies on gross domestic product (GDP) in Wales being below 75 per cent of the UK average. This has been described as 'a badge of failure' (Hill, 2000, p. 1); it marks Wales as one of the poorest regions in Europe prior to the recent addition of the eastern European succession states. Regrettably, the use of this initial round of European funding did not significantly change the level of GDP in Wales and a new round of funding, totalling £3.5 billion, was allocated for 2007–2013. Now referred to as 'convergence funding', this is being deployed more strategically than the Objective 1 programme. With Convergence funding, the WAG plays a central role in how the money is used, in contrast to the more devolved model that saw local government and third-sector organisations heavily involved.

However, despite such interventions the economic performance in Wales remains poor. A key reason for this is the second major problem in the contemporary Welsh economy: the low employment rate. This figure is distinct from the unemployment rate, which simply measures the numbers of people seeking work. Instead, the employment rate measures those in work as a proportion of the full population of working age. The employment rate informs us about all forms of economic inactivity, including unemployment, premature retirement and those prevented from working by illness or incapacity. Wales consistently has the lowest employment rate in the UK, with the exception of the north-east of England. This simply means that more people of working age in Wales are economically inactive and are not currently seeking work. This is a critical weakness in the Welsh economy and prevents improvements in output. The social consequences of high rates of economic inactivity are explored later in this chapter.

The final key problem in the Welsh economy is the general prevalence of lower wage levels than elsewhere in the UK (see Figure 3.1). Although there is variation between different sectors of the economy, the overall pattern is that average earnings in Wales reach only 88 per cent of the UK level. In the UK in April 2007, average gross weekly earnings were £456.70, in comparison with the Welsh average of £404.70 (Bryan and Roche, 2009). In April 2008 this had risen to £478.60 in the UK generally and to £412.00 in Wales, demonstrating a slight widening of the gap. Low wages have become the primary cause of poverty in Wales, rather than unemployment – which triggered poverty for the majority of people in the 1990s. However, the effects of the recession that began in 2007 have yet to be seen in the statistical evidence on poverty and it is likely that unemployment will return as a major cause of poverty.

Figure 3.1

Low-paid work in the Welsh service industry

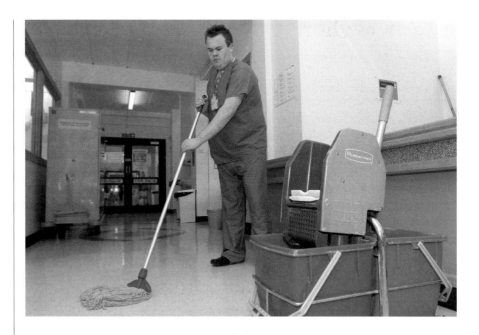

To return to our images of Wales and the pattern of work, we can see that the economy of Wales is now far more complex than we might have imagined and that there are core structural problems in the Welsh economy which present major challenges for the government in Wales, but most critically for the people who experience worklessness and low wages. The images of miners, steelworkers and farmers no longer adequately describe the contemporary world of work and employment in Wales. The image of the Welsh 'Mam' also belongs in the past, as the economic activity rates of women continue to rise. In order to fully understand the transformations that have taken place it is necessary to trace the major changes in economic activity in Wales since the Second World War. The economy we experience today and the patterns of work we observe are the legacy of major processes of economic and social change. These are considered in the next section of this chapter.

Summary

- The manufacturing industry remains significant in Wales, although it has been overtaken in importance by the distribution and finance sectors.

- The service sector is now the biggest employer in Wales.

- Despite funding from the EU, Wales is one of the poorest regions in Europe.

- Wales has the lowest employment rate in the UK.

- Low wages are a primary cause of poverty in Wales.

3   The evolution of the Welsh economy

The stereotypical images presented in the previous section of the chapter have some foundation in reality. It is the very real history of work in Wales that has given rise to these powerful images which have survived long after the social and work conditions that created them. Wales was at the forefront of the industrial revolution, and the twin industries of coal mining and metal production drove not only the Welsh but also the UK economy for over a century and a half.

This section looks in detail at the economic and work trends that have been evident in Wales since the end of the Second World War, a period that has seen a radical transformation of UK society and economy. In Wales these changes had a significant impact on patterns of work and associated family and community life. By the 1950s there was a buoyancy and optimism about the future economy and prosperity of Wales.

Activity 3.2

Read Extract 3.1, which describes south Wales's economy in the mid 1960s.

- Identify the key reasons for the optimism described.

- Note the problems pointed to in the last paragraph and assess their implications for the contemporary economy.

Extract 3.1

South Wales in the 1960s

The last twenty years have been remarkable ones for the [south Wales] region in many ways. The inertia and gloom of the pre-war depression have disappeared, the basic industries have been modernised almost beyond recognition, the highest annual level of unemployment has been around 4 per cent compared with 38 per cent in the depths of the depression, emigration has been considerably reduced, and jobs have been significantly diversified through the introduction of new and expanding industries and services. 'The redevelopment of South Wales has been one of the great success stories of the past thirty years', commented a *Times* leader in March 1963, and two years later the *Investors Chronicle* (9 April, 1965) spoke of 'the spirit of confidence one finds among the industrialists, the businessmen, the financial community (in South Wales)'. The Sunday colour supplements have 'covered' the area: 'South Wales likes to spend. It has never had money before. It has waited a long time. It is determined to enjoy'. ...

There are some reflections of truth in this new image of South Wales, but it is also true that the salad days of the steel industry appear to be over. Away from the prosperous costal strip, the coal industry is reducing manpower rapidly. In the economic downturn after the credit squeeze of July 1966 the percentage of unemployed in Wales rose higher than in all other regions except Northern Ireland. Too much of the post-war industrial growth has resulted from government protection rather than from a positive desire by industrialists to move to the area. After thirty years of policies designed to strengthen its economy, South Wales still has one of the highest unemployment rates in Britain, low activity rates, continuing migration, and too limited a range of labour skills. These problems and their solutions do not come readymade. They are inevitably influenced by the physical resources, industrial history, and economic characteristics of the region.

Source: Humphrys, 1972, pp 12–14.

Comment

The overall optimism in the UK at this time clearly influenced feelings in Wales and it is perhaps only in retrospect, writing in the early 1970s, that Graham Humphrys, the author of Extract 3.1, was able to identify some of the weaknesses in the Welsh economy, even at this time of prosperity. You will also have noticed that these are the very weaknesses that continue to affect the Welsh economy.

I grew up in this period in a south Wales that enjoyed full employment and the rising affluence of the post-war reconstruction period. Perhaps epitomised by Harold Macmillan's phrase 'You've never had it so good', deployed in the 1959 general election campaign, the period saw British society emerging from the privations of war rationing into a time characterised by the greatest levels of economic equality and social mobility experienced in its history. On the large council estate where I grew up, men were employed in local mines, factories and steelworks, while women remained largely confined to their domestic role of managing the household. The rite of passage to adulthood for men was marked by their entry into the world of work; the influence of their chosen occupation on their self-identity was fundamental. For women, adulthood arrived with marriage and motherhood (not always in that order) and the establishment of a family unit which had its foundation in the pattern of work that for over a century had been dominated by male occupations in mining, steel production and heavy manufacturing.

These work patterns created powerful social and political identities linked to lifestyles that shaped the culture of industrial Wales.

Fifty years later Wales is a very different place, with radically transformed patterns of work and forms of family and social life shaped by different experiences in the workplace and wider society. In that fifty years the industries that had dominated Wales for over one and a half centuries have all but disappeared. Coal mining, steel making, heavy manufacturing and agriculture have given way to light manufacturing, electronics, media, tourism and financial and service industries, although manufacturing remains a component of the Welsh economy. The work patterns associated with the coal and steel industries in particular have been replaced by factory, office and shop working. Agriculture in rural Wales is creating roles for farming communities more associated with tourism and a stewardship of the landscape than with animal husbandry and food production.

This transition of the Welsh economy and associated patterns of work has been a highly complex process, as successive changes in the Welsh economy have promoted specific industries only to see them replaced with new alternatives as global economic forces make themselves felt in Wales. Textiles in the 1960s, electronics in the 1970s, service industries in the 1980s, financial services in the 1990s and call centres in the 2000s: all illustrate the waves of economic change that have washed over the Welsh workforce. As in other parts of the old industrial Britain, adapting to change has become a speciality of Welsh workers.

The historical Welsh economy with its traditional patterns of work has made way for increasing diversification of economic activity. In order to understand the detail of the complex process of transformation in the Welsh economy, it is useful to break down the time since the Second World War into a number of periods when certain patterns of change tended to dominate. There are of course no clear dividing lines between these periods; rather they represent the times when the central features of the Welsh economy and the pattern of work associated with it changed in balance and character. At key times, a point is reached when a new set of conditions outweighs the preceding set.

The three periods are:

■ industrial Wales: 1945–75

■ modernising Wales: 1976–95

■ post-industrial Wales: 1996 to the present

3.1 Industrial Wales: 1945–1975

The first of these periods represents the establishment of the modern economy in Wales, characterised by increasing state involvement, both in public ownership of industry and in the development of major public services. The period also witnessed a process of diversification of economic activity and the emergence of new patterns of production alongside the already declining coal and steel industries.

Figure 3.2

Two miners lighting a cigarette after a shift down a mine in Tonypandy, 1955

The **Labour settlement** refers to the development of the welfare system and the nationalisation of industries by the Labour government from 1945 to 1951.

The election of a Labour government in 1945 signified a radical mood in the aftermath of the war which aspired to a more egalitarian and open society than the hierarchical class divisions of the inter-war years. In a programme of legislation often referred to as the post-war **Labour settlement**, the government instigated a twin approach to the transformation of British society. First, a raft of social reforms established the Social Security system, the National Health Service (NHS) and free education for all. Based on the 1942 Beveridge Report, the new welfare state established a safety net to protect British citizens from the 'cradle to the grave'. On the economic front the government also introduced a rapid programme of nationalisation of what were seen as the 'commanding heights' of the economy. The coal industry, steel production, the utilities and later the transport industries were all brought into state ownership. This process was instigated in part in realisation of the original Clause 4 of the Labour Party constitution and its belief in state ownership, and partly in the belief that key industries were too important to the rest of the economy to risk in private hands.

Both of these aspects of the Labour settlement had an enormous impact on the Welsh economy and the employment patterns of those working in key industries in Wales. The creation of the welfare state expanded employment in the massive support structures required for universal health care and mass education. The Education Act 1945 provided the right to free education for all children up to the age of 15, creating considerable demand throughout the UK for teachers to staff the extended school system. It is often said that Wales's major export in the 1950s was of teachers into the wider UK education system. The establishment of the NHS in 1945 also created a wide range of secure jobs, from direct medical personnel to the support staff required in a large-scale heath service. At the same time local government was expanding in size and in the range of functions it performed in society and contributed significantly to employment in the personal and social services it was establishing at that time. Therefore, it is easy to see how in this immediate post-war period the state emerged as the largest employer in Wales. This prompted Humphrys to comment that Wales was 'the closest to a nationalised region that existed in Britain' (Humphrys, 1972, p. 64).

The passing of key industries from private to state ownership also had a huge political significance for the trade union movement in Wales and was seen as introducing a new era of higher wages, better working conditions, improved workplace safety and generous pensions on retirement. This gave a huge political and social confidence to the working class in Wales. It also brought comparative affluence and provided the basis for new consumption patterns associated with the highly paid workers in the key industries. The programme of nationalisation ensured that a pattern of secure lifetime employment developed for workers in the new state sector. Additionally, a secure economic base in the hands of the state had associated effects in private industry as companies emerged to supply the state sector with the ancillary products and services required to secure coal and steel production.

This immediate post-war period has been extensively commented on by academics. Most notably, the 'affluent worker' thesis identified a process in which working-class male employees began to enjoy relatively high wages and to establish patterns of consumption based on a more privatised family model. This included home and car ownership and possession of consumer durable goods (Goldthorpe et al., 1969). The post-war period has also been seen as a 'golden age' as welfare provision, healthcare, universal education and high levels of employment transformed the lives of workers in the UK in comparison with the common experience before the war (Hobsbawm, 1994).

Many of the new employment opportunities in the emerging state bureaucracies and services were filled by the products of the new education system itself. The opening up of grammar schools to children from working-class backgrounds through the 11-plus 'scholarship' examination filtered what were seen as the most able working-class children in to an education which prepared them for senior roles in the developing state sector as well as the expanding private sector. For those who failed the iniquitous 11-plus exam, a passage through secondary modern school into trades and skilled occupations in the coal, steel and manufacturing industries secured lifetime pensionable patterns of employment. Many cohorts of workers entering the labour market in the 1950s and 1960s subsequently retired on good pensions and a financially secure passage through old age. These conditions were the basis for the optimism evident in Humphrys' account of the period in Extract 3.1.

However, the caveats towards the end of Extract 3.1 also point to some of the fundamental weaknesses of the Welsh economy which were to emerge within two years of Humphrys' description of the boom years of the modernising economy.

The 'golden age' identified by Hobsbawm (1994) was severely shaken by the oil crisis of 1973–4 which demonstrated the fragility of the economies of the developed nations and their dependence on imported crude oil. Often seen as the trigger of inflation in the UK economy, this point in history is marked as the first sign of the economic crisis that was to destabilise the British economy for the next ten years. By 1975 the British economy was demonstrating symptoms of severe structural weakness.

3.2 Modernising Wales: 1976–1995

The late 1970s saw the rate of inflation rise dramatically at the same time as economic growth stagnated. This combination triggered a considerable economic crisis which prompted the Labour government of then Prime Minister James Callaghan to attempt to curb inflation with a public sector pay freeze. The resulting conflict with the trade unions and the disruption to public services that followed became known as the winter of discontent (1978–9). Major public services collapsed and the disruption to social and public life set the scene for the election of a Conservative government with a radical agenda to reform the British economy and curb the power of the trade unions.

This period reflects the impact of a major economic crisis which became intertwined with radical political change in the UK. In 1979, for the first time since the Second World War, the newly elected Conservative government abandoned the **Keynesian** economic policy which had prioritised full employment, and instead adopted a neo-liberal approach to politics which saw the key priority as the reduction of inflation. The doctrine of neo-liberalism adopted by the government of Margaret Thatcher held that the state had grown too large in the post-war period and had taken on too many roles in society. Alongside this, trade union power was seen as challenging the efficiency of the economy.

Together, these factors were believed to be preventing the free market from working efficiently. As a consequence, policies were pursued which reduced the role of the state and related public expenditure and that promoted major cuts in public services. This occurred at a time of economic recession when the economy was already contracting. This combination of ideological, political and economic factors caused high levels of unemployment and the effective shrinking of the state. There was also a general collapse of key industries like mining, steel production and heavy manufacturing, which had an enormous impact on the patterns of work in the old industrial areas such as south Wales.

There is a considerable body of opinion in Wales that many of the policies of the period derived from old antagonisms between the Conservative Party and organised labour, and that the reductions of capacity in coal and steel were symptomatic of a desire to reduce the influence of the historically powerful trade unions associated with these industries. A historical overview, however, demonstrates that similar policies were followed in other coal- and steel-producing economies in Europe, including France and Germany. In part this was caused by the pursuit of neo-liberal policies across the developed nations, but it was also the result of overproduction in both coal and steel at a time of worldwide recession. Consequently, it can be concluded that the major economic problems of the time resulted in part from global economic circumstances and in part from the specific response of a UK government influenced by a strong belief in a small state, vehemently opposed to economic interventionism and naturally predisposed to reducing the role of the state and associated public expenditure.

The major issue for us here is the huge impact of this period on the Welsh economy, the availability of work and the resulting challenge to the integrity and social sustainability of many communities in Wales, which effectively lost almost all sources of livelihood and employment. This impact is considered further in Section 5 of this chapter.

Keynesianism refers to John Maynard Keynes's approach to managing the economy, practised by governments from 1945 until Thatcher's policy of monetarism in the 1980s. The core of Keynesianism is to reduce the impact of the economic cycle of boom and bust by using taxation and government spending to either slow or stimulate the economy.

3.3 Post-industrial Wales: 1996 to the present

The third period is characterised by economic recovery and significant reduction in the unemployment rate, together with a raft of UK policies to renew state responsibility for economic management and to redefine the welfare responsibilities of government. However, the election of a Labour government in 1997 did not see a simple return to the pre-Thatcherite policies of 'Old Labour'. Rather, policy was developed from a perspective characterised by 'New Labour' and a policy programme referred to collectively as the 'Third Way'. This was an attempt to avoid both the excesses of state ownership and the uncontrolled effects of the free market. The Third Way balanced ideas of state responsibility with those of the obligations of citizens to work and provide for themselves. Policies such as the New Deal programme promoted the return to work of people who had experienced long-term unemployment and provided a range of support mechanisms to ease the passage from welfare to work.

The political change also coincided with the upturn in the economy that had been building from the mid 1990s. The wider British economy experienced a long period of sustained growth, and unemployment fell significantly from a peak of 13 per cent in 1984 to a low of 4.1 per cent in early 2008. This period saw the level of unemployment in Wales fall below the UK average for the first time. Despite this, the legacy of the 1980s has ensured that significant numbers of people in Wales remain economically inactive, with a continued problem of high levels of Incapacity Benefit claimants.

This brings us to the pattern of economic production outlined at the start of this chapter. It is during this period that we see the major diversification of the economy leading to the complex patterns of employment described above. Now we can identify major nodes of economic growth along the M4 corridor in south Wales and the A55 in north Wales. Key developments in manufacturing include aircraft components manufacture and aircraft servicing, automotive components and car engine production and electronics manufacturing. These were matched in the service sector by developments in the retail, leisure and tourism industries, call centres and financial services sector. Wales also excels in the development of the creative and cultural industries, with international successes in film, television and music production. Much of this development has focused on Cardiff and the establishment of a nexus of production for S4C, BBC and ITV (this is discussed further in Chapter 10). It is also in this period that the term 'the knowledge economy' came into use to define the development of research and product development in 'high-tech' industries associated with information and communications technology, pharmaceutical and medical products and future 'green' technologies.

Figure 3.3
Dr Who in Cardiff

This period also sees perhaps the most fundamental political change, in the form of devolution in 1997 and the creation of the WAG. Economic development is a devolved area of policy and for the first time the steer and management of the Welsh economy are located in Wales. Key policy documents (WAG, 2002; 2005; 2007) have defined the vision for a Welsh economy which promotes prosperity and equality and the eradication of poverty. The WAG has firmly linked economic policy to social policy, and the promotion of economic development is seen in terms of its regenerative capacity and its ability to challenge the long-term inequalities between regions in Wales and to increase the prosperity of Wales in comparison with the UK as a whole.

The division of the post-war period into three key phases helps to delineate times of major change and to categorise the pattern of the Welsh economy into critical phases. However, as well as the major shifts in economic activity in Wales there have also been a number of themes that have remained constant. The next section examines a number of processes which have in many ways been a constant response to the changing economic context in Wales and are still evident in the evolution of work in Wales.

Summary

- The period 1945–75 was characterised by the nationalisation of key industries and the development of major public services, leading to an expansion in jobs and comparative affluence in Wales.

- The period 1976–95 saw high unemployment, a great reduction in state ownership and a collapse of heavy industries such as mining and steel production; many communities in Wales lost their livelihoods.

- The period from 1996 to the present has seen an economic recovery, with unemployment rates in Wales falling and new industries being set up.

4   Work in Wales: key features in the post-1945 period

The last section considered the different phases of the development of the Welsh economy since the Second World War. Evident in each of these periods are several key processes which continue to shape the response of the Welsh economy to changing global economic conditions. This section identifies these key processes and will help you understand some of the social patterns of change that have occurred.

4.1 Decline of the traditional industrial base

The first of these is the decline of the primary industries which so centrally defined the opening years of this period. To understand this process we begin with a brief examination of the coal industry.

Activity 3.3

Read Extract 3.2, which describes the conditions affecting coal production in the period 1979–87. As you read, identify the combination of global pressures and the specific conditions of the south Wales coalfield.

Extract 3.2

The decline of coal production in south Wales

The period of 1979–84 was notable for several developments. Firstly a severe contraction in economic activity depressed the total energy market considerably. Second, the world price of coal fell and imports became much more competitive with NCB [National Coal Board] coal. Third, a much harder line was taken by the Conservative government and the NCB over pit closures.

Between 1979/80 and 1982/83 *total* energy consumption fell from 350 million tonnes of coal equivalent to 310 million tonnes, and consumption of coal itself from 128 million tonnes to just 110 million tonnes. In south Wales the main effect of the slump was ... in the market for coking coal, where demand fell by over a third. With over half of south Wales's pits producing coking coal this hit the coalfield very hard ...

Initially, attempts in 1981 by the Conservative government to push through a period of rapid pit closures were thwarted by the National Union of Mineworkers (NUM) with industrial action. Eight pits were closed in the south Wales coalfield through this period, five of them in 1983/84. Further plans surfaced when the Board let it be known that it wanted to speed up closures and shed 20,000 of its 175,000 labour force, closing 4 million tonnes of capacity. This was the starting point for the 1984/85 strike.

The strike lasted over a year at considerable cost to the miners, the NCB and the economy. When it finally collapsed in March 1985 the NCB was able to proceed with its restructuring plans with little opposition.

Source: George et al., 1988, pp. 163–7

Extract 3.2 outlines the decline in the market for coal as well as the pit closures in the south Wales coalfield. It also mentions the 1984–5 miners' strike. Although the final demise of coal production occurred after this strike, the industry had long been in decline. Coal production peaked in 1913 with 57 million tons; a figure which constituted 40 per cent of British coal production. The particular value of Welsh 'steam' coal was its clean burning characteristics and high calorific output, which had been in particular demand during the age of steam. Additionally, the anthracite coals from the west of the Welsh coalfield had been particularly suited to domestic use in an era when domestic heating was almost exclusively provided by coal burning. However, as electrification of industry occurred, and with the development of oil-burning engines in the British naval and merchant fleets, the demand for coal fell considerably even before the First World War. The number of miners employed at the peak of production was 280,000 and this had declined to 100,000 in 1947 at the point of nationalisation (George et al., 1988).

Further decline in the numbers employed in mining occurred continuously until the 1984–5 miners' strike. Table 3.2 charts the gradual demise of the industry.

Table 3.2 Deep-mine output and employment in the south Wales coalfield

	1960	1972–3	1979–80	1986–7
No. of pits	118	51	36	14
No. of wage earners	87,000	35,000	27,000	10,200
Saleable output (mn. tonnes)	19.4	11.0	7.6	6.5

Source: George et al., 1988, p. 161

A complex range of factors caused the fall in demand for coal in the post-war era. Notably, the development of nuclear power reinforced the generally falling demand for coal from industry. The rise of oil as a primary fuel in rail transport and manufacturing was mirrored in domestic consumption, which increasingly moved to smokeless fuels and, in particular, North Sea gas. Another challenge was the emergence of cheaper imported coal from countries including Germany, France and South Africa, which commanded more and more of the shrinking market. Additionally, falling steel production after 1973 further reduced the demand for coal as the twin pillars of the Welsh economy entered a parallel decline.

The process of decline in steel follows a different trajectory but arrives at a similar depressed state by the early 1980s. Steel production in Wales benefited from the general rise in domestic consumption during the 1960s and 1970s, providing steel and tinplate products for the car industry, the food industry and the manufacture of consumer durable goods. By 1975, steel production constituted 20.8 per cent of all manufacturing in Wales and employed nearly 70,000 workers. However, the period 1973–5 was to be a turning point for the fortunes of steel production in Wales, and between 1974 and 1984 over 50,000 steel jobs were lost (Baber and Mainwaring, 1988). Since 1984 there has been a more gradual but further loss of steel capacity. The most damaging aspect of the loss of jobs in the steel industry was the rapidity with which it occurred. The large number of job losses over such a short period of time made it difficult for the wider economy to absorb the redundant workers into other areas of economic activity. The loss of high-earning employment to the general economy created a multiplier effect which suggests that over half of all job losses in Wales between 1974 and 1986 resulted from the contraction of the steel industry (Baber and Mainwaring, 1988).

The combined losses of employment in coal and steel production had a devastating impact on the patterns of work in Wales. Both the industrial areas of south Wales and the smaller industrial enclave of north-east Wales saw the employment patterns of over a century largely disappear as the two principal industries declined.

While the decline of coal and steel production has led to major social and economic problems in the industrial communities of Wales, there has been a parallel decline in agriculture – with equally devastating consequences for rural communities. Although agriculture has long been in decline in Wales as a significant source of employment at the national level, its role in rural communities is far greater, for here it constitutes up to 10 per cent of employment. Its significance also goes beyond its role as a source of employment; it is a key component of rural life, contributing to cultural, linguistic and landscape reproduction. The industry has experienced major challenges in recent years. Perhaps best known are the crises associated with livestock infection with BSE in the 1980s and the foot and mouth epidemic of 2001. The latter episode also had a major impact on the tourism industry, as strict quarantine controls effectively barred visitors from the countryside. The complex interaction between farming and tourism is also underlined by the diversification of farming since 2000, with 20 per cent of farms reporting diversification activities in 2006/07.

As well as the rural problems associated with livestock infections, the general rural economic climate has presented challenges to Welsh farming. With the exception of parts of west Wales, the border areas and the Vale of Glamorgan, the majority of Welsh farms are relatively small and have not secured the economies of scale associated with modern agriculture. The region has also failed to derive major income from the European Union Common Agricultural Policy (CAP). Supermarket procurement policies have also ensured low farm prices, with particular consequences for the dairy-producing farms in Wales. Two key problems characterise the rural economy (Midmore et al., 1996). The first relates to the low wage levels, coupled with the higher costs of travel to work and to access public services. The second is a high rate of unemployment for young people and a consequent pattern of outward migration in which young people leave to seek employment in urban areas. This is exacerbated by the high costs of housing in rural areas, where house prices are inflated by the retirement- and second-homes markets, effectively pricing young people out of housing in their home communities. These problems are closely associated with falling farm incomes (these no longer support family employment) and a corresponding increased need for farming households to supplement their income through non-agricultural work.

In summary, the decline of the major historical industries in Wales has had a fundamental impact on the economy and work experience of the people of Wales. In both industrial and rural communities the pace of economic change has been rapid and has presented major challenges to patterns of work and social experiences which were taken for granted and formed the basis of the stereotypes considered earlier in this chapter. The reality of economic diversification is explored in the following section.

4.2 Diversification of the Welsh economy

The second key process evident in the changing Welsh economy is a gradual diversification, as government policy has sought to challenge the 'regional specialisation' that made Wales so dependent on two main industries.

> Thus it was possible in 1965 for Government to claim that, of the manufacturing industries listed in the Standard Industrial Classification (SIC), only three – sugar, jute and lace – were not listed in Wales. This increasing diversification was also shown in a very changed employment pattern from pre-World War II days: then the two out of every five employed males worked in coal, steel and tinplate, as compared with one in four in 1965.
>
> (Wanhill, 1980, p. 1)

This diversification had been consciously promoted by government since 1934, when the Special Areas Act brought assistance to the areas of highest unemployment in Wales. The Act created the industrial estate in Treforest, south Wales, which remains to this day an important source of employment. It also offered a range of incentives for companies relocating to Treforest and smaller factory sites at Dowlais, Cyfartha, Dinas, Cwmbran, Brynmawr and Ynyswen (Wanhill, 1980). This policy in many ways set the direction of later regional policy, with loans, grants and other inducements to promote a programme of relocation of employment within the UK. These same strategies formed the major approaches adopted by government in the late 1970s as an inducement for foreign direct investment (FDI), an issue returned to in the following section.

The over-dependence on two key industries had badly affected unemployment levels during the years of the Great Depression, and locations such as Merthyr Tydfil earned a reputation that persists to this day for high levels of unemployment and economic inactivity.

Consequently, much of government policy since the 1930s has attempted to overcome the persistent structural economic problems of Wales. In the immediate years after the Second World War the Special Areas Act was replaced with the Distribution of Industry Act 1945, establishing development areas which underlined the earlier practice of providing incentives for industrial development. One notable outcome of this policy was the establishment in 1948 of the Hoover factory at Merthyr Tydfil, where 2,000 people were employed manufacturing washing machines to meet the demand for consumer durable goods emerging in the UK at that time. The closure of this plant in 2009 signalled the end of this early attempt to bring employment to an area characterised by high unemployment. The closure adds a further chapter to the history of a community that burst into existence in the first nineteenth-century phase of industrial development in Wales, but since the years of the 1930s' Great Depression has faced difficulties in finding a role in the Welsh economy.

These early government policies attempted to attract industry from other parts of the UK to the development areas. Initiatives included the relocation of key government departments to Wales. These included the Driver and Vehicle Licensing Centre at Swansea in 1964, tax offices at Llanishen and the Passport Office at Newport. However, by the late 1960s the emphasis was moving to FDI as the primary strategy to increase economic activity in areas of unemployment in the UK. Wales was very successful at this activity and a significant number of large-scale employers were brought there by combinations of ready-made factories and major financial incentives, with up to 40 per cent of costs covered. The success of this policy was hailed throughout the 1960s and 1970s as the saviour of the Welsh economy with an almost direct replacement of jobs lost in the traditional industries. However, in retrospect a number of issues have emerged that suggest that the long-term reliance on FDI was almost as damaging as the reliance on coal and steel it replaced.

In particular, critics were concerned about the quality of the jobs that often resulted from the investments by companies based overseas. Jobs were generally limited to the assembly of components manufactured elsewhere and the term 'screwdriver' economy began to be applied to Wales. Such jobs were generally low-skill, with correspondingly low wages. Relocation conditions often included the banning of union organisation in the plants, and workers' bargaining power was further restricted by the tendency to employ largely female workforces with no previous history of employment or trade union membership and activity. Jobs were also often precarious and casual, as Japanese companies in particular used 'just in time' production techniques which adjusted the size of the workforce in direct relationship to the orders received. Consequently, a pattern emerged of the stable employment of a small 'core' group of key skilled workers and the casual and temporary employment of a larger group of 'peripheral' workers who would be employed and laid off as the production levels promoted adjustment in the numbers of unskilled production workers required (McNabb, 1980).

A further concern about the quality of jobs was the absence of higher-value employment in areas such as research and development and administrative functions within these incoming companies. This promoted the use of the term 'branch plant economy' to delineate a pattern of industrial production which saw the high-value activities of a company retained within its country of origin. The implications were that such companies were attracted as much by the ability to complete the assembly process in a region characterised by low wages as by the financial incentives provided. An additional incentive, following the UK's entry to the European Union in 1973, was the ability to escape import taxes and tariffs by manufacturing goods in the UK. Recent experience has demonstrated the rapidity with which such companies can quickly relocate operations when wage conditions create a cheaper workforce elsewhere. As a consequence, many of the Japanese electronic companies which were heralded as the central success of the FDI strategy have now relocated to countries that have recently joined the European Union. Key names including Sony, Hitachi and National Panasonic have transferred their activities from Wales to countries such as Poland.

There were also critics who identified the mismatch of skills between these new industries and the skills of the men made redundant from coal and steel production. The very specific work skills associated with mining, steel production and heavy manufacture were not required in the new industries and there was a general failure by the state to retrain the workforces shed by the older industries. There was also a cultural mismatch with the work expectations of men who had enjoyed high wages for hard physical work in coal and steel production. The low wages and manual dexterity associated with, for example, electronics manufacture were commonly perceived as 'women's work'. Men rejected the possibility of employment in the new industries and relatively young men who lost their jobs in the traditional industries remained unemployed until retirement age. There was also a tendency for the new production plants to locate to the coastal belts along the M4 corridor in south Wales and the A55 in north Wales. These new centres of production were some distance away from the traditional centres of employment, particularly in the south Wales Valleys. Poor transport links added to the difficulties of working in the new industries, as did a cultural reluctance to travel to work developed by workers who had historically lived and worked in virtually the same location. Collectively, these factors ensured that there was no direct transfer of employees shed by the old industries into the newer patterns of employment.

The dominance of regional policy by an attachment to the FDI approach was most severely challenged by the failure of the LG investment at Newport in south Wales. Championed at the time as the largest FDI ever in the UK, the then Welsh Office in 1996 allocated a huge level of resource to the South Korean giant LG to bring production of electronic goods to Newport. However, before the investment could be realised the collapse of the South Korean economy effectively put an end to the project and the significant expenditure never created any permanent jobs. This in many ways invalidated the FDI approach, and there is now far more caution in this area of regional policy and more focus on the growth and support of indigenous enterprises.

4.3 Feminisation of the workforce

The third process evident in the changing Welsh economy is the gradual feminisation of the workforce, which accelerated considerably as the primary industries were replaced by light manufacturing, textiles and electronic sectors of production from the late 1960s onwards. Before the war the pattern of work in Wales was dominated by industries almost solely populated by male workers. The Factory Acts of 1842 had effectively removed women and children from employment in the mines and in their wake created a domestic role for women that was largely based on maintaining the male workforce. However, this domestic role was challenged by the Second World War and the development of major armaments manufacturing capacity in Wales. Although many women in the immediate years after the war simply returned to the domestic role, the war experience had challenged the traditional attitudes to women working and the economic changes of the thirty years after the war saw the numbers of women in work increase dramatically.

Activity 3.4

Read Teresa Rees's account of women and work in Wales (Extract 3.3). Consider the connections between changes in working patterns, changes in the social experience of women, and the impact of these on patterns of family life.

Extract 3.3

Women and work in Wales

In 1994, *Our Sisters' Land: The Changing Identities of Women in Wales* was published. It includes a collection of 'voices' of women in Wales, illustrating a diverse range of private and public identities (Aaron *et al.*, 1994). The voices show women as both crucially embedded in supporting their families but also involved more and more in public life, in paid work, politics, the voluntary sector, campaigns, the arts, business, education and initiatives whereby they create their own businesses and organisations.

From contributing to the economy largely in indirect and unrecognised ways in the 1970s, half the women of working age in Wales in the late 1990s are now themselves in the workforce. Moreover, while the proportion of women who are in the workforce has increased, that of men has decreased. However, despite predictions based upon changes in the industrial structure, women have not become breadwinners. Wales remains unfortunately characterised by low-paid work for women. While the Equal Pay Act means that from 1975 it was no longer legal to pay men and women different rates for the same work, many women in Wales today are employed in relatively low-skilled work with few prospects for training and promotion, earning considerably less than rates paid to men for 'men's jobs' (Istance and Rees, 1996). Indeed, in Britain as a whole the hourly rates of women working part-time have fallen as a percentage of full-time women workers' wages (Walby, 1997) and pay rates are lower in Wales than elsewhere. This is directly linked to patterns of industrial restructuring and is a key issue to be tackled in Wales for the future. ...

There have clearly been substantial job losses in coal and steel, although manufacturing, while in decline, remains more significant in the UK. It is the development of the service sector, however, that has created employment opportunities for women. Young well-qualified women are gaining entry to the professions. However, very few reach senior managerial or decision-making positions compared with women elsewhere in Britain. Less-qualified and unqualified women find it extremely difficult to secure employment that offers training, prospects or a decent wage.

References

Aaron, J., Rees, T., Betts, S. and Vicentelli, M. (eds) (1994) Our Sisters' Land. the Changing Identities of Women in Wales, Cardiff, University of Wales Press.

Istance, D. and Rees, T. (1996) 'Escaping the low wage/ low skill syndrome: the case for investing in women's skills', British Journal of Education and Work, vol. 9, no. 1, pp. 43–58.

Walby, S. (1997) Gender Transformations, London, Routledge.

Source: Rees, 1999, pp. 7–8

Comment

In Extract 3.3 Rees paints a picture of major changes in the role of women in Welsh society and the resulting demise of the Welsh 'Mam' rooted in a solely domestic role. Instead women are a major presence in the workplace and the economy. The growth of light manufacture and the development of the service sector in particular provided women with many opportunities to enter the workforce for the first time. Women performing these new roles were often the principal wage earners in families where men were made redundant from the primary industries but did not identify themselves with the skills and attitudes required for employment in these newly emerging sectors of the economy. Feminisation of the workforce accelerated throughout the 1990s with the development of more service-based industries, particularly retail and financial services. The transfer of key government departments to Wales in the 1970s and 1980s also increased the potential for female employment. The advances in telephony technology in the late 1990s paved the way for the transfer of many business functions to call centres, particularly in banking and insurance services. The growth of call centres was rapid and much of the work was feminised. In the 2001 census rates of female economic activity reached over 52 per cent of women of working age: a figure that could not have been imagined in 1945. Today female workers constitute 45 per cent of the workforce in Wales.

Figure 3.4
Worker at a Japanese assembly-line factory in Wales

However, it is worth noting that this still represents one of the lowest female economic activity rates in Europe. Additionally, much of the employment for women in Wales is 'relatively low-paid, low-skilled and often part-time employment' (Istance and Rees, 1994, p. 17). Furthermore, women are under-represented in senior roles in both the public and private sectors in Wales.

Summary

- The sharp decline of traditional industries in Wales (coal, steel, agriculture) has had a significant impact on both the economy and society.

- Newer industries have been established in Wales, some with backing from the UK government, but with mixed success.

- Increasing numbers of women have entered the workforce in Wales, especially with the setting-up of new service industries, but much of this employment is low-paid and low-skilled.

5   Work, worklessness and poverty

This chapter has been concerned to outline the relationship between the Welsh economy and patterns of work and work experience in Wales. Regrettably, one of the more negative outcomes of the Welsh economy is the existence of high levels of poverty. In recent years this has been measured largely in relation to **child poverty**: 'The child poverty rate in Wales is 32 per cent, currently the highest in the UK where the average is 31 per cent. In comparison, Scotland and Northern Ireland have child poverty rates of 25 per cent' (Kenway et al., 2008).

Child poverty is measured by the proportion of children living in families with a household income of less than 60 per cent of the national average household income. This is usually measured after housing costs are deducted.

There are two ways in which the pattern of economic activity influences the level of poverty in Wales. The first of these is the way in which low wages, discussed in Section 2 above, depress family incomes. To be employed in Wales is no guarantee against poverty. In 2007, 13 per cent of men and 19 per cent of women in Wales earned less than £6.50 per hour, leading to the conclusion that 'Wales remains a low-pay economy' (Kenway et al., 2007, p. 4). There are also spatial patterns associated with the distribution of low wages, with rural areas experiencing a higher incidence of low-wage occupations. The second influence the economy has on the extent of poverty is through the consequences of high levels of economic inactivity.

In this respect Wales reflects a wider experience of worklessness in areas previously dominated by mining, steel production and heavy industry. The period of collapse of the industrial base in Wales in the early 1980s was marked by rapidly rising levels of unemployment and economic inactivity. This latter term is more useful to employ as it includes many more categories of worklessness than simple unemployment. For example, it covers all those of working age who are not in work, including people with long-term sickness and disability and those who have retired prematurely as well as those who are currently seeking work. A clear pattern that emerged in the 1980s was the large number of people who were assigned to either Incapacity Benefit or Severe Disability Allowance. Figure 3.5 shows the rates of economic inactivity in Wales since 1984 and the contradictory gradual rise for men and fall for women. This is in part explained by increasing employment opportunities for women, as employment in retail and services (traditionally employing more women than men) generally has increased in significance in Wales. However, the large numbers of Incapacity Benefit claimants in Wales is a major cause for concern and an increasing focus of government policy.

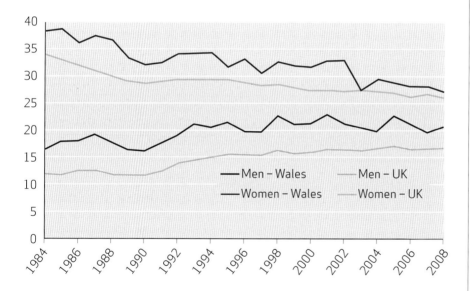

Figure 3.5
Economic inactivity in Wales, 2007 (Source: WAG, 2008b, p. 1)

Activity 3.5

Examine Figure 3.5, which is drawn from a WAG statistical bulletin about economic activity. As you do so:

■ compare the rates of activity for men and women

■ remember some of the processes you have read about in this chapter and note why the rate of economic inactivity continues to fall for women.

Comment

This graph shows the simple numerical measurement of economic inactivity. You will have noticed that the rate of inactivity for men continues to rise, while for women there is a gradual fall in inactivity rates. This is a consequence of the feminisation of work we discussed in Section 4.3. While it is important to understand statistically the levels of economic inactivity, it is also important to understand the social impact of high levels of long-term worklessness. In many communities in Wales three generations of economically inactive individuals can be found within single families.

Critically, worklessness and low wages can become concentrated in particular communities and families. The consequences both for the individual and for family cultures can be considerable. Additionally, in localities where low wages and economic inactivity are the dominant experience, a major cultural shift can occur which disconnects the community from the wider cultural values that underpin a commitment to work. Low levels of economic opportunity can create a fatalistic attitude which accepts a future of worklessness as the norm. Moreover, economic inactivity can become a rational choice in circumstances where low wages are coupled with precarious patterns of employment and a predominance of part-time and casual work. In such areas young people in the education system often lose motivation and a culture can emerge that rejects the academic values of the school and undermines educational performance. Peer pressures to conform to worklessness can develop and a general collapse of aspiration and confidence can dominate the local social experience.

These social and psychological adjustments to worklessness and low wages overlie the structural causes of underemployment in such localities. Intractable barriers to employment include geographical distance and isolation from places of work, poor transport links and, fundamentally, the low skills base of the population. To this can be added individual and communal values that reject travelling to places of work and which develop an acceptance of a lifestyle of poverty as normal and even satisfactory.

Just as the world of work has influenced Welsh culture in the past, the world of worklessness exerts a corrosive influence on engagement and participation in the wider community. Communities characterised by worklessness can become isolated and culturally marginalised, a process usually referred to as **social exclusion**. The social horizons of people living in such communities can become confined to the immediate area and the boundaries of the estate or community become the furthest social horizon for residents. Local cultural experience can become compressed and whole communities can lose their social and cultural links to the economy and the world of work.

Summary

- Low wages are one cause of poverty, especially in rural areas of Wales.

- Worklessness rates are particularly high in areas where mining, steel production and heavy industry used to be dominant.

- Rates of economic inactivity are rising among men, but falling among women.

- One consequence of economic inactivity is the marginalisation of the individuals and communities affected.

6   Conclusion

In this chapter you have examined the major features of the contemporary Welsh economy and the work patterns that emerge from it. You have also considered some of the key underlying patterns of change which have brought us to the present. Central to these have been the decline of the traditional economic activities of mining, steel production and agriculture, and their replacement by a more diverse and complex economic structure. Profound social changes have occurred in response to changing economic patterns, notably the increased role of women in the workplace and the experience of worklessness. Both of these have impacted on family and social life; indeed the social and cultural experience of living in Wales has changed considerably from the experience of my youth, which I briefly outlined in Section 3. Taking the Welsh economy forward into a more prosperous future presents major challenges to the WAG. As well as overcoming some of the structural weaknesses in the economy identified in this chapter, policy will have to successfully challenge the social and cultural impact of both low wages and long-term economic inactivity if Wales is to reach standards of living for all its citizens that compare favourably with the rest of the UK.

Social exclusion refers to the economic, cultural and social marginalisation of individuals, families and communities. It describes the long-term consequences of poverty where people experiencing poverty suffer poor educational attainment, poor health outcomes and low housing quality.

References

Baber, C. and Mainwaring, L. (1988) 'Steel' in George, K. D. and Mainwaring, L. *The Welsh Economy*, Cardiff, University of Wales Press.

Bryan, J. and Roche, N. (2009) 'The Welsh economy: 2008 under review', *Contemporary Wales*, vol. 22, pp. 62–94.

George, K. D., Mainwaring, L., Shorey, J. S. and Thomas, D. R. (1988) 'Coal' in George, K. D. and Mainwaring, L. (eds) *The Welsh Economy*, Cardiff, University of Wales Press.

Goldthorpe, J. L., Lockwood, D., Bechhofer, F. and Platt, J. (1969) *The Affluent Worker in the Class Structure*, Cambridge, Cambridge University Press.

Hill, S. (2000) 'Wales in transition' in Bryan, J. and Jones, C. (eds) *Wales in the 21st Century: an Economic Future*, Basingstoke, Macmillan Business.

Hobsbawm, E. (1994) *The Age of Extremes: the Short Twentieth Century 1914–1991*, London, Michael Joseph.

Humphrys, G. (1972) *Industrial Britain: South Wales*, Newton Abbot, David and Charles.

Istance, D. and Rees, T. L. (1994) *Women in Post-compulsory Education and Training in Wales*, Manchester, Equal Opportunities Commission.

Kenway, P., MacInnes, T. and Palmer, G. (2007) *Monitoring Poverty and Social Exclusion in Wales 2007* York, Joseph Rowntree Foundation and New Policy Institute.

Kenway, P., MacInnes, T. and Palmer, G. (2008) *Monitoring Poverty and Social Exclusion in Scotland 2008,* York, Joseph Rowntree Foundation and New Policy Institute.

McNabb, R. (1980) 'Segmented labour markets, female employment and poverty in Wales' in Rees, G. and Rees, T. L. (eds) *Poverty and Social Inequality in Wales*, London, Croom Helm.

Midmore, P., Haines, M. and Sherwood. A. (1996) 'A national policy for the Welsh countryside' in Midmore, P. and Hughes, G. (eds) *Rural Wales: an Economic and Social Perspective*, Aberystwyth, Welsh Institute of Rural Studies.

Rees, T. (1999) *Women and Work: 25 Years of Gender Equality in Wales*, Cardiff, University of Wales Press.

Wanhill, S. (1980) *An Econometric Model of Wales*, Bangor Occasional Papers in Economics, no. 18, Cardiff, University of Wales Press.

Welsh Assembly Government Statistical Directorate (2008b) 'Farm diversification in Wales 2006/10', *Statistical Bulletin SB 35/2008*, June, Cardiff, WAG.

Welsh Assembly Government Statistical Directorate (2008a) 'Economic inactivity in Wales 2007', *Statistical Bulletin SB 61/2008*, November, Cardiff, WAG.

Welsh Assembly Government Statistical Directorate (2009) 'Workplace employment by industry for Wales 2001–2007', *Statistical Bulletin SB 45/2009*, July, Cardiff, WAG.

Welsh Assembly Government (2002) *A Winning Wales: the National Economic Development Strategy of the Welsh Assembly Government*, Cardiff, WAG.

Welsh Assembly Government (2005) *Wales a Vibrant Economy: the Welsh Assembly Government's Strategic Framework for Economic Development*, Cardiff, WAG.

Welsh Assembly Government (2007) *One Wales: a Progressive Agenda for the Government of Wales. an Agreement between the Labour Party and Plaid Cymru Groups in the National Assembly*, Cardiff, WAG.

Further reading

Contemporary Wales University of Wales Press, Cardiff. This annually published journal always includes a chapter examining the contemporary Welsh economy. It provides an update of the key features of economic activity in Wales derived from the most recently available statistics.

For an excellent overview of the key sectors of the Welsh economy as it entered the twenty-first century, see Bryan, J. and Jones, C. (eds) *Wales in the 21st Century: an Economic Future*, Basingstoke, Macmillan Business.

Monitoring Poverty and Social Exclusion in Wales, Joseph Rowntree Foundation and the New Policy Institute York, is a series of reports on the conditions of poverty in Wales. First published in 2005, it was updated in 2007 and 2009 and provides the most recent statistics of key indicators of poverty in Wales.

Dave Adamson's 2009 article 'Still living on Edge?' (in *Contemporary Wales*, 21, pp.47–66) reviews the primary causes of poverty in Wales today.

Chapter 4
Gender and 'race'

Sandra Betts and Charlotte Williams

Contents

1   Introduction

In building up your picture and understanding of contemporary Wales you have already begun to see that Wales is an increasingly diverse and complex society characterised by change and by a range of differences and divisions. Indeed group differentiation is a key organising feature of all societies. Many such differences are taken for granted and relatively inconsequential; for example, variations between groups according to hobbies, interests or preferences. But differences become socially significant when they lead to social divisions. Differences between people that are given importance and made significant start to play a crucial role in shaping society, such that societies become divided into distinctive social groups that 'unite people through their particular and shared experiences and interests [and] that mark them as different from, and possibly in conflict with, other groups' (Braham and Janes, 2002, p. ix). Differences can lead to divisions and social divisions can result in social inequalities, social exclusion and discrimination.

It is not surprising, then, that social scientists have shown a keen interest in the way society is divided into different and distinctive social groups, in examining the resultant inequalities and disadvantages and in exploring how divisions persist, are reproduced and are also subject to change over time. This chapter focuses on just two social differences: differences of 'race' and differences of gender. Space does not allow us to talk about other differences, such as those of age, sexuality or disability. Our focus on gender and 'race' reflects the political and social attention that has been given to these issues and enables us to explore in some depth the extent to which these differences are significant in shaping contemporary Wales, and in impacting upon people's life chances and life experiences.

The aims of this chapter are to:

■ introduce the concepts of 'race' and gender and highlight the importance of understanding the ways in which racialised and gendered divisions are part and parcel of the structural arrangements of a society

■ look at some of the ways in which 'race' and gender have been thought about, represented and discussed in Wales over recent decades

■ present some key demographic data concerning gender, 'race' and ethnic diversity in Wales today

■ consider the key question: to what extent do racial and gender differences in Wales today result in inequality and disadvantage?

■ examine post-devolution policies designed to achieve greater equality and produce more equitable outcomes for all citizens.

1.1 Racial differences

Early thinking on racial difference focused on variations in people's physical appearance – skin colour, hair colour and texture, and facial features. The assumption was that it was possible to describe scientifically and classify the world's population into racial groups. '**Races**' could be seen and therefore they existed. Even more troublingly, these categories gave rise to **racism**: the belief in the superiority of some 'races' or one 'race' over others.

Over the last century ideas about 'race' have mutated and developed and it is now widely accepted that these categories have little scientific basis, despite having immense social significance. To understand 'race' in contemporary society we must see it as a social construct far removed from its original formulation. Nevertheless, it has important meaning in respect of how we view certain groups of people and categorise or racialise them, and how this construction of them as different has implications for their material realities. Thus the use of the term 'race' today permits social scientists to stress the political significance of 'race' and ethnicity; placing the term in inverted commas shows that it is not a fixed, biological category, but a dynamic, changing social concept. 'Race' is not now used in the social sciences to describe biological make-up, but the term is retained in order to hold on to the historical and political dimensions of difference, while 'racialisation' is the term used to refer to the processes by which understandings of 'race' are used to classify individuals or groups of people.

As with 'race', the term 'ethnicity' is highly contested and used to mean different things. Nevertheless we all have an ethnicity and this encompasses a range of factors fundamental to our identities, such as language, culture, religion, place and national origin. Welsh and English, Pakistani and Polish can be seen as ethnic groups. An ethnic group is one whose members share a distinct awareness of a common cultural identity separating them from other groups around them.

The link between 'race', nation and nationalism should also be noted. Nation and nationalism are important to an understanding of 'race'. Like the communities discussed in Chapter 2, nations mark out a boundary between those who belong (insiders) and those who do not (outsiders). Ideas about the national character and national identity are communicated and sustained through the culture of a society. These ideas have a bearing on the treatment of 'race' and on the manifestation of racism within any given society. Nationalism is about membership of a community and can be, but is not necessarily, underpinned by racism and racialised exclusions. Racism and nationalism are thus not necessarily bedfellows, but nation building has often been characterised

'Race' signifies the division of humans according to physical characteristics (notably skin colour) into different racial groups.

Racism is the attribution of characteristics of superiority or inferiority to a population sharing certain physically inherited characteristics.

by racist practices and discourses and racist thinking has informed some debates about national identity and citizenship.

1.2 Gender differences

From the mid twentieth century onwards social scientists, among others, have drawn attention to the distinction between sex and gender and to the significance of gender in understanding social differences, social divisions and inequalities in society. Social scientists have investigated and theorised how different social relationships and different institutions and processes distinguish between women and men and create meanings about femininity and masculinity, and how gender distinctions are linked to inequalities, hierarchy and power relations.

The term 'sex' (denoting whether someone is male or female) refers to the natural or biological differences between men and women, such as differences in genitals, internal reproductive organs and body hair.

Gender roles are the patterns of behaviour that society expects from a man or a woman.

The term 'gender' (denoting whether someone is masculine or feminine) refers to the social, cultural and psychological characteristics associated with maleness and femaleness in particular cultures and societies. These culturally created differences between men and women are learned through socialisation and lead to the adoption of different **gender roles**. Today it is increasingly recognised that gender is a crucial factor in shaping individual experience and identity as well as in shaping social institutions. Gender shapes the experiences of women and men differently and, as you will see later in this chapter, remains a key basis of inequality in Wales.

Summary

- 'Race' and gender are two of the key social differences that impact on people's life chances and life experiences in Wales.

- 'Race' is not a fixed biological category but a dynamic and changing social concept. Certain groups of people are categorised or racialised, and this has implications for their life experiences.

- Gender refers to the social and cultural expectations about behaviour regarded as appropriate for males and females. Gender is important in shaping individual experience and identity.

2   Thinking about 'race' and gender

The main focus of this chapter is on racial and gender differences in contemporary Wales, but it is important to set that discussion within a historical context. To this end, this section looks at some of the ways in which 'race' and gender have been thought about, represented and theorised over the course of the twentieth century and up to the present day.

2.1 Thinking about 'race' and Wales

Race relations literature and policy have tended to focus on areas of ethnic minority concentration in the UK. For a number of reasons Wales has been largely off the race relations map of Britain. This is curious, because Wales is home to one of the oldest black, or more appropriately multicultural, communities in Europe (see Figure 4.1).

Figure 4.1

Images of 1950s Bute from *Down the Bay*, photographs by Bert Hardy

In the 1940s Kenneth Little studied 'the coloured people of Cardiff' and thus opened up a social science of race relations in Wales (Little, 1948). The somewhat 'exotic' reputation of the area of Cardiff known in the early twentieth century as Tiger Bay that was the focus of Little's study had been well established even before the turn of the century. Accounts by novelists, newspaper columnists, social workers, civil servants, social reformers and others had contributed to the rather ambivalent representation of the area as dirty, diseased, violent and immoral, but at the same time fascinating and a world-leading example of harmonious race relations.

Against this backdrop, Little set about conducting a meticulous social survey that captured the socio-economic circumstances of some of Wales's earliest 'coloured' (a post-war term) immigrants:

> We can proceed to consider the coloured community itself. The main elements consist of Arab, West African and West Indian seamen, but it has been estimated that altogether in this Loudoun Square quarter [in Butetown] some fifty different nationalities are to be found. ... The square itself serves as a convenient centre. Here the density of the coloured population is greatest – with perhaps eight out of every ten persons.
>
> (Little, 1948, p. 68)

Summarising the employment situation in the area at the outbreak of the Second World War, Little comments that 'the community may be expected to undergo further vagaries of economic hardship' (1948, p. 75), and in reviewing the state of race relations between the coloured community and the majority white population at the time he notes that 'the community is segregated with some considerable degree of rigidity from the rest of the city in the geographical, social and psychological senses; in the last respect the existence of strong patterns of colour prejudice among residents of the town is the main causal factor' (1948, p. 183).

Migration to Wales and the consequent ethnic diversity it produced need to be seen in historical context. The mid-nineteenth-century boom in the coal industry and merchant shipping attracted black seamen from Africa, America and the West Indies. By the time of the Second World War this community was well established; there was considerable intermarriage and a clear presence of second- or third-generation 'mixed-race' people. Wales did not experience the West Indian immigration of the *Windrush* era so characteristic of a number of cities in England (Evans, 2002). Little's study identifies four important issues surrounding 'race' in Wales. This settlement represents something quite different from other parts of the UK, where pre-war settlement in major towns such as London, Bristol and Liverpool was largely a product of the economics of shipping and the business of transporting slaves. Second, and significant for understanding contemporary racial divisions, Little's study illustrates the geographic containment of the issue of 'race' in Wales to an area a little short of one square mile in the dockland area of Cardiff. Third, the work documents the nature of discriminations, racisms and exclusions faced by these individuals and their descendants which have had an enduring impact to the present day. Fourth, and of particular interest, the study raises the question of whether there is something distinct or different about Wales in terms of an understanding of 'race' and racism.

In the historical encounter between the majority Welsh population and black and ethnic minority settlers to the country, there is evidence of both amicable race relations and trenchant ethnic conflict, and yet a predominant myth of Welsh national identity portrays Wales as a tolerant nation, particularly in comparison with its neighbour, England. In any reading of Welsh race relations history it will be clear that the fate of the Welsh themselves as an ethnic minority within the wider context of Britain is a significant factor in understanding this popular myth of Welsh tolerance.

Wales, Scotland and Ireland were the first (internal) colonies of the great imperial project of Britain. This has led to an ongoing sense of national oppression. For example, the experience of cultural domination by the English in which self-rule was lost, the language and culture of Wales were subjugated and the Welsh themselves were racialised, has led to a pervasive and continuing sense of national oppression. The politics of self-rule and the reassertion of the Welsh language and culture in public life have been a key focus of the politics of ethnic conflict in Wales. It is this form of ethnic conflict, between the Welsh and the English, that has been foregrounded and this has served to displace any focus on other racialised divisions.

A widely held, but perhaps misplaced, belief is that this historical experience has produced a strong empathy and sense of tolerance towards other racialised minorities. The argument runs that as an oppressed people themselves the Welsh are more understanding of the oppression of others, including the oppression of black people. In this sense the Welsh national character is portrayed as anti-imperial, tolerant and internationalist, by contrast with the English, who are perceived as colonialist and racist. This is, of course, a part of national myth making and cannot be supported by available historical or contemporary evidence. However, it is a deeply held and powerful belief. This type of thinking has been mobilised in varying degrees in contemporary Wales to cast the Welsh as a non-racist nation. One consequence of this myth is to view 'race' issues and racism as a non-issue for Wales. The idea that 'race' is 'no problem here' has provided a powerful discourse even in the face of considerable evidence to the contrary.

The legacy of this set of ideas meant that prior to devolution 'race' was not considered to be an issue for public policy interventions. The assumption was that the relatively low numbers of people from ethnic minorities meant there was little need for such policy. In the absence of perceived need, racism was not recognised by government, and complacency on the part of civil servants and policy makers meant that little or no attention was directed towards 'race' issues. The idea of Wales as a multicultural society was barely acknowledged in public life.

At the same time, lack of political clout among minorities led to an inability to push their concerns onto the political agenda. The black and ethnic minority population is very diverse, dispersed and isolated and this has militated against their establishing any kind of strong collective political identity able to forge change. What grassroots activity existed was poorly coordinated and organised more around social support than political lobbying. Effectively, minorities across Wales remained largely disenfranchised, powerless and hidden. The idea of multicultural Wales was associated only with a tiny area of Cardiff and the lack of inter-ethnic conflict in this small area of Wales contributed to the myth of harmonious race relations.

Access to identification with and membership of the national community is important to the exercise of citizenship rights and to equality. If you feel that you belong, then you may also feel entitled to some of the opportunities of that society. This feeling has been frustrated for the majority of people from black and ethnic minority groups in Wales. The sense of belonging to the national community is signalled in a number of ways and communicated through ideas about 'Welshness': who is and who is not considered Welsh. The marginalised position of ethnic minorities has been compounded by dominant constructions of Welsh national identity that figure in the popular imagining and political discourse. The way in which the nation tells its story via its cultural representations, how it presents who is seen as Welsh and who isn't, can operate to exclude. There is inevitably some tension between the aspirations of a country wishing to advance itself as a distinct nation and one that wishes to portray the image of a country welcoming and accepting of all ethnicities.

Activity 4.1 explores this tension: how at one and the same time to build a sense of the national collective and a distinct national identity and also to incorporate an increasingly ethnically diverse population. These are issues that have much concerned politicians and scholars particularly in post-devolution Wales.

Activity 4.1

Extract 4.1 comes from a public lecture to the Honourable Royal Society of Cymmrodorion, in London, by one of the authors of this chapter.

Read the extract and consider the following questions:

■ What is meant by the 'paradox' of how to square diversity with national integrity?

■ Why is this a contemporary dilemma?

Extract 4.1

Can we live together? Wales and the multicultural question

Addressing a multicultural audience at the Global Britons Conference in Cardiff, the First Minister, Rhodri Morgan, spoke of the 'ultimate paradox of a country'. On the one hand, there is the recognition of huge diversity and long standing diversity as a product of Wales' industrialised and globalised past. On the other hand, he referred to the 'Celtic nature of Wales' – the Celtic essence, Wales' cultural integrity 'as maintained through its language' (Morgan, 2003). This is the paradox: how to square diversity and national integrity.

The First Minister is, of course, correct in his acknowledgement of long standing diversity. Cultural diversity is not a new phenomenon to Wales. Wales has always been in one sense multi-cultural. ... However, it is the era of modern globalisation coinciding with the emergence of the nation state that brings a more complex encounter with difference to Wales. It is no longer reasonable to think of nation states as ethnically homogenous entities. Economic expansion, technological and information advance and increased migrations mean that modern nations are increasingly and consciously diverse. However, as the world is opened up to us, so we feel insecure and try to shrink it back to size. Thus, the potential for ethnic conflict increases as the assertion of who we are becomes all the more important ...

The idea of multiculturalism is nevertheless popular. Most people would argue that multiculturalism is a good thing. But what if it isn't?

When the First Minister spoke about the paradox of nation he raised the core elements of the multicultural question – how to reconcile increasing diversity with national identity. National identity is of course a construction and his construction of nation was by reference to something called 'The Celtic Essence'. What is clear is that these indices of identity as presently constituted are proving rather too inaccessible or meaningless for the majority of ethnic minorities. I would argue that instead of formulating the paradox in this way, that is, how to fit together two potentially incompatible forces, we need to consider how we are constructing these notions. Is not, for example, diversity/migration, movement and change, a fundamental element of the Celtic essence and integral to it? Some commentators would argue that we need to dispense with the idea of nation altogether because in an era of globalisation the idea of nation becomes more and more anachronistic. The discourse of nationality itself creates barriers, antagonisms and renders marginal those who do not fit the predominant constructions of national identity.

Reference

Morgan, R. (2003) *Speech to the Global Britons Conference*, 11 February, Cardiff, Foreign Policy Institute, available at http://fpc.org.uk/articles/195.

(Williams, 2005, pp. 216–30)

Wales is changing both within and because of pressures beyond it. It is increasingly diverse as a result of the ebbs and flows of inward and outward migrations. Ideas of nation and national identity that cling to narrow, traditional and exclusive definitions of who is Welsh and who is not Welsh are increasingly being challenged. To link national belonging to membership of a distinct ethnic group will always act to exclude people and limit the project of nation building. The paradox is how not to lose the distinctiveness of Wales as a nation, its history, culture and traditions, while at the same time recognising and embracing its ethnic diversity.

To be genuinely inclusive, the 'integrity' of the nation must be built on factors that cut across ethnic boundaries. In post-devolution Wales, politicians, popular culture and minority peoples themselves are contributing to redefining national identity, asserting a variety of national identities and claiming belonging based on a more inclusive rights-based citizenship (some of these ideas will be developed in Chapter 8).

2.2 Thinking about gender and Wales

If thinking about 'race' in Wales has been characterised by notions of 'no problem here', then thinking about gender has been influenced and characterised by women's gradual emergence 'out of the shadows' and by perceived shifts in gender roles.

Thinking about gender, and particularly about women, has changed since the start of the twentieth century. For much of that century, thinking was dominated by the doctrine and practice of 'separate spheres':

> Separate spheres meant separate worlds for men and women. Man's sphere was the public domain of work and politics; woman's sphere was the private world of home and family. Man's duty was to provide financially for his wife and family through money earned in the outside world. Woman's duty was to be a wife and mother and to

create a home which was a refuge from the forces of darkness outside its walls: under her care home would be a centre of Christian virtue, moral purity and sobriety.

(Beddoe, 2000, p. 12)

This doctrine dominated the early years of the century, an era in which 'women wore long skirts and large hats, travelled in horse-drawn vehicles, worked as live-in domestic servants (or employed them) and were denied the basic rights of citizenship' (Beddoe, 2000, p. 13), and it retained much of its power and significance through the course of two world wars. The period 1914–39 saw little fundamental change in gender roles. The First World War did see gender barriers in employment break down a little, but the role of women was still fundamentally in the home. Cardiff-born Ivor Novello's wartime song urged women to 'Keep the Home Fires Burning' and after the war women were expected to resume their roles as wives, mothers and dutiful daughters.

The period of the Second World War again saw women come out of the home and into work – both 'war work' and civilian jobs vacated by men – but this war too 'did little more than superficially dent the notion of separate spheres' (Beddoe, 2000, p. 133). In post-war Wales, women remained custodians of the home and family, and men remained the breadwinners.

This picture of gender roles in the early years of the twentieth century is arguably one that could apply to many western societies, and certainly to other parts of Britain. But is there a Welsh dimension to the account?

Figure 4.2

Young women at a cookery class at the Juvenile Unemployment Centre in Cardiff, September 1937

Activity 4.2

■ Can you think of anything about Wales and Welsh culture that might explain why separate spheres, ideas and practices were so well entrenched in Welsh society for much of the twentieth century? Make a note of your ideas.

■ Then read Extract 4.2 by Deirdre Beddoe below, and compare your ideas with what she writes.

Extract 4.2

Clearly the lives of women in Wales have been shaped by a distinctive Welsh culture, which has largely been defined by Nonconformity ... ministers of religion, politicians and other male public figures zealously promoted the domestic ideology and the role of women as a civilizing force within the home. This, in turn, imposed on women in Wales a whole set of prescriptive rules: they were to be 'respectable', with all that word entails. The chapel policed their behaviour: women were cast out of chapels as late as ... the 1960's for becoming pregnant while unmarried or on reports of adulterous behaviour. ... In terms of women's paid employment there has also been a distinctive Welsh dimension ... the nature of industrialisation in Wales meant that there was very little paid work for women in the mining valleys before 1939 ... the war identified factory work as women's work and post-war opportunities meant that women began to enter the workforce in increasing numbers, despite a great deal of male hostility. ... It can be argued too that Welsh women were subjected to a particularly 'virulent strain' of patriarchy. The nature of men's work in Wales, in heavy, dirty and dangerous jobs ... meant not only that women's unpaid work was essential in the home, but that in Wales, work itself was defined in exclusively macho terms: only men's work was real work. ... In Wales there was a particular male pride in being able to support a 'non-working' wife. The legacy of the nineteenth-century notion of separate spheres lingered longer in Wales, keeping women, with few exceptions, out of the public sphere.

(Beddoe, 2000, pp. 180–1)

Comment

In this passage, Beddoe identifies four factors in Welsh culture and society that shaped the lives and experiences of women:

■ a strong Nonconformist culture

■ the role of the chapel

■ the nature of industrialisation

■ a virulent strain of **patriarchy**.

Such factors lie behind the Welsh 'Mam' representation of Welsh women as hard-working, pious and clean: responsible for the home and the well-being of her family, she was immortalised in Richard Llewellyn's novel *How Green Was My Valley* (1939).

But women's wartime experiences had enhanced their confidence and raised their expectations, and the period from 1945 onwards was to witness much tension and unease as women sought to reconcile notions of supposed freedom and equality with experiences of oppression, unease and frustration. Yet it was not until the 1970s that these 'feelings' found expression and new ways of 'thinking' about gender emerged. As Beddoe puts it: 'a growing feminist consciousness and influences from the USA, together with a rising tide of anger about equal pay, would turn vague stirrings of discontent into a new mass feminist movement in the 1970's' (2000, p. 158).

The last decades of the twentieth century saw many changes in the lives of women in Wales. Women became more visible, in work, in education, in organised religion, in social movements and eventually in politics. The new Welsh post-industrial economy with its expanding service sector provided the conditions for women's increased participation in the labour market and trade unions. The Women's Liberation Movement (WLM) brought attention to the oppressed position of women and campaigned tirelessly for change on a wide range of issues. Strongest in the urbanised south-east, there were WLM groups throughout Wales, particularly in university towns. Thinking about women and the particularities of women's experiences came to assume an academic profile. Courses in women's studies developed in all of the higher educational institutions in Wales in the 1980s and 1990s. Research was undertaken and new publications appeared with the aim of filling the huge gaps in knowledge and playing a part in the ongoing struggle to change attitudes and improve opportunities for women in Wales.

One such text was *Our Sisters' Land* (Aaron et al., 1994), which highlighted the tension between the old images and stereotypes of gender roles and the transformations that were currently occurring. The editors suggest the book shows that

> Welsh women are ... to a greater or lesser extent, in the process of change ... in both the private and public sphere, a growing diversity of patterns of women's lives and identities challenges popular images of women in Wales; at the same time, structures which perpetuate gender divisions at home and work remain stable.
>
> (Aaron et al., 1994, p. 8)

Patriarchy means the dominance, power and authority of men over women.

This recognition of both change and continuity at the end of the twentieth century is endorsed by Beddoe, who writes: 'there can be no doubt that the last thirty years have seen substantial gains for women, but on the other hand, in the year 2000 it is certainly premature to talk of equality between the sexes in Wales. The old gender hierarchy remains – with men on top' (2000, p. 178).

So what of the twenty-first century? What progress has been made; what remains to be done? Has our thinking about gender and gender divisions changed? These questions will be explored in the remaining sections of this chapter.

Summary

- Despite the fact that Wales is home to one of the oldest multicultural communities in Europe, 'race' has not been considered an issue for public policy.

- Thinking about 'race' in Wales has been dominated by the idea that 'there is no problem here'.

- Thinking about gender in Wales has been characterised by an understanding of changing gender roles and women's gradual emergence 'out of the shadows'.

- A distinctive Welsh culture with a strong emphasis on the 'separate spheres' ideology meant that women in Wales were firmly located in the domestic sphere for much of the twentieth century.

- The last decades of the twentieth century saw many changes in the lives of women. Barriers were dismantled and women became more visible in public spheres.

3   Demographic factors: 'race' and gender

Demography is the study of populations, including their location, their age, gender and 'racial' make-up, and how they change over time.

The previous section explored some of the ways in which gender and racial differences have been thought about, represented and understood in Wales over recent decades. This section introduces some basic **demographic** data about the structure and composition of the population of contemporary Wales, with particular reference to gender and to black and ethnic minority groups.

3.1 'Race' and place

Contemporary Wales is a multiracial, multi-ethnic and multi-faith society. On one measure, birthplace, Wales has by far the most diverse population of the four UK countries, with around a quarter of the population born outside Wales. This of course includes a large number of people (80 per cent) of various ethnicities born in England. According to the 2001 census, the number of people from black and minority ethnic backgrounds in the UK was 4.6 million (almost 8 per cent of the population); in Wales the figure was 62,000 (2.1 per cent). This was an increase from 41,551 people in Wales (1.5 per cent) in the 1991 census.

A consideration of ethnic diversity today must include newly 'racialised' groups such as eastern Europeans, asylum seekers and refugees, as well as those who have historically been the subject of racial discriminations – such as Gypsies and Travellers. The 2001 census data does not capture these groups, so there may well be an underestimation of the extent of ethnic diversity in Wales. In the 2011 census the ethnicity question will be extended to include a variety of mixed ethnicities as well as migrations from other parts of Europe. However, based on the 2001 data, Asians (including Asian British) are by far the largest ethnic minority group in Wales, accounting for 41 per cent of the total ethnic minority population. Interestingly, the next largest group comprises those who categorise themselves as 'mixed' (29 per cent). This group reflects the long settlement of ethnic minorities in parts of Wales.

Figure 4.3
Somali pupils being taught their language at a Cardiff high school

Activity 4.3

Most people from black and ethnic minority backgrounds live in or around the Cardiff area. However, there is no single local authority area in Wales that does not have an ethnic minority presence. Table 4.1 provides evidence of this.

Examine Table 4.1 and answer the following questions:

■ Roughly what proportion or percentage of the total population of Cardiff consists of non-white residents?

■ What do you think might be some of the issues affecting black and ethnic minority individuals living in rural areas of Wales?

Table 4.1 Ethnic dispersal by local authority, 2001

Area	All people	Non-white
Wales total	2,903,085	61,580
Cardiff	305,353	25,729
Newport	137,011	6,603
Swansea	223,301	4,806
Rhondda Cynon Taff	231,946	2,673
The Vale of Glamorgan	119,292	2,576
Bridgend	128,645	1,767
Carmarthenshire	172,842	1,623
Caerphilly	169,519	1,548
Neath Port Talbot	134,468	1,448
Wrexham	128,476	1,403
Gwynedd	116,843	1,389
Flintshire	148,594	1,194
Conwy	109,596	1,157
Powys	126,354	1,086
Denbighshire	93,065	1,073
Ceredigion	74,941	1,037
Pembrokeshire	114,131	1,026
Monmouthshire	84,885	964
Torfaen	90,949	852
Blaenau Gwent	70,064	581
Merthyr Tydfil	55,981	564
Isle of Anglesey	66,829	481

Source: adapted from census data (ONS, 2001)

Comment

The geographic concentration of the ethnic minority population reflects the history of migration in Wales. Over half of the minority population live in cities in the south: Newport, Cardiff and Swansea. In Cardiff the minority population almost matches the UK figure; it is about 1 in 12 or, to be precise, 8.4 per cent. Elsewhere, there is a very much lower ethnic minority population – for example, Gwynedd, has about 1 in 85, which is just over 1 per cent. Nevertheless, demographic transformations are taking place even in the rural areas of Wales, with diversity becoming more visible.

A number of studies highlight the experiences of ethnic minorities living in more rural areas of Wales where racism, both institutional and personal, is well documented and support for victims of racist violence and attacks is weak (Robinson and Gardner, 2004; Scourfield et al., 2004). Isolation and exclusion can contribute to a sense of un-belonging for many members of ethnic minority groups in rural areas of Wales. At the same time, the fact that they do not have a strong visible presence in many areas means that too often service providers operate with an assumption that low numbers equal low need. Service delivery to meet particular needs is often sluggish, poor or non-existent, and access to justice in cases where people are seeking redress from discrimination or racist victimisation can be fraught with difficulty (Williams, 2004). The low visibility and the dispersal of minorities in these areas have made amassing statistical evidence of their needs very difficult (see Section 4.2).

Rural communities are changing rapidly. They are becoming increasingly diverse and this in itself brings with it new challenges to the creation of an inclusive society. There will inevitably be some tensions in contemporary Wales between the advancement and development of the country as a bilingual nation and one that wishes to attract and retain in-migrations from people of all ethnicities. This tension is hotly debated and acutely played out in more rural areas of Wales, which are considered by many to be the heartlands of Welsh language and culture. The perception that incomers pose a threat to the community life, culture and spoken language of small towns and villages is one that has given fuel to debates about the decline of the Welsh language and the loss of Welsh traditions and culture. While the exclusionary force of the 'language issue' has perhaps been overstated in the past, there are some very real tussles to be acknowledged. Language requirements, perceived or real, that are attached to key resources such as jobs, local housing, education and training opportunities, and opportunities for participation and representation on local decision-making bodies, have had an impact on people from black and ethnic minority groups. This has been particularly experienced in relation to their lack of representation in the public life of Wales (see Section 4.2).

3.2 Gender

The population of Wales is nearly 3 million (one in 20 of the UK population): just over half that of Scotland and nearly double that of Northern Ireland.

Figures from the 2001 census show that 48.4 per cent of people living in Wales are male and 51.6 per cent are female. So the overall ratio of male to females is 0.94:1 (that is, 94 males for every 100 females), but this ratio varies between age groups. In Wales more boys are born than girls, but the ratio falls very slightly as children get older – possibly due to a higher death rate from accidents in young males. There are equal numbers of men and women around the age of 20, and then slightly more women than men up to the age of 70. At this point the differences become more significant, because women live longer than men. For people aged between 70 and 80, there are 13 women for every 10 men. Between the ages of 80 and 90, there are 19 women for every 10 men, and among the over-90s there are 36 women for every 10 men.

Life expectancy (at birth) for males is 76 years; for females it is 80.5 years. Both figures are significantly higher than thirty years ago, and the gap between males and females is narrower. Thirty years ago men could expect to live to 68 and women to 74.5 years.

Women make up just over half of the population in contemporary Wales, and as they live longer than men this trend is likely to continue. However, not only are there more women in the population today, but women are to be 'found' in more places, locations and settings throughout Wales than used to be the case. Women in contemporary Wales are more evident and more visible in education, employment and public and political life.

Girls are more likely than boys to leave school with qualifications, and to get five or more good GCSEs. More girls than boys aged 16–18 are in full-time education, and girls are also much more visible in the corridors of higher education today. In the 1960s the number of men at university was double the number of women, and numbers were about equal in the mid 1990s, but there are now more women students than men (55 per cent women, 45 per cent men) (WAG, 2007b).

Up to the 1960s only one quarter of women of working age in Wales had paid work. A woman's chief occupation was that of housewife and mother. Those who did have a job tended to give it up when they married, and they rarely returned to work. By the 1980s, however,

55 per cent of women were economically active and this figure rose to 68 per cent in the early years of the twenty-first century (ONS, 2004).

It is also the case that women are more visible in at least some positions and places of power. In 2009 women made up 40 per cent of the WAG's Cabinet and 47 per cent of National Assembly Members. This pattern, however, is not repeated at local authority level, or with respect to public bodies or the private sector (EHRC, 2009).

Today women not only form the majority gender group in Wales; they also occupy a greater number of roles than was the case in the past. Women have become more 'visible' in Wales and are to be found in more 'places'. This, however, begs the question of how extensive or radical these changes have been, and how much of a challenge to conventional gender roles and conventional gender stereotypes they constitute. These issues are discussed in Section 4.2.

Summary

- Contemporary Wales is a multiracial, multi-ethnic society.

- There is a geographic concentration of the ethnic minority population in the cities of south Wales, but there is an ethnic minority presence in every local authority area in Wales.

- Women in Wales today are better educated and more evident and visible in public and political life.

4   Inequality, 'race' and gender

This section examines the extent to which the differences of 'race' and gender already identified translate into divisions and inequalities, and the extent to which opportunities and life chances are affected by differences of 'race' and gender.

4.1 Inequality and 'race'

Research on inequalities in health, housing, economic activity and labour market participation among ethnic minority groups in Wales exists, but it should be noted at the outset that much of it is small-scale and needs to be viewed with caution. The inadequate nature of the data on issues of ethnicity is the result of a number of factors, both practical and political. The legacy of neglecting issues of 'race' in political circles meant that data collection and data monitoring of ethnic group need was given a low priority at all levels of government. That said, low numbers of ethnic minorities and their dispersal across the country make it difficult to produce statistically robust data at ward level while protecting anonymity. Additionally, much of the evidence should be read with care because using the term 'ethnic minorities' generically to determine life chances is to miss what can be quite significant diversity between different ethnic minority groupings. It should also be recognised that other factors and differences, such as class, gender and age, may intersect with 'race' to produce distinct outcomes. We must therefore exercise some caution in interpreting data relating to ethnic minority groups in Wales.

With respect to health, the available evidence suggests that members of ethnic minority groups have poorer health than their white counterparts. People from white groups and black ethnic backgrounds have the highest percentage of limiting, long-term illness: 24 per cent and 19 per cent, respectively. However, these ethnic groups also have the highest proportion of older people in their communities. In contrast, there is less limiting, long-term illness in the 'Chinese and other ethnic' group (8 per cent), which also has a low proportion of older people within its community. Looking at people who reported their health to be 'not good' on the 2001 census form, the white Irish group was most likely to state this (18 per cent) and the 'Chinese and other ethnic group' the least likely (4 per cent). The overall figure for Wales was 13 per cent. However, there is a close relationship between ethnic groups reporting ill health and their age structures.

Turning to housing, evidence from the 2001 census showed that people from the white groups and those of Pakistani and Chinese origin are more likely to own their home than to rent; the lowest rate of home ownership is among the Black or Black-African group. Bangladeshi- and Black-African-headed households are much more likely to be overcrowded than households headed by people of white origin. Ethnic minority communities disproportionately live in some of the most economically deprived areas and in some of the poorest-quality housing (WAG, 2005). Overall, ethnic minority households experience a higher rate of housing deprivation than white households, but this, it must be remembered, hides a picture of considerable diversity as some ethnic groups have relatively advantaged positions in the housing and labour markets.

With respect to economic activity and labour market participation, a number of studies have found that the overall economic activity rate for almost all ethnic minority groups in Wales is lower than for white groups (Winkler, 2009).

However, there are variations in the economic activity rates of different ethnic minority groups in Wales. For example, people of Bangladeshi origin are least likely to be economically active – only 53 per cent are in employment, or are unemployed but looking for work. People of Chinese origin have an activity rate of over 80 per cent. (The activity rate for

Figure 4.4
Ethnic restaurants in
Cardiff's City Road

white groups is 76 per cent.) It should also be noted that gender
differences play a large part in accounting for the different activity rates
of ethnic minority groups. The economic activity rate for Bangladeshi
men is 83 per cent, which is actually slightly higher than the average for
the male population as a whole (82 per cent); it is the very low activity
rate of Bangladeshi women (22 per cent) that accounts for the low
overall figure. According to Victoria Winkler:

> The difference in the overall economic activity rate of Black
> Caribbeans and Black Africans (74 per cent and 63 per cent
> respectively) is also attributable to differences in women's activity

rates. However, gender differences only partly explain the lower overall activity rate of the Black or Black British group as a whole, which was noticeably below the figures for the white group.

(Winkler, 2009, p. 55)

The literature also shows that there is segregation in the labour market by ethnic group. While it is the case that a higher proportion of people (nearly 20 per cent) from all ethnic minority groups work in professional occupations compared with people from white groups, it is also the case that ethnic minority populations in Wales are overwhelmingly concentrated in sectors associated with poor terms and conditions and low pay – in health and social work (20.4 per cent), in hotels and catering (16.9 per cent) and in wholesale and retail trades and the repair of motor vehicles (16.8 per cent) (Sullivan et al., 2005). The biggest employment sector for ethnic minority groups in Wales is health and social work. Over a third of Indian women and men work in this sector, as do more than one fifth of the Black-African and Black-Caribbean populations (28.0 and 20.3 per cent, respectively). Half of both Black-Caribbean and Black-African women are employed in public sector services.

While economic activity and participation in the labour market are important measures of citizenship and inclusion, substantive citizenship also extends to participation and representation in the organs of governance. The WAG acknowledges that there is a need for all citizens to be empowered to determine their own lives and to shape the communities in which they live (WAG, 2007a). However, examination of evidence concerning the participation and representation of ethnic minority groups in public and political life in Wales suggests that the politics of Wales is a very white affair. There are currently no Welsh Members of Parliament from ethnic minority groups and the Welsh Assembly gained its first and only ethnic minority member in 2007. In terms of local councillors, only 0.8 per cent are from ethnic minority groups and they have a shorter average length of service than white councillors (WLGA, 2005).

Ethnic minority groups are also under-represented in terms of appointments to public bodies. The proportion of people from ethnic minority groups holding public appointments increased from a very low level at the start of the twenty-first century to 0.5 per cent in 2004/05, and rose again to 3.9 per cent in 2005/06, but fell to 1.3 per cent in 2006/07 (Winkler, 2009).

4.2 Inequality and gender

In Section 3 you saw that in contemporary Wales women are achieving at record rates in the school system, are more visible in higher education and constitute nearly half of the workforce. There is therefore a temptation to assume that equality reigns, that women are no longer an oppressed group and that to all intents and purposes we have 'solved', or are well on the way to solving, the 'gender problem'. On the surface the lives of men and women have become or seem to have become more similar. However, it would be a mistake to assume that 'all is well'. In several key areas notable differences and inequalities remain.

Health status scores are lower for women than men, indicating worse health and well-being among women. A higher percentage of women than men report being treated for a specific illness.

With respect to housing, figures show that in Wales there are many more women than men over the age of 60 who live alone, and that this difference increases with age. WAG statistics show that there are three times as many women than men over the age of 70 living alone, and four times as many over the age of 85.

Statistical information is also collected on the number of households applying to local authorities to register as homeless. Data for the period October to December 2007 indicates that women are more likely than men to fall into this category: there were 1,714 applications from women (56 per cent of the total), compared with 1,369 from men (44 per cent).

There is a link between employment (economic activity and participation in the labour market) and education. Thus, in considering gender differences and divisions in employment, we should begin by looking at differences in educational achievement. There is strong evidence to suggest that girls are outperforming boys at all stages of the education system. WAG data shows us that more girls than boys reach the expected levels in Key Stages 1, 2 and 3 for languages and slightly more for science and mathematics. More girls (56.9 per cent) get five good GCSEs than boys (46.2 per cent) and girls get higher average scores than boys. Girls also do slightly better at 'A' levels, and more girls aged 16–18 (62 per cent) are in full-time education than boys of this age group (53 per cent). Throughout the 1960s, the number of men at university vastly exceeded the number of women, but there are now proportionately more women students (55 per cent) than men (45 per cent). However, major differences remain with respect to course, subject and discipline choices. Girls and boys make stereotypical choices of options and subjects at all stages of education, as Table 4.2 illustrates in relation to higher education.

Activity 4.4

Examine Table 4.2.

■ Calculate the percentages of men and of women studying each of the following four disciplines: subjects allied to medicine; engineering and technology; social studies; and computer science.

■ Consider some of the implications of these gender divisions for women's and men's life chances.

Table 4.2 Higher education students by subject and gender, UK, 2006/07

Subject	Women	Men	Total
Subjects allied to medicine	232,145	48,660	280,805
Engineering and technology	14,640	82,790	97,430
Social studies	109,780	61,330	171,115
Computer science	18,860	67,210	85,890

Source: HESA, 2008, Table 2e

Comment

Table 4.2 provides evidence of strong gender difference between key academic disciplines. Men are clustered in engineering, technology and computer science, where they constitute 82 per cent of all students studying these disciplines. Women predominate in subjects allied to medicine (SaM) and social studies, where they constitute 76 per cent of all students in these disciplines. Their domination of this category is because 67 per cent of all female SaM students are studying nursing.

Although women dominate social studies as a broad discipline, men dominate in the 'hard sciences' within that category, for example in economics and politics. Such subject choices, apparent throughout the education system, facilitate particular career pathways and impact on the value of the occupations and rewards available to men and women.

Turning to the area of employment, although women in Wales comprise just under one half of the working population, their ability to participate fully in the Welsh economy continues to be seriously affected by the persistence of occupational segregation, different patterns of work and the gender pay gap. As you have already seen, girls/women and boys/men make different choices and follow different education and training pathways. This has an impact on the occupational profile – men and women tend to do different jobs. Table 4.3 shows the occupational pattern for Wales in 2004. It shows major differences in the occupational distribution for men and women.

Table 4.3 Percentage of men and women in different occupations, Wales, 2004

	Men	Women
Managers and senior officers	16	9
Professional occupations	11	10
Associate professional and technical occupations	12	15
Administrative and secretarial	5	21
Skilled trades occupations	22	2
Personal service occupations	3	14
Sales and customer service occupations	5	13
Process, plant and machine operatives	15	3
Elementary/unskilled occupations	12	12

Source: ONS, 2004

The proportions of men and women in professional or managerial jobs (the first three categories) are similar for men (39 per cent) and for women (34 per cent). The proportions of men and women in unskilled jobs are equal (12 per cent). But there are big differences in the proportions of men and women in skilled trades and semi-skilled manual work (process, plant and machine operatives), where men make up 37 per cent and women 5 per cent of the total, and in administrative and service work, where men account for 13 per cent and women for 48 per cent of the total. People in skilled trades and semi-skilled manual work get higher pay than those in administrative and service work. This goes a long way to explaining the pay gap between men and women.

The evidence on occupational segregation also suggests that while women are undoubtedly more visible in the labour market in contemporary Wales, many of the jobs they do in the formal economy are a continuation of their roles and responsibilities at home and do not present much of a challenge to conventional gender stereotypes. Women predominate in occupations that involve serving, caring, cleaning, and assisting (usually male) superiors.

Patterns and forms of work have changed significantly in recent decades (see Chapter 3). Of particular significance has been the rise in part-time work. The Annual Population Survey 2006 shows that there are 390,000 part-time employees, of whom 298,000 are women. Women comprise 76 per cent of the part-time workforce in Wales. They also comprise the majority of those who request flexible working in order to provide childcare and/or adult dependent care in their working age years.

Four in ten working women work part-time, compared with fewer than one in ten men. Women working part-time are nearly twice as likely as men to say that they do not want full-time work. Women are five times more likely than men to give family reasons for working part-time (WAG, 2007b. This reflects women's continuing disproportionate role in family and caring responsibilities and has implications for their opportunities in respect of promotion, pensions, occupational training and pay.

The gender pay gap in Wales has been narrowing over recent years but continues to be a cause for concern. The pay gap is the difference in average earnings between men and women. This is a thorny area because there are semantic issues here as well as statistical ones, and 'earnings' are measured in different ways. The WAG uses a measure of mean earnings, according to which, in 2006, women's average hourly pay (excluding overtime) was 10.9 per cent lower than men's pay. This relates to full-time employees and refers to gross pay. Using a different measure, the Bevan Foundation (2006) looked at gender equality in earnings by taking women's average gross weekly earnings as a percentage of men's average gross weekly earnings. The Foundation included full-time and part-time workers in order to take account of different working patterns and chose to base its analysis on weekly earnings rather than hourly earnings as it is this that 'influences people's ability to support themselves and their families' (Bevan Foundation, 2006, p. 11). The Foundation reports a steadily narrowing gap between women's and men's gross weekly earnings: in 1998 women's pay averaged 57.7 per cent of the amount men were paid; in 2005 this had increased to 63.9 per cent.

The final area for consideration is that of gender differences in public and political life. In 2009 the Equality and Human Rights Commission (EHRC) published the document 'Who Runs Wales?' This looks at gender balance in the boardrooms and in the corridors of power and concludes that 'progress towards getting more women into positions of power is far too slow' (EHRC, 2009, p. 3).

While women comprise nearly half the members of the National Assembly, they make up only 20 per cent of Welsh Westminster MPs, nine per cent of Welsh council leaders and 25 per cent of local councillors. In other key areas of life in Wales the picture is much the same. Women comprise only 23 per cent of chief executives of NHS trusts, 16 per cent of heads of further education colleges, 16 per cent of secondary school head teachers, 25 per cent of chief constables, 15 per cent of editors of daily and weekly newspapers, and none of the chief executives of Wales's top 100 private companies.

According to the EHRC, these findings suggest that we 'are stuck in second gear 'and 'progress towards gender equality remains far too slow' (2009, p. 8).

Activity 4.5

The *'Who Runs Wales?'* report paints a picture of life in Wales in which boardrooms are overwhelmingly male and it is largely men who take the big decisions that impact on everybody's lives.

■ Do you think this matters and, if so, why?

■ What could be done to speed up progress towards gender equality?

Consider your own views on these questions and then look at the position of the EHRC below.

> If those making the decisions are drawn from a narrow section of society, most people's needs will be overlooked ... Research tells us that greater diversity at our top tables leads to different issues being put on the agenda and discussed at meetings ... Diversity helps organisations to be more in tune with the people they serve. Evidence shows that women bring with them a determination to reach decisions that have broader support ... Every employer [should] advertise all vacancies openly ... be more creative in seeking applications from under-represented groups and in removing the barriers in their recruitment and promotion procedures. ... Wales' long working hours culture can prevent women from progressing [; this needs] rethinking ... managing home and work is a challenge to us all but women are especially hard-pressed in Wales where there are few childcare options ... employers that are innovative in offering support for working parents and carers, and real flexible working opportunities, report that more women take on senior roles and that retention rates improve.
>
> (EHRC, 2009, pp. 6–7)

Summary

■ Although the available research is small-scale and the data not very robust, evidence suggests that with respect to health, housing, economic activity and participation in public and political life, there are profound inequalities between the white population and ethnic minority groups in Wales.

■ Despite the many changes that have occurred in the lives of women in Wales over past decades, notable gender differences and inequalities remain in the areas of health, housing, education, employment and economic activity, and in participation in public and political life.

5 'Race', gender and post-devolution responses

This section examines how post-devolution Wales is progressing in terms of seeking to achieve greater equality. In Wales devolution marked a shift away from a laissez-faire approach to equalities, towards a concerted approach to establishing a robust framework for the pursuit of an equalities agenda.

One of the strongest rationales for devolution was to increase citizen involvement, inclusiveness and participation. Equalities provided a powerful driver in the run-up to devolution (see Chapter 8). The women's movement in particular played a key role in discussions and debates pre-devolution and in the drafting of the Government of Wales Act 1998. The principle of equality of opportunity was enshrined in the constitutional framework of the newly devolved administration as an 'absolute duty'. The Assembly, in all of its business and functions, must make appropriate arrangements with due regard to the principle of equality of opportunity for all. Equality is to be 'mainstreamed' on the political agenda in that it is no longer something to be 'added on'; rather, equal opportunities are the bedrock of all phases of policy development and of the very thought processes and actions of all institutions.

The National Assembly has developed a number of equalities policies and strategies and has sought to pursue its equalities duties with some vigour. But while it is certainly the case that equality issues have a higher profile in the Assembly than in other equivalent institutions, there are nevertheless concerns about whether the political commitment to mainstreaming is being backed by an adequate level of resources or institutional capacity and expertise. Some studies have noted that on many indicators progress towards equality in Wales leaves much to be desired (Chaney, 2009). The evidence considered in Section 4 of this chapter lends support to this claim.

In concluding this discussion of gender and 'race' differences, divisions and inequalities in Wales today, this section looks briefly at the current situation in the post-devolution setting.

5.1 'Race'

The Parekh Report of 2000 on the future of multicultural Britain acknowledged the potential impact of devolution on questions of 'race' and ethnicity. The report challenged the new institutions to 'rethink the national story', to review their understanding of themselves and to take responsibility for racial inequalities. Nations can no longer ignore the challenges posed by increasing multiculturalism.

From a very low starting point, the then National Assembly for Wales (NAW) Equality of Opportunity Committee's audit acknowledged the magnitude of the task ahead and has steered a course of action aimed at demonstrating leadership in developing 'race' equality and good race relations. There is no doubt that ethnic minorities and equality issues have received unprecedented attention in post-devolution Wales. 'Race' equality is explicitly on the policy agenda. Efforts have been made to improve data collection to provide for evidence-based policy making. Attention has been given to issues of recruitment and retention of ethnic minority workers in public services and public appointments, and ongoing efforts are made to improve consultation with a wide range of groups. For example, the government has established an Inter Faith Council, an All Wales Ethnic Minority Association and other mechanisms to open dialogue with individuals and groups.

However, the extent of change post-devolution should not be overstated. The greater involvement of ethnic minorities in the operation of government does not necessarily mean a change in outcomes. The new politics of dialogue and interchange have proved difficult for many ethnic minorities who remain weak partners in these exchanges. A plethora of policy papers may indicate a more active and engaged government, but being able to demonstrate inclusion and involvement in the policy process is not the same as being able to demonstrate that benefits are accruing to minority groups in terms of impacts, outcomes and life chances (see Chapter 8 for further discussion).

5.2 Gender

The women's movement in Wales played a key role in the run-up to devolution and gender was high on the equalities agenda. The gender balance in the Assembly following the first election was highly significant and could be seen to herald a new style of politics and representation. Several of the women Assembly Members (AMs) came from voluntary sector women's organisations and these organisations found, from the early days of devolution, that they had good access to the Assembly and were able to make representation and be consulted on equal opportunities issues and policies. Other women's organisations – including Merched y Wawr, Women in Agriculture and the Women's Royal Voluntary Service (WRVS) – were more marginalised and felt that their voices were not being heard.

One of the key gender issues in Wales, both pre- and post-devolution, has concerned women in the economy. The evidence reviewed in Section 4 above suggests that while the gap in economic activity rates between men and women is narrowing, occupational segregation by gender is marked, with women working in very different industries and

Figure 4.5
Female Community
Support Officers at a
protest in Aberystwyth

occupations from men, being located at different levels in work hierarchies and having very different types and conditions of work. In Wales gender has had more of an impact on life chances than elsewhere in Britain and patterns of segregation are particularly rigid. Chwarae Teg (Fair Play), an organisation tasked and funded by the WAG to provide advice to ministers and policy makers on matters related to women's contribution to the Welsh economy, raises questions about equality at work:

> Gender differences and their effects are clearly evident across training and skills, pay, poverty, occupational segregation, career choices and organisation of our labour markets, influencing by gender who works where and under what conditions ... for Wales to fully embrace gender mainstreaming, there is a need to ensure that all legislation, policies or programmes, in all areas, and at all levels ... leads to a more inclusive policy making process.
>
> (Chwarae Teg, 2009, p. 16)

The Chwarae Teg report makes a number of policy recommendations to the WAG and sums up its overall message thus:

> A balance needs to be created where women and men are equally represented within the skills and higher paid sectors, but to achieve this aspiration, it is essential that stereotyping in schools and education is challenged as a priority to encourage more women into science, engineering and technology to meet the future skills needs of Wales and drive the engine of the economy.
>
> (Chwarae Teg, 2009, p. 4)

Summary

- Devolution established a strong framework for the pursuit of an equalities agenda.

- The Welsh Assembly has an 'absolute duty' to provide equal opportunity for all.

- 'Race' and gender equality issues are now explicitly on the policy agenda in Wales.

- It is premature to suggest that the new politics of dialogue and structures of consultation have yet led to real material change or to genuine inclusion in society for women and for ethnic minority groups.

6   Conclusion

Wales has a long way to go towards achieving multiculturalism, 'race' equality or gender equality. Some progress has been made. Women are more visible in public, political and economic life and there is a more visible celebration of difference in the representation of the nation and in national identity. Some would argue that these changes are superficial rather than signalling real change and that much remains to be done.

As the UK moves to implement the Single Equality Act (2010), the WAG will have to respond, preparing a single equality scheme laying out its intentions and operating processes for the coming decade. Questions remain about whether the Assembly has laid the foundation for sustainable work on equalities, or whether the progress to date will be halted or reversed by future changes in government.

References

Aaron, J., Rees, T., Betts, S. and Vincentelli, M. (eds) (1994) *Our Sisters' Land: the Changing Identities of Women in Wales*, Cardiff, University of Wales Press.

Beddoe, D. (2000) *Out of the Shadows: a History of Women in Twentieth Century Wales*, Cardiff, University of Wales Press.

Betts, S. and Chaney, P. (2004) 'Inclusive and participatory governance? The view from the grass roots of women's organisations in Wales', *Wales Journal of Law and Policy*, vol. 3, no. 2, pp. 173–87.

Bevan Foundation (2006) *Measuring up: Progress towards Equality between Women and Men in Wales*, Tredegar; Bevan Foundation/Equal Opportunities Commission.

Braham, P. and Janes, L. (2002) *Social Differences and Social Divisions*, Oxford, Oxford University Press.

Chaney, P (2009) *Equal Opportunities and Human Rights: The First Decade of Devolution in Wales*, Cardiff, Equality and Human Rights Commission.

Chwarae Teg (2009) *Policy Briefing: Women in the Economy in Wales* [online], available at www.chwaraeteg.com.

Equality and Human Rights Commission (2009) *Who Runs Wales 2009?*, Cardiff, EHRC.

Evans, N. (2002) 'Immigrants and minorities in Wales 1840–1990' in Williams, C., Evans, N. and O'Leary, P. (eds) *A Tolerant Nation? Exploring Ethnic Diversity in Wales*, Cardiff, University of Wales Press.

Higher Education Statistics Agency (2008) *All Higher Education Students by Level of Study, Domicile and Gender at the UK Level 2006/07*, Cheltenham, HESA.

Little, K. (1948) *Negroes in Britain: a Study of the Racial Relations in English Society* (reprinted 2002), London, Routledge.

Office for National Statistics (ONS) (2004) *Labour Force Survey*, London, HMSO.

Office for National Statistics (ONS) (2001) *UK Census*, London, HMSO.

Parekh, B. (2000) *The Future of Multi Ethnic Britain*, London, Profile Books.

Rees, T. (1999) *Women and Work: 25 Years of Gender Equality in Wales*, Cardiff, University of Wales Press.

Robinson, V. and Gardner, H. (2004) 'Place matters: exploring the distinctiveness of racism in rural Wales' in Neal, S. and Agyeman, J. (eds) *The New Countryside? Ethnicity, Nation and Exclusion in Contemporary Rural Britain*, Bristol, Policy Press.

Scourfield, J., Evans, J., Shah, W. and Beynon, H. (2004) 'The negotiation of minority ethnic identities in virtually all white communities: research with children and their families in the South Wales valleys', *Children and Society*, vol. 19, no. 3, pp. 211–24.

Sullivan, M., Clutton, S. and James, E. (2005) *How Does Race and Gender Influence Wealth and Well-being in Wales?*, Swansea, National Centre for Public Policy, University of Wales.

Welsh Assembly Government (2007a) *One Wales: a Progressive Agenda for the Government of Wales*, Cardiff, WAG.

Welsh Assembly Government (2007b) 'Statistical focus on men and women in Wales', *Statistical Bulletin*, 38/2007, Cardiff, WAG.

Welsh Assembly Government (2006) *Annual Population Survey*, Cardiff, WAG.

Welsh Assembly Government (2005) 'A profile of the housing and socio-economic circumstances of black and minority ethnic people in Wales in 2001', *Housing Research Report HRR 4/05*, Cardiff, WAG.

Welsh Local Government Association (WLGA) (2005) *Census of Local Authority Councillors 2004*, Cardiff, WLGA.

Williams, C. (2005 'Can we live together? Wales and the multicultural question', Lecture to the Honourable Society of Cymmrodorion, 2004, *Transactions*, vol. 11, pp. 216–30.

Williams, C. (2004) 'Access to justice and social inclusion: the policy challenges', *Journal of Social Welfare and Family Law*, vol. 26, no. 1, pp. 53–68.

Winkler, V. (ed.) (2009) 'Equality issues in Wales: a research review', *Research Report 11*, Cardiff, Equality and Human Rights Commission.

Further reading

For a historical account of the black presence in Wales, see Alan Llwyd (2005) *Cymru Ddu/Black Wales: a History*, Cardiff, Butetown History and Arts Centre. For a literary account, read the memoir: Charlotte Williams (2002) *Sugar and Slate*, Aberystwyth, Planet Books.

There are a number of books published by Butetown History and Arts Centre that tell the story of Butetown in the post-war period. See, for example, Neil Sinclair (2003) *The Tiger Bay Story*, Cardiff, Dragon and Tiger Enterprises.

Jane Aaron, Teresa Rees, Sandra Betts and Moira Vincentelli (eds) (1994) *Our Sisters' Land*, Cardiff, University of Wales Press, provides a collection of accounts on the changing identities of women in Wales.

For a detailed account of gender and employment in Wales, see Teresa Rees (1999) *Women and Work: 25 years of Gender Equality in Wales*, Cardiff, University of Wales Press.

Chapter 5
Class

Neil Evans

Contents

1 Introduction

Class is not something that crops up very often in polite conversation. Most people would not ask someone they had just met what their social class was. It would be seen as rude and an obstruction to getting to know the person as an individual. But sociologists and historians commonly use the word and most of us understand generally what it means. It helps us to think about the general pattern of our society and how we place ourselves within it. Class is certainly something that is often asked about in social surveys, and market researchers like to place people in groups according to what they are likely to buy and consume. Interviewers have some licence to ask impertinent questions!

The aims of this chapter are to:

- discuss the way in which class is viewed in Wales, and whether this view has changed

- examine shifts in the class structure in Wales since the end of the Second World War, such as polarisation and social mobility

- consider whether there are differences between the class structures in urban and rural areas in Wales.

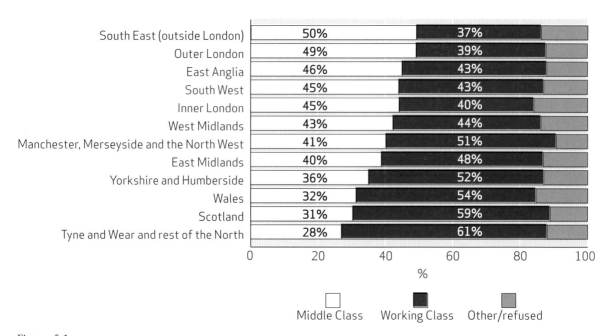

Figure 5.1
Self-identification of social class in Great Britain by area
(Source: wales.gov.uk/firstminister/reports/futures/SOCIETY-e.pdf?lang=en)

Activity 5.1

First, answer these two questions:

■ What social class do you think you belong to?

  – upper class

  – middle class

  – working class

  – I don't think classes exist any more

■ Why did you give that answer?

Now look at Figure 5.1, which provides answers (gathered from the various regions and nations of Britain) to the first question.

■ What is distinctive about the answers given in Wales compared with other parts of Britain?

Comment

In this survey, reported in 2008, 54 per cent of people in Wales identified themselves as working-class and 32 per cent as middle-class. The remaining 14 per cent either refused to answer (it's a rude question!) or identified themselves as belonging to another class. Wales has one of the highest percentages in Britain of people identifying as working-class; in south-east England and London around 50 per cent of people think they are middle-class and less than 40 per cent see themselves as working-class – more or less reversing the percentages in Wales. Only Scotland and the far north of England have a greater percentage of people who identify themselves as working-class: around 60 per cent.

So most people in Wales can place themselves in a class and think of themselves as working-class.

Answering the second question in Activity 5.1 is much more difficult; and we don't know why the people in Wales who were surveyed answered the way they did. But we do have the answers that some people in Swansea gave to interviewers around 2002.

A female head teacher from Morriston, aged 58, identified herself as middle-class but added:

> I was obviously born working class. I obviously have, if you are thinking in more, sort of, social categories, typical of the Welsh working class, aspired to be a teacher and so on ... I'm not a fan of class. It's one thing I don't like really.

> (quoted in Charles et al., 2008, p. 86)

Behind the simple answer to a question lies a very complex personal history, which is often the case. Like many people, the respondent is uncomfortable with the idea of class in some ways. A 31-year-old woman from a deprived area of social housing said this:

> I wouldn't think I'm better than anybody else, you know, if somebody is, you know, better off than me, or hasn't got as much or whatever, I wouldn't say, "Look I've got more than you so I'm better than you." No, I wouldn't have thought so.
>
> (quoted in Charles et al., 2008, p. 87)

Many of us call ourselves working-class or middle-class because both are seen as 'ordinary' categories rather than placing ourselves in a superior position to others (Savage, 2000). This is exactly what this woman is doing.

Why might so many people in Wales opt to call themselves working-class, rather than middle-class – especially compared with people in the south-east of England? Here is a possible clue from a study of redundant steelworkers in the 1980s:

> Southern English middle-class readers, like the present writer, may have difficulty in grasping that to be working class (at any rate in South Wales) is not to ... lack ... the 'badges of achievement' which all others possess, but is, rather, to occupy an honourable status which gives you dignity and entitles you to respect. As one of our respondents who had been out of work for over a year put it: 'I used to be working class, but I can't claim that any more. I've fallen below that'.
>
> (Harris et al., 1987, p. 15)

This is similar to the answer given by a 34-year-old woman from a deprived estate in Swansea almost twenty years later: 'Not working class any more, common' (quoted in Charles et al., 2008, p. 87). By becoming unemployed she thought she had lost her social standing. A couple in their late 60s living in Oystermouth (which most people would see as a solid middle-class area) and in comfortable circumstances saw no reason to reject the label of working-class:

> Wife: I wouldn't like to say I'm not working class because we come from strong Labour working class backgrounds. ... My father was a miner. Leighton's [her husband's] father was a red.
>
> (quoted in Charles et al., 2008, p. 86)

How we see ourselves in terms of class is influenced by our past lives as well as by our current circumstances. While some people may revel in feeling 'superior', others will be uncomfortable with the idea. We may be generally uncertain about where we stand in society and don't like to place our very individual lives in little boxes made by others. The idea of class involves a sense of hierarchy. The term 'social stratification', another way to refer to class, is borrowed from geology where each stratum of rock is laid over another.

How would I answer the questions posed in Activity 5.1? I'm middle-class, I suppose.

Why do I say that? I had a professional job which was paid at a level comfortably above the average wage. I had much freedom within it; I was trusted to do it without detailed supervision. That put me in what some sociologists call the 'service class'; that is, I was paid quite well, could look forward to annual rises in my salary and promotion, and was expected, in return, to not limit myself to simply being in work at fixed times but in some ways to invest much of my life in it (i.e. to serve). My working conditions were pleasant and safe. To get a job like that I needed two university degrees. Now I'm retired, I have a reasonable pension. Most of my close friends are in a similar position and our children have both got good degrees and achieved similar social positions. My wife's father was a university professor. We live in a fairly large house and have some savings. I listen to Radio 3 and Radio 4, like classical music and jazz and read what are usually regarded as serious books, not to mention the *Guardian* and the *Observer.*

In placing myself like this, I'm drawing on the kinds of criteria that social scientists use to assess class. Education is usually a critical factor in this, as is your job and the networks of people that you're part of. Class is also related to culture; Radio 4 is often seen as the middle-class (and middle-aged!) station. We've had advantages which have been passed on to our children. Less often raised in talking about class is the fact that I'm a man. Certainly in the past class was seen as a status that male 'heads of household' conferred on the whole family. Despite the gains achieved by feminism and equal opportunities legislation, men still tend to have advantages over women in gaining opportunities, as you saw in Chapter 4. Gender raises issues about class to which I'll return later.

So if I can place myself in a social position in this way, why did I add that grudging 'I suppose' at the end of my answer? My reasons are very much like those of the interviewees from Swansea quoted above. To say you're middle-class, at least in Wales, might seem pompous and pretentious. I was trying to be honest and realistic – and to use what I know about the way in which sociologists discuss class.

More important, I grew up in the south Wales Valleys where everybody seemed to be working-class; my father was a coach driver for part of his working life. That meant long hours, low wages and no occupational pension. In jobs like that people tend to leave work behind them once they are at home; they do a fixed amount of work for a fixed wage and often don't have prospects of advancement. They are expected to earn but not really to serve. I was the first in my family to go to university; and in the village I come from, education and 'getting on' were valued at the very least because (as many miners told me) they could save you from going down a hole in the ground every day of your working life. But I grew up with comics rather than books, the old Light Programme (effectively Radio 2), pop music, ITV and Cardiff City football club. I still like lots of those things, too. Indeed, it is much too simple to imagine that our class positions equate with whether we like so-called 'high' or 'low' culture. Many of us appreciate mixtures of the two.

So they might have taken the boy out of the Valleys but they haven't taken the Valleys out of the man. If I'd grown up in a middle-class home I would probably have had advantages from that background, such as accent, connections, books, musical education: things referred to as **social capital** and **cultural capital**. These ideas are associated with the work of the French sociologist Pierre Bourdieu (1930–2002), whose work explored the cultural dimensions of class in particular. As he stressed, social and cultural capital can be passed on through the generations and clearly give advantages; my children have had these to a greater extent than I had.

So my life – like those of the people whose interviews were quoted above – raises questions about *social mobility*; that is, that people might end up in a social class different from the one in which they started. Usually we mean moving up in the social scale when we talk about this, but it is important to know that people can go down as well as up. Moving up in society often means moving to another place. A study of middle-class people conducted in the 1960s opened by observing: '[Swansea's] role in social and geographical mobility is that although it may appear in the first chapters of the autobiographies, it rarely appears in the last. Provincial Britain is somewhere to get away from ... ' (Bell, 1968, p. 10). This alerts us to an important facet of Welsh society: many people have moved out of Wales in order to advance their careers and opportunities. Far fewer have moved in to do so.

Social capital means the networks to which people belong that produce resources for achieving their ends.

Cultural capital means the knowledge, skills and education that individuals have.

Summary

- People in Wales are more likely to identify themselves as working-class than those in most other parts of the UK.

- This self-identification is influenced by people's pasts as well as by the positions they find themselves in now (people can move from one class to another over their lifetimes).

2 Conceptions of class in Wales

When we talk about class we are placing ourselves in relation to others in society. All our individual cases are complex and none of us are identical. But we usually have some idea of where we fit in and some sense of the overall shape of our society: its class structure. So how does the idea of class help us to understand Wales? What is the overall shape of Welsh society?

Activity 5.2

What do you think of when you think about class in Wales?

- Wales is a place where people engage in militant class conflict; class means the picket line, solidarity.

- Wales – unlike England – is classless.

- Wales is run by the English upper class – white settlers – who take all the best jobs.

- Wales is run by a Welsh-speaking middle class: the 'Taffia'.

I want to discuss each of these responses in turn to see what, if any, truth there is in them.

2.1 Class as organisation and conflict

Class conflict provides a powerful image of Wales. It has been projected across the world. The most-read book and most-seen film about Wales, ever, is Richard Llewellyn's 1939 *How Green Was My Valley?* John Ford directed a film of it in 1941, winning five Oscars (see Figure 5.2). It contains many scenes of industrial conflict and its strongly projected images endure. Of course it is an image that is most associated with the mining valleys of south Wales, but a hundred years ago south-east Wales contained three quarters of the population of Wales and mining was the largest occupation there by far. In the rest of Wales there were small pockets that were similar, like the slate-quarrying communities of Gwynedd and the mining and other industrial communities in Clwyd which also had a sometimes bitter industrial history.

You have already seen that being working-class in Wales has often been regarded as a positive identity and that this may have something to do with why so many people tend to identify themselves as working-class. Our images of class in Wales start in the era when large-scale and usually heavy industries were the dominant form of employment and tended to shape the nature of the communities around them. A hundred years ago the vast majority of the population of Wales was engaged in manual

Figure 5.2

Miners come out on strike in John Ford's *How Green was My Valley?*

labour, and that was seen as a positive thing because civilisation was regarded as resting upon this work. Moreover, working people achieved respectable lifestyles for themselves through their creation of chapels, trade unions, choirs and many other organisations. They created communities, social and cultural capital, for themselves and were proud of the achievement. Many people were also proud of having a tradition of standing up for their rights; being radical is a way that many people think of themselves as Welsh.

An important aspect of class has been the creation of organisations that recruit mainly from one class and may be in opposition to others.

Trade unions are very different from the craft guilds which preceded them, as guilds were run by master craftsmen (they were almost always men) but included the people they employed as well. Trade unions were formed on a class basis; those who were employed organised around their common interests and this meant not including the boss. The Labour Party, unlike similar European parties, identifies itself with a class rather than with a political viewpoint. The equivalent party in Germany calls itself the Social Democratic Party. The Labour Party owes its origins to the trade unions, though it now seeks votes far beyond the working class and claims to represent the people in general rather than one class in particular, but its name looks back to a time when the idea of class was central.

Strikes and massive industrial conflict have been rare in Wales since the mid 1980s. Like many images of places, it is a rather dated one. Indeed, it has been seen as dated for a long time. When social scientists began to take a strong interest in the nature of working-class communities and culture in the 1950s and 1960s they already talked about a 'traditional' working class. Miners, railway workers, dockers and steelworkers, the groups which dominated the working class in Wales at the time, were central to this group. They lived in communities side by side with other miners, railway workers, dockers and steelworkers. But there was also talk of a 'new' working class: workers in new mass production industries like car and white goods manufacture who faced assembly lines in their daily working lives. Their lifestyles were seen as being much more influenced by the boom in consumer goods in the period, and they were much less likely to live alongside others who worked in the same industry and to share their leisure time with workmates than were the 'traditional' working class. Both groups now seem rather like a vision from the past.

Being working-class was in many ways a masculine identity. To stand up to the boss was to be a *man*. Boys entered manhood by entering the work of work. In *How Green Was My Valley*, the central character, Huw, goes to a grammar school but ultimately rejects the office job he might have had in order to go down the pit with his father and brother. Women were much more confined to the home than they have been since the Second World War. Men were seen as being heads of household and so as giving the whole family its class position. Women, of course, did take part in strikes and politics, but often as supporters of men in their disputes. Most recently this was the case in the miners' strike of 1984–5, but such support was a feature of many areas of Wales throughout the twentieth century.

Do any of these attitudes still influence our view of the world now? The strength of Labour voting in Wales suggests something about this and is considered in Chapter 7. What about trade unions? To what extent do

Welsh people still join them and is there anything distinctive in their support for them?

In 2008 just over a third (37.4 per cent) of all employees in Wales were members of trade unions. This represents a considerable decline compared with the past, when heavy industry dominated the Welsh economy. But it is the highest level of any region or nation in the UK. It is also rising slightly, while the trend over the whole of the UK is for a slight decline. In the south-east of England, only a little over one in five employees (21.5 per cent) are in trade unions, while the Welsh figure is slightly above the level of the old industrial regions of England, like the north-east and north-west. Trade union membership in Wales totals almost half a million and these days the new recruits are more likely to be women than men.

Generally, trade union membership is concentrated among people who work in the public sector and tends to be higher for managerial, professional and technical employees and lowest in sales and customer service occupations (Barratt, 2009). Much has changed in the trade union movement from the days when it had the image of men in flat caps and on picket lines. In the summer of 2009 the website of the Wales Trades Union Congress showed the changes. There were no references to strikes, but there was a welcome for a proposed government measure to promote equal rights for women and concern about the impact of the recession on women's jobs. But those who join trade unions probably think their interests are different from those of their employers.

So seeing class as being rooted in particular kinds of organisation has been important – and this view persists. Those who grew up in the era when such matters were more central to people's lives (and there are a lot of them, because of the high birth rate immediately after the war) may find it difficult to adjust their perceptions, and family traditions affect behaviour. But this view is bound to be affected by changes in the nature of society, especially by the far greater numbers and proportion of women who leave the home in order to work. The old view of class resonates far more if we think of men working underground than if we think of women working in offices.

2.2 Classlessness

This seems like a direct contradiction of the first image of class in Wales, but perhaps it is not as flatly opposed to it when we consider it more deeply. Seeing Wales as essentially working-class means starting our analysis with the ordinary people and stressing what they have in common. By contrast, in England people often refer to the class system as being a central feature. By this they generally mean that some people are born with major advantages and they hold on to them through going to the right school and mixing with people who have power and money – acquiring social and cultural capital. Class often, in this case, means snobbery and it starts our story at the top of society. When we say Wales is classless we mean that people have many values and attitudes in common, and come from similar kinds of small communities. We see Wales as 'a community of communities', as was discussed in Chapter 2. In some ways it is another way of saying that we are all working-class.

Activity 5.3

Read the following passage.

■ What does it claim to be the nature of Welsh society, and what makes this different from English society?

It had often been remarked that class divisions between those living in Wales are less marked than in parts of England – in terms of the origin of income (most of the owners of land and capital are resident outside Wales), the distribution of income, and the differences of life-style. There is also a stress on locality – where one comes from – which masks status differences between wage workers and the few professional and managerial families in the 'urban villages'. ... Even in towns as big as Swansea who you are (i.e. your place in the kin network) is often as important as what you are. In local affairs this leads to (what outsiders regard as) nepotism and a preference for locals.

(Leonard, 1980, p. 26)

Comment

Part of what is being said here is that there are relatively few rich people in Wales; Wales is controlled by people who live in England, so Wales can be relatively classless *and* have a history of social conflict. The 'enemy' of the 'classless' Welsh is seen as living outside Wales. Nepotism ('jobs for the boys' – and it usually was boys) is based on kin and locality rather than institutions ('the old school tie').

But this argument of classlessness is most often used about the rural areas of Wales, rather than the industrial ones. An influential account of the Aberporth area after the Second World War argues that local people did not think in terms of upper, middle and lower classes but of 'people of the chapel' and 'people of the pub':

The distinctive characteristics of each group are its *buchedd*. ... The Welsh term *buchedd* (plural *bucheddau*) denotes behaviour, either actual or ideal, and thus corresponds broadly to the English term 'way of life'. The same overall pattern of social life is found within each *buchedd* group. ... The two groups have a great deal in common ... The significance of the family and kindred is the same for both groups; ... Many members of both groups have the same occupations, the same working conditions, the same wages, leaving their houses at the same time in the morning and returning at the same time in the evening.

(Jenkins, 1960, pp. 13–14)

David Jenkins's point is that local understanding of the society is based on moral criteria and lifestyle and has little or nothing to do with people's occupation and income. Respectability is the key. However, this argument is not supported by the evidence of his own survey or of other studies of Welsh society (Day and Fitton, 1975). The respected people, the leaders of the chapel and the community in general, tended to be the better-off and more established residents. Indeed, one reason for the decline in religious observance in twentieth-century Wales was that the middle classes took such positions of power and prestige and were seen as forming an exclusive group.

The idea that the rural areas were classless probably arises from the fact that Nonconformity was once a mass religion and the basis of politics. The social distinctions within the countryside were overlain with a widespread adherence to the Liberal Party, and subsequently in many cases to Labour. The owners of large estates, from which farmers rented their land, stood outside this. They were identified as English in culture, Anglicans in religion and Conservatives in politics. There was an alliance of the other classes against them and for many people what they had in common seemed more important than what divided them. But there were still differences in income, farmers employed labourers, and there was a middle class of teachers and professional people.

There are other ways of assessing classlessness. One measure of class is income. There are very large differences in incomes between the best-off and the worst-off in Wales – it is far from classless. Differences of income on this scale mean that some people are able to afford very lavish lifestyles, often involving forms of conspicuous consumption (the display of wealth and standing through material goods). Their culture is bound to be different from that of people on the lower levels of income, who will often struggle to afford necessities and for whom all that is conspicuous about their consumption is the lack of it.

However, the scale of inequality is rather less in Wales than it is in the rest of Britain. The richest 10 per cent have a share of incomes that is rather less than the British average, while the poorest 10 per cent have incomes that are rather above the average share for Britain. The gap is

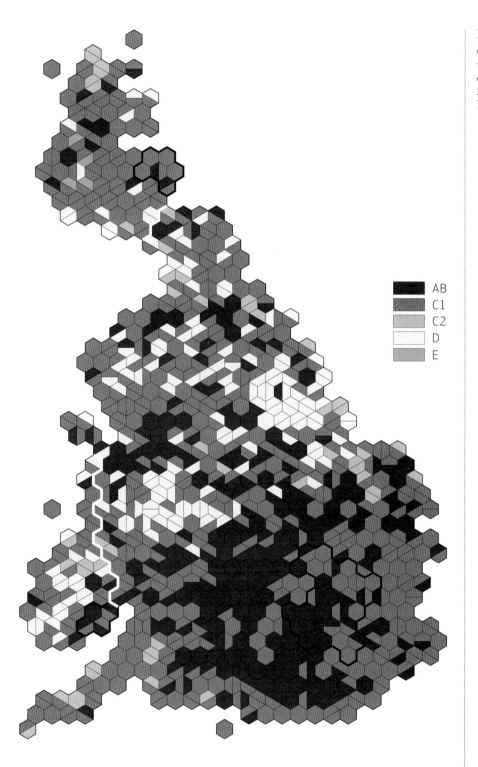

Figure 5.3
Cartogram of Britain by
the dominant social
class of people aged
25–39 in 2005 (Source:
NGCA (2009), p. 54.)

still very large, however, and we would surely notice the differences of income, culture and status if we saw the two groups side by side. As you will see, we don't observe the differences as we don't often see the two together.

Why is the share of income of the richest groups in Wales less than that of their equivalents in England? The answer is related to the *class structure* of Wales – that is, the numbers of people in the various social groups into which people are divided by census takers and sociologists. In Wales there tends to be a smaller proportion of the population in the better-off groups than is the case in England, and a higher proportion in the less well-off groups. This has been so for some time, at least going back to the 1960s.

Activity 5.4

Figure 5.3 is a cartogram. A cartogram is a map on which statistical information is presented in diagrammatic form. Although this cartogram has roughly the same proportions of Great Britain that a map would, it's really just a geometrical design to visualize the distribution of social classes in Britain: population differences distort the geographical shape, but you can still recognise the three distinct countries and their capitals. As each hexagon represents 100,000 people, no one area will be entirely one social class – but in each area one social class is dominant. The numbers in the key refer to the social classes used in the census to categorise people. Earlier letters in the alphabet and lower numbers mean higher social classes.

■ What does this tell us about the structure of classes in Wales in comparison with the rest of Britain?

Comment

Figure 5.3 shows how small the concentrations of people in the higher social classes are in Wales – especially when we compare the situation in the south-east of England. There are also significant differences between areas of England. Some areas, like the north-east, are quite similar to parts of Wales. It might be misleading to compare England as a whole with Wales. We may need to think more about the divisions within England.

But there are very significant differences between social classes in Wales. So far we have concentrated on the average of Welsh society. What do we know about the small, well-off and powerful groups? The next two sections address these issues.

2.3 White settlers

You have already come across the idea that much of the wealth and power in Wales is possessed by people who live elsewhere. The key financial institutions in Britain are in London. New York and Tokyo are the other major financial centres in the world. Many of the companies that employ people in Wales are multinational and have their headquarters outside Wales. But what about English people who live in Wales? Do they form an **elite**? Do they take most of the top jobs? Is there a **cultural division of labour**? Might being English provide an advantage of some kind? At one time, in some political discussions in Wales these people were referred to as 'white settlers' – that is, they were compared with the European elites in African countries who ruled over native populations. This is, of course, an inflammatory way of expressing the idea.

About one in five of the population of Wales was born in England. They cannot all hold elite positions – there are simply too many of them – but do they take a disproportionate number of the best-paid and most powerful positions? The short answer is that we don't really know. An English (Geordie) sociologist explains one reason for this: 'Social science has been, rightly, accused of adopting a posture of palms up to the rich for the receipt of funding and eyes down to the poor as part of the surveillance necessary for their control' (Byrne, 2005, p. 5).

As you will see, there is a good deal of research in Wales on the poor. Studies of the rich and powerful are much harder to come by and are not very conclusive on this issue. What evidence there is suggests there is some advantage for those who are not Welsh by birth. From data in the 1991 census it can be shown that 6.2 per cent of those born outside Wales are employed in professions, compared with 2.2 per cent of non-Welsh-speaking people born in Wales and 3.5 per cent of Welsh speakers. That is, they are almost three times more likely to be in the top jobs than Welsh people who do not speak Welsh and almost twice as likely to be so than Welsh speakers. At the managerial level, Welsh speakers and the non-Welsh are level (around a third of each group is so employed), but both do better than non-Welsh-speaking Welsh people (around a fifth of them hold such jobs). At the skilled manual level, the groups are almost equal, with around a fifth of each one in these occupations. Below this level, the non-Welsh-speaking Welsh begin to predominate; among the unskilled they are almost twice as well represented as the other groups (Aitchison and Carter, 2000, pp. 123–7). So there is some truth in the view that there is an incoming elite. But this data also reveals significant differences between Welsh people according to whether or not they speak Welsh. This issue needs to be addressed to obtain a fuller understanding.

An **elite** is a relatively small dominant group within a large society, having a privileged status and possessing power.

A **cultural division of labour** means that people's jobs are related to their ethnic or national origins.

2.4 The 'Taffia'

The idea of English domination tends to be stressed by people of a nationalist persuasion. Those who are opposed to nationalism and devolution in Wales often think that the country is run by a tiny group of Welsh speakers, sometimes known as the 'Taffia': a loaded term suggesting there are Godfathers everywhere. Again there is little actual evidence of this, though there are frequent assertions:

> The Welsh-language scene itself at that time [in the early 1990s] was a tightknit community with everyone knowing everyone else. If you went regularly to gigs at Cardiff's Welsh club, Clwb Ifor Bach, then you would inevitably see the same faces, and it didn't take long to get to know them.

> ... many ... were artists or ... worked in the arts or ... were employed at S4C or ... were involved at the local media. HTV and the BBC in Wales are notoriously populated by the 'Taffia' – an exclusive clique of Welsh speakers whose backgrounds in Welsh-speaking schools and Welsh universities, coupled with their ability to speak the language, has led to the sort of nepotism notorious amongst Oxford and Cambridge graduates in London media circles.
>
> (Owens, 2000, pp. 33–4)

More considered analysis finds some basis for this argument. Cardiff has developed a Welsh-speaking community since the Second World War, prompted by the growth of national institutions that are located in the city. The Welsh Office was created in 1964, there are other institutions like the National Museum of Wales and the former Welsh Folk Museum at St Fagans (now the National History Museum), and media production is concentrated in the city, with the BBC, ITV and S4C all having facilities there. One study has found evidence of a renewal of the Welsh-speaking middle class of teachers, preachers and writers through broadcasting and argues that a tightly knit group has used language issues as an avenue of social advancement (Bevan, 1984). Meanwhile, devolution has meant that civil service jobs that were once in London have been moved to Cardiff, so Welsh people may need only to move within Wales and not out of Wales to advance themselves. The London Welsh community has suffered considerable decline because of devolved government. And many of these positions require a fluency in the Welsh language, which gives Welsh speakers certain advantages in some areas.

The Welsh-speaking population of Cardiff tends to cluster in particular areas:

> the majority of Welsh speakers have settled either in the traditional middle to high status residential districts of the city (e.g., Llandaff) or in select suburban and rural fringe areas (e.g., St Fagans, Radyr). ... the

Welsh-speaking population of the city is largely composed of young
to early middle-aged families. Not surprisingly, having established
themselves in Cardiff, such families have sought to ensure that ample
facilities would be available for children to pursue their education
through the medium of Welsh ... [there has been] ... a highly
significant growth in the number of bilingual schools in the region.

(Aitchison and Carter, 1987, p. 490)

You have seen already that Welsh speakers are well represented in the
upper reaches of Welsh society, though not at the very top level. Welsh
speakers and the non-Welsh are both over-represented in the better-off
groups; non-Welsh-speaking Welsh people have the least effective social
and cultural capital. There are some interesting variations in this,
according to region. In the areas that were once seen as the heartland of
the Welsh language, Anglesey, Gwynedd, Ceredigion and
Carmarthenshire, the non-Welsh are over-represented at the top. In the
more economically dynamic areas of south-east Wales, Welsh speakers
are over-represented in elite positions compared with the non-Welsh.
This shows the effectiveness of the formation of a Welsh-speaking
middle class in urban south Wales and reveals something about the
patterns of migration within Wales.

This is linked to the quality of education in Welsh-medium schools,
which have been a clear success story in post-war Wales. The
commitment of parents, pupils and teachers to the cause of language
renewal has ensured that they produce well-qualified pupils. The
children benefit from effectively having two first languages and from a
wide range of extra-curricular activities. Better cultural capital is
especially important when, in general, schools in Wales have not
performed particularly well; whether there are benefits from the social
capital of the networks of the 'Taffia' is less clear (Reynolds and Bellin,
1996). Welsh-medium schools are open to the children of non-Welsh
speakers and now educate some 20 per cent of children. This does not
make them especially exclusive.

Summary

■ A history of class conflict means that many people in Wales are
   proud to describe themselves as working-class.

■ Wales is often perceived as classless, in comparison with many other
   parts of Britain, in the sense of people holding similar values and
   coming from similar communities.

■ People born outside Wales are more likely to have jobs in the
   professions than those who are Welsh-born, but there are also

differences between Welsh-born people according to whether or not they speak Welsh.

■ There is a widespread view that Welsh speakers dominate the most influential tiers of society.

3   Changes in the class structure of Wales

Wales has changed a good deal since the Second World War. These changes have been charted in a series of studies of Swansea and its region, which offer a convenient perspective. The authors of a recent (2006) major study of the area sum up the changes in the class structure of Swansea since the 1960s thus:

> The shape of the occupational distribution taken as a whole has changed dramatically. The traditional distribution was shaped like a pyramid. It was composed of a small elite group at the top, a large mass of 'ordinary working people' at the bottom and a medium sized stratum composed of people who were 'in between'. The 2001 male occupational distribution echoes this: manual workers still constitute the largest group, though it is much shrunken, and the other two groups are enormously enlarged and are of equal size. What makes the overall 2001 distribution depart so dramatically from the traditional is the distribution of women. Nearly two thirds of women are 'in between', thereby creating a bulge in the middle of the occupational structure. Their distribution is therefore 'oval', as is the distribution of the whole work force when the distributions of the two sexes are added together.
>
> (Harris et al., 2006, para. 4.14)

There is a decline in both the 'traditional' and the 'new' working classes and a great expansion of non-manual jobs. But perhaps the greatest change here is that there are now so many women in waged work that it is no longer possible to ignore them, as was done in the past. Women's employment has been an important element in changing the nature of Swansea's class structure.

3.1 Polarisation

These changes might be thought of as positive changes in the class structure of Wales. Men have moved away from dirty and dangerous jobs into cleaner and safer ones. More women are earning wages for their work. But are there any negative features? Swansea is located in one of the more prosperous parts of Wales; while it has its impoverished areas, much of the city has benefited from recent redevelopment. It is firmly a part of the M4 corridor, where the fruits of economic change have concentrated. The same is broadly true of the A55 corridor in north Wales. But it is not necessary to travel very far inland from either road to find a very different picture. Wealth and poverty are often located in very different geographical areas. Poverty is often hidden from the view of the better-off and can easily be overlooked.

Ever since the 1920s the coal-mining areas of south Wales have suffered from pit closures and population decline. The same is true of the industrial areas of north Wales, while in slate quarrying decline started a generation earlier. This decline reached its nadir in the late 1980s, and by then there were also massive job losses in the steel industry and in the lighter manufacturing industries which had developed after 1945 to replace heavy industry. The new economic developments in south Wales concentrated in the valley mouths, the major cities of the coastal belt and the developing suburban sprawl that filled in many of the gaps between them. In the 1980s decline was accelerated as the Thatcher government rejected any support for heavy industry and encouraged the growth of service industries. This had profound implications:

> ... whereas the UK in the 1970s had a relatively flat hierarchy of income inequality akin to the continental European countries (partly as a result of tax redistribution mechanisms and social welfare provision), by the 1990s the UK resembled the US's more elongated spectrum. ... [In Wales] ... polarisation does have spatial dimension, and ... it is creating new 'ghettos' of poverty and prosperity. This may be termed the Los Angelization of the Welsh socio-economic terrain. ... The evidence ... is suggestive of a polarization of socio-economic fortunes between the different regions of Wales and, equally alarmingly, within Wales's towns and cities. The drawing of parallels with the well-known disparities and inequalities in American cities such as Los Angeles is hence increasingly justified.
>
> (Morris and Wilkinson, 1995, pp. 29–30)

Social divisions and divisions between prosperity and poverty are not new, of course, but new areas of wealth and deprivation have been created in the recent past:

> What has emerged over recent decades are new areas of prosperity and deprivation. Typically the latter are the post-war council estates such as Ely in Cardiff or ... in part of Tylorstown, in Glyncoch (Pontypridd) and Penderry in Swansea. The obverse is the rise of the lower middle/ upper working class estates throughout urban Wales, but particularly in the southern Valley districts of Taff Ely, Islwyn, Torfaen, the Rhymney Valley and in the west, Lliw Valley. Creigiau, located between Llantrisant and Pontypridd in Taff Ely, typifies this

phenomenon. Home to the burgeoning Welsh lower middle class and the emergent upper working class ... it has pleasant, spacious housing, extremely low unemployment, a low sickness rate, a high percentage of social class I and II types and extremely high car ownership. Moreover it is extremely spatially and socially isolated from the areas of deprivation.

(Morris and Wilkinson, 1995, p. 44)

The jobs in heavy industry and engineering that have declined were relatively well paid and did not require formal educational qualifications. Not enough alternative jobs have been created and those that have been are often low-paid and offer few prospects. Many people in these jobs need to claim Family Income Supplement from the state in order to survive. Whereas from 1945 to around 1980 the differences in income between people generally narrowed, since 1980 they have widened. Taxation has been changed in important ways. But the benefits of reduced income tax have been felt more clearly by those who earn more, as rates of tax for those on higher incomes have been reduced much more than for those on average or low incomes. These reductions in income tax have been compensated for by increased taxes on goods and services, particularly value added tax (VAT). At the same time, many who once worked in industrial jobs have been classified as medically unfit to work and survive on state benefits. State benefits in general have not risen as fast as have the salaries of the better-off, so the gap has widened. Spending on social housing has been reduced and very little new social housing built, while the best of the stock of such houses has been sold. What is left is often the worst-maintained and least desirable of the stock and only those with no option about where they live will accept them. Some areas have therefore become stigmatised and seen as undesirable.

All these changes combined have produced clear winners and losers. The sociologist Dave Adamson describes it as a crisis:

One of the features of the crisis in Welsh society is its near invisibility. You won't see it on the High Street, you won't experience it at the local rugby match. You won't find it in the out-of-town shopping centre or the latest heritage museum celebrating Welsh tradition. You may see it shuffling along the street of a Valley town in a shabby track-suit and worn-out trainers or searching for bargains in Hypervalue and Pound Stretcher. You won't find it teeing-off in one of the host of new golf-courses which are appearing along the coastal belt in South Wales and you're unlikely to see it in St David's Hall or Theatr Clwyd. You will see it if you stand outside a comprehensive at 3.30 p.m. or speak to the young people who congregate on street corners in Porth or Bangor. The crisis is hidden from the eyes of mainstream Wales; from the traditionally affluent and educated elites who have been joined in recent years by a new-working class which has benefitted from the diversification of economic activity in Wales.

(Adamson, 1996, p. 6)

The key to the crisis, according to Adamson, is the stark division in Welsh society. People in Wales can live such different lives that those at the more prosperous end of income levels will rarely encounter those at the other end. The differences are not just in income but also in what people consume, where they can afford to shop and their culture. Golf clubs and Pound Stretcher are the ends of Adamson's social spectrum. He is describing a class divide, but, as we have seen already, class involves much more than income and jobs. It permeates people's whole ways of life.

Figure 5.4
Rhyl West is one of the most deprived wards in Wales. Underused holiday accommodation is sometimes rented by housing benefit claimants.

Advertisers recognise this in the ways they target their sales pitches. The ACORN classification of the population is based on the small areas covered by postcodes. While it groups the population into five broad bands according to income, these are subdivided into no fewer than fifty-six categories which recognise different areas of housing, age, family size, ethnicity and jobs. On this basis the classification claims to be fairly accurate in predicting what people are likely to consume (ACORN, 2009). The detailed picture may not be quite as stark as Adamson paints it, but the complex ACORN picture shows both broad contrasts and detailed differences.

Activity 5.5

Turn to the map of areas of deprivation in Chapter 2, Section 4.2 (Figure 2.4).

■ How would you summarise the geographical pattern of inequality in Wales?

Here is the answer given by two social scientists in 1995 (little has changed in the general pattern since then):

> ... four features would seem to emerge from this study; the continued prosperity of the rural suburbs; the continued prosperity of the truly rural areas, but largely based on 'new English' wealth; the continued decline of the old core northern Valley areas; and the 'ghetto-ization' of the new prosperous middle and upper working classes into 'Brookside' developments and the reverse 'ghetto-ization' of an underclass into inner cities and, more especially, the council estates of urban Wales.
> (Morris and Wilkinson, 1995, p. 44)

3.2 Poverty and marginalisation

Since the 1980s, much attention has been given to poverty and deprivation in Wales. Poverty has often been blamed on the poor themselves, as when in 1994 John Redwood, the then Conservative Secretary of State for Wales, placed the blame for poverty on single mothers on council estates. Commentators on the right of the political spectrum referred to an 'underclass' which allegedly had different values from the rest of society. Its members wanted to avoid work and responsibility and their moral values had been undermined by the easy availability of welfare benefits. Most sociologists reject the description of these people as an 'underclass' and stress the ways in which changes in Welsh society since the 1970s have reduced opportunities and produced casualties. They refer, instead, to a marginalised working class which is excluded from many of the benefits of modern society by a range of disadvantages which add up to social exclusion. Social exclusion is more than poverty, although poverty is a central component. Just as class is more than income, social exclusion affects politics, culture and society. It is the inability to participate fully as a citizen (Byrne, 2005).

Rachel Trezise is a talented writer who takes us into the lives of the casualties of economic and social change (see Box 5.1). She writes vividly from direct experience of the social problems of the Valleys. In one story she describes a character on the railway station in Cardiff:

> He was standing motionless at the front of the platform, his face another ambiguous expression. This time he raised his eyebrows so his eyeballs widened and wrinkles appeared in his forehead. Her mother would have called them Valley Lines, like laughter lines, but caused by stress, strife, poverty, alcohol, drugs, chain smoking; anything a Welsh person endured in order to stay alive, pessimistic old cow, her mother. The train screamed into the station ... Valley Lines, it said on the map in front of her.
>
> (Trezise, 2005, p. 103)

Martin Luther King once observed that the thoughts of the poor went unheard – unless riot gave them a voice. Trezise offers us a voice that does not involve urban disorder. Trezise's account is very bleak – quite the opposite of the warmth and family support shown in the highly romantic *How Green Was My Valley*, for instance. She sets the tone by describing the Rhondda Valley as a place 'where poverty surrounded you like a neck brace' (Trezise, 2005, p. 17). Her mother's relationship with her biological father broke up when she was a small child; at the age of seven she lived in a council house which faced private terraced houses on the other side of the street. Her mother's new relationship was with a miner and his income, along with her mother's as a cleaner at Treorchy Library, allowed them to buy a house in another part of the village. She could read books in the library her mother cleaned. 'Each aspect of her family life was healthy and happy. A Mam, a Dad, a big brother, two cats, a dog and a goldfish' (Trezise, 2000, p. 15).

This brief happy period was based on two incomes; a new relationship is often a way in which women are lifted out of poverty, if they live with a man in a job. But it was clearly a precarious state. Her new father was made redundant and took to drinking for much of the day in the pub where her mother worked in her other job. Her mother took to spending more of her time on the other side of the bar and the child spent her non-school time in the pub as well. The newly formed family disintegrated in an alcoholic haze, with sexual abuse proving the final straw. Mother and daughter then found themselves on the Penrhys estate:

> ... the drug and crime capital of the Valleys; and the most mentioned location on the subject of poverty and trouble anywhere in Wales. ...

The police avoided Penrhys because it made their lives safe and generally less stressful. It was a prison for the innocent and a haven for the criminal ...'

(Trezise, 2000, p. 29)

Box 5.1   Rachel Trezise

Figure 5.5   Rachel Trezise

Born Cwmparc, Rhondda, 1978
Works:

- *In and out of the Goldfish Bowl* (2000), autobiographical novel
- *Fresh Apples* (2005), short stories
- 'Dial M for Merthyr: on the road with Midasuno' (2007), documentary
- *I Sing of a Maiden* (2007; with Charlotte Grieg), musical play
- 'The Lemon Meringue' (2008), Radio 4 play

Sixteen Shades of Crazy (forthcoming), novel

Awards:

- Orange Futures Award (2001)
- inaugural Dylan Thomas Prize (2006)

Even when she moved back to the less marginal Valley floor community – Penrhys was built on the exposed hillside between the two Rhondda valleys in the 1960s – her view of her surroundings is unrelievedly bleak and often, understandably, hostile (Penrhys History, 2009). Trezise depicts the Valleys inhabitants as narrow, parochial and often defeated. But her central character's life is improved by her own efforts in education at the local college of further education and (in real life) at the University of Glamorgan. A grandmother from the 'traditional' working class clearly helped, too.

Clearly there are problems in taking just one, distinct, case. Graduates from this background are rare and those who win major literary prizes are much rarer. But it chimes with much of what is known more generally about the lives of the marginalised poor (Byrne, 2005). There is a good deal of movement from poorly paid jobs to unemployment, from poor housing to relatively good, and back again. Poverty is always a state of precariousness; possible to escape with two incomes but always a yawning chasm if one of them is lost. The precariousness does not allow much political and social organisation to counter deprivation, as was once the case. What has emerged since the late 1990s, often promoted by the Welsh Assembly Government, are a number of initiatives to counter social exclusion, a major focus of New Labour policy. These have often promoted community organisation, to produce active citizenship. Some deprived areas have been greatly improved by the experience and latent talents mobilised. But the organisation is simply on a community basis, not the wider class mobilisation that was created in the past. Local councillors and trade unions have shown little interest in the process, according to the leading expert on these developments (Adamson, 2001).

3.3 Social mobility

If the gap between the rich and the poor is increasing, it will probably become more difficult to leap across it. Of course most social mobility does not span huge divides. Some people can move from great poverty to fantastic wealth, from 'rags to riches', but this is a rare thing. Most social mobility is of more modest dimensions: the factory worker who becomes a foreperson, the miner's daughter who becomes a university lecturer, or the office cleaner's child who becomes a manager.

One reason for social mobility is related to changes in the social structure. If more jobs for managers and professionals are being created, not all of them can be filled by the sons and daughters of managers and professionals. It will be necessary to take in people who come from different social origins – say miners' daughters and sons – to fill the gap. In the 1950s novels and films were full of this movement; the title of one of them, *Room at the Top*, symbolised the era when merit seemed to open the way to social advancement. That this happens does not mean that it becomes more difficult for the children of managers and professionals to reach such positions or that opportunities are the same for everyone. Indeed, the children of managers and professionals will usually have advantages in getting there. If you aspire to be a doctor or a vet the most important asset to have is a parent (preferably two) who practises that profession. Similarly, if you want to go to university your chances are much improved if you have a parent who did so. Cultural capital and the social capital of connections are vital resources.

So in some ways it is not very surprising that there was considerable social mobility in the thirty years following the end of the Second World War. The economy was expanding rapidly for most of the period and there was opportunity for many in new white-collar and technical jobs. Access to secondary and higher education was improved with the expansion of provision; it was easier for those of humbler social origins who had ability to use and develop their talents. There were also opportunities within the workplace for those who did not go into higher education. Banks tended to have a promotional ladder (though it was much easier for men to climb it than women) which could lead from being a clerk to becoming a manager. Mining and steel making had systems of apprenticeships and training which allowed some to develop their skills and abilities and to be rewarded for this with promotion. There is not a lot of specific research on this in Wales, but it was generally true of Britain and educational opportunities for talented children were good (in terms of population, the provision of grammar school places in Wales was three times that in the south-east of England). There is also anecdotal evidence: London's schools were said to be full of Welsh teachers in the 1960s, and of course there was a flourishing London Welsh community (and rugby team).

But what has happened in the period since the decline of heavy industries, with increasing polarisation in Welsh society? Again we do not have a great deal of direct research on this, but what we do know tends to suggest that opportunities have declined. The training systems that were produced by heavy industry have collapsed along with the industries themselves. Many organisations now look for graduate entrants for their higher levels and this means there are fewer chances for those who have started at the bottom. More often they remain there, now. Qualifications have become far more important than in the past – though of course far more people go to university than in the past. Many of the new jobs created are part-time, temporary and dead-end. Often they offer few prospects.

Activity 5.6

Table 5.1 shows the results of an analysis of social mobility in Wales in the post-war period. How does the balance between the upwardly mobile, the downwardly mobile and those who remain in the class of their birth change in the post-war period? How do the prospects of the latest group for whom we have figures (1967–1976) compare with those of the generation born immediately after the war (1947–1956)?

Table 5.1 Social mobility by date of birth for people born in Wales (percentages)

Years	1937–1946	1947–1956	1957–1966	1967–1976
Down	29.8	29.8	32.4	33.8
Same	21.1	17.3	29.5	23.0
Up	49.1	52.9	38.1	43.2

Source: Patterson and Iannelli, 2007, Table 6

Comment

Here are some conclusions that can be drawn:

■ Relatively few people remain in the class of their birth. The proportion is always under a third of the population, and usually about one in five. There has been a slight increase in the prospects of staying put, but the most striking thing is the greater likelihood of this among those born in the later 1950s and early 1960s.

■ The degree of downwardly mobility is perhaps surprising. We tend to think of social mobility as being a one-way process. But always almost a third of people are downwardly mobile, and the proportion has increased.

■ Upward mobility has been high – the largest group throughout – but has declined. I was born at the best time to be able to take advantage of improved opportunities: between 1947 and 1956.

■ The 1967–1976 group have increased chances of downward mobility and staying in the same position, and decreased chances of upward mobility compared with the 1947–1956 group.

Social polarisation has led to the development of a marginalised working class. It is also associated with a decline in social mobility. To what extent are these trends paralleled in rural Wales, or are there particular issues in the countryside?

3.4 Rural Wales

You have seen that in the past the countryside was often regarded as a place that was relatively classless, even if the reality was different. Throughout the twentieth century employment in agriculture declined and rural areas, especially those close to small towns, were affected by suburban growth. This has implications for class and it has been suggested that there has been a 'middle-class capture' of the countryside. We can see this from the pattern of wealth and deprivation discussed in Section 3.1. In Wales this has distinctive features. 'Middle class' is a very broad term and includes diverse social groups. In Wales there are relatively few members of the managerial or service class in rural areas (though rural areas close to conurbations are an exception). In the remoter rural areas the middle class is predominantly professional or self-employed.

There has also been a growth in second-home ownership, because of both retirement and tourism, including as a result of the diversification of farms away from agriculture. Population levels which had been falling in rural areas from the 1840s began to rise again in the 1970s. Many locally born people moved out and larger numbers of incomers moved in to produce the modest rise. Eddying movements have led to some social turbulence. The population has concentrated in the larger rural settlements and this leaves the remoter ones with poor transport and other services, because of the costs of providing these for fewer people. Cars become virtually essential because of the lack of efficient public transport. In Gwynedd in 2007 households with incomes of £7,500–£10,000 a year were spending 10 per cent of this on fuel; car ownership was proportionately higher in rural wards than urban ones. Houses are expensive because of competition from better-off locals and incomers and housing has become one of the key issues producing social conflict. Social housing has been sold off and very few new houses are built. Many people in rural areas have low incomes and face a struggle to live in their beautiful surroundings. About a fifth of all jobs in rural areas are in distribution, hotels and restaurants; this sector had earnings of just over half the UK weekly average in 2007. Furthermore, over a quarter of the population of these areas are pensioners, a group which is at high risk of falling into poverty.

Does this amount to polarisation as detected in Wales generally, and in urban areas in particular? Here is a description by three social scientists of four communities which they studied in depth in the rural areas of Wales:

> Not only was there a significant presence of low-income households in the rural Wales study areas, but the presence of 'have-nots' in these places was not in any way receding. Poverty and low income are not

yesterday's problems in rural Wales. Each of the study areas had recently received a significant proportion of lower income in-migrants, and it may, therefore, also be suggested that the problems associated with low income and poverty were being reproduced more generally across rural Wales. Nevertheless, our respondents were, on the whole, reluctant to admit the existence of poverty and deprivation in their areas. Although an average of 43.7 per cent did perceive that disadvantage and deprivation existed in their areas, the qualitative comments from our survey suggested that the notion of deprivation was stigmatic for some of our respondents and often 'out of sight was out of mind' for others. It would seem that the perceived benefits of living in the countryside were felt to offer some compensation.

(Cloke et al., 1997, p. 135)

You have already seen that poverty can be 'invisible' in urban areas. People who live in affluent areas of Cardiff or Swansea may never need to confront it in their daily lives. It is, of course, much more apparent on a deprived council estate. But in the rural areas, social deprivation is much more concealed. Perhaps this is all the more so as the prominent political issue in rural Wales is not class but in-migration – especially of English people, with their impact on the Welsh language and indigenous culture. Deprivation is sidelined as an issue. As the authors of the above extract point out, not all the in-migrants are affluent by any means but they tend to be seen as such.

In a report of the WAG in 2008 it was recognised that 'Rurality and sparsity can be significant elements in the social exclusion and deprivation suffered by people living in rural Wales' (WAG, 2008, p. 3). Half of the 'income-deprived' people in Wales live in rural areas; the other half are more concentrated and noticeable. Policies aimed at tackling social exclusion are based on community development, which means that they are ineffective for the dispersed poor of the countryside (WAG, 2008, p. 5).

Summary

- Polarisation – the gap between rich and poor – has intensified as new areas of wealth and deprivation have been created in Wales since the 1980s.

- There has been considerable social mobility in Wales since 1945, but this means people moving down the social scale as well as up it.

- Problems of poverty and marginalisation in rural areas are particularly significant, but often go unacknowledged.

4 Conclusion

Class can seem like an old-fashioned thing. Many of the images that it brings to mind are old ones, whether they are of miners or top-hatted aristocrats. Some social scientists claim that class is fading and lacks the centrality in people's lives that it once had; that it no longer helps us understand society today. Certainly the forms it assumes have changed, but we should be wary of dismissing its significance.

There are four particular arguments for the continuing relevance of class in Wales which emerge from this discussion:

- First, there is no evidence that social distinctions or differences in income are declining. Wealth still provides people with status, prestige and power, while poverty carries a deep stigma. Not only have social divisions not declined, some of them have grown. Class in the form of social and cultural capital has a clear influence on people's life chances.

- Second, we are influenced by the past. Much of the population of Wales was born and grew up in a time when the older stereotypes of class were still very much apparent. In any society there is not just the here and now and the new but a persisting influence of the past. The strength of the Labour Party in Wales, however much its position has been eroded, reflects that past and so perhaps does the relative enthusiasm with which Welsh people join trade unions. The people quoted at the beginning of this chapter thought of themselves as working-class because of their past, not their present. The living are haunted by ghosts of the past. Outsiders' images often adjust even more slowly to changing realities.

- Third, class is one of the things that make Wales distinctive, in the sense of a pattern of social relationships which are significantly different from those in England – or at least London and the south-east of England. Think of the balance of rich and poor in Wales, the rate at which Welsh people join trade unions, and the ways in which the Welsh think about class. The pattern of class is very much a part of what makes Wales distinctive, part of what makes its inhabitants Welsh.

- Finally, class is something that gets into our very being. It is part of our make-up and something we carry around with us. 'Class is something beneath your clothes, under your skin, in your reflexes, in your psyche, at the very core of your being' (Annette Kuhn quoted in Sayer, 2005, p. 22). This is why to ask about class is a rude question. It is intensely personal.

Class is, of course, only one of the divides in Welsh society. The time when it could be seen as the only important form of stratification, or at least the one that structured all the others, has passed. Gender, 'race' and sexuality have vied with class for attention in recent years. Arguments about class, in the past, made assumptions about all these things, rarely considering that there was a perspective other than that of white men. Thinking about difference involves thinking about all these things, too. But class will not simply dissolve before our eyes if we do.

References

ACORN (2009) 'ACORN classification map' [online], available at www.caci.co.uk/acorn/acornmap.asp (accessed 15 October 2009).

Adamson, D. (2001) 'Social segregation in a working-class community: economic and social change in the South Wales Coalfield' in Van Gyes, G., de Witte, H. and Pasture, P. (eds) *Can Class Still Unite? The Differentiated Workforce, Class, Solidarity and Trade Unions*, Aldershot, Ashgate.

Adamson, D. (1996) *Living on the Edge: Poverty and Deprivation in Wales*, Llandysul, Gomer.

Aitchison, J. W. and Carter, H. (2000) *Language, Economy and Society: the Changing Fortunes of the Welsh Language in the Twentieth Century*, Cardiff, University of Wales Press.

Aitchison, J. W. and Carter, H. (1987) 'The Welsh language in Cardiff: a quiet revolution', *Transactions of the Institute of British Geographers*, new series, vol. 12, no. 4, pp. 482–92.

Barratt, C. (2009) *Trade Union Membership 2008*, National Statistics Publication; Department for Business, Enterprise and Regulatory Reform, available at http://stats.berr.gov.uk/uksa/tu/TUM2008.pdf (accessed15 October 2009).

Bell, C. (1968) *Middle Class Families: Social and Geographical Mobility*, London, Routledge & Kegan Paul.

Bevan, D. (1984) 'The mobilisation of cultural minorities: the case of Sianel Pedwar Cymru', *Media, Culture and Society*, vol. 6, pp. 103–17.

Byrne, D. (2005) *Social Exclusion* (2nd edn), Buckingham, Open University Press.

Charles, N., Davies, C. and Harris, C. (2008) *Families in Transition: Social Change, Family Formation and Kin Relationships*, Bristol, Policy Press.

Cloke, P., Goodwin, M. and Milbourne, P. (1997) *Rural Wales: Community and Marginalization*, Cardiff, University of Wales Press.

Day, G. and Fitton, M. (1975) 'Religion and social status in rural Wales: "Buchedd" and its lessons for concepts of stratification in community studies', *Sociological Review*, vol. 23, no. 4, pp. 867–92.

Harris, C., Charles, N. and Davies, C. (2006) 'Social change and the family' *Sociological Research Online*, vol. 11, no. 2 [online], available at www.socresonline.org.uk/11/2/harris.html (accessed 6 November 2009).

Harris, C. C. and Swansea Redundancy Group (1987) *Redundancy and Recession in South Wales*, Oxford, Blackwell.

Jenkins, D. (1960) 'Aberporth' in Davies, E. and Rees, A. D. (eds) *Welsh Rural Communities*, Cardiff, University of Wales Press.

Leonard, D. (1980) *Sex and Generation: a Study of Courtship and Weddings*, London, Tavistock.

Morris, J. and Wilkinson, B. (1995) 'Poverty and prosperity in Wales: polarization and Los Angelization', *Contemporary Wales*, vol. 8, pp. 29–45.

Northern Gallery for Contemporary Art (2009) 'Rank: picturing the social order, 1516–2009', Sunderland, NGCA.

Owens, D. (2000) *Cerys, Catatonia and the Rise of Welsh Pop*, London, Ebury.

Patterson, L. and Iannelli, C. (2007) 'Patterns of absolute and relative social mobility: a comparative study of England, Wales and Scotland', *Sociological Research Online*, vol. 12, no. 6 [online], available at www.socresonline.org.uk/12/6/15.html (accessed 15 October 2009).

Penrhys History (2009) 'Penrhys' [online], available at www.penrhys.com/history.asp (accessed 15 October 2009).

Reynolds, D. and Bellin, W. (1996) 'Welsh medium schools: why they are better', *Agenda*, summer, pp. 19–20.

Savage, M. (2000) *Class and Social Transformation*, Buckingham, Open University Press.

Sayer, A. (2005) *The Moral Significance of Class*, Cambridge, Cambridge University Press.

Trezise, R. (2005) *Fresh Apples*, Cardigan, Parthian.

Trezise, R. (2000) *In and out of the Goldfish Bowl*, Cardigan, Parthian.

Welsh Assembly Government (2008) 'Poverty and deprivation in rural Wales', report of the Rural Development sub-committee, July, available at www.assemblywales.org/poverty_deprivation_in _rural_wales.pdf (accessed 6 October 2009).

Further reading

There are two excellent introductions to class analysis in the UK:

Crompton, R. (2008) *Class and Stratification* (3rd edn), Cambridge, Polity Press; and Savage, M. (2000) *Class and Social Transformation*, Buckingham, Open University Press.

On Wales, the most up-to-date analysis of poverty and marginalisation is Adamson, D. 'Still Living on the Edge?' *Contemporary Wales*, vol. 21, 2008, pp. 47–66.

On elites in Wales, there is little that is up to date, but there are useful pointers in Aitchison, J. W. and Carter, H. (1987) 'The Welsh language in Cardiff: a quiet revolution', *Transactions of the Institute of British Geographers*, new series, vol. 12, no. 4, pp. 482–492.

Much relevant material can be found on the website of the Welsh Assembly Government (www.wales.gov.org.uk) and The Poverty Site maintained by the Joseph Rowntree Foundation (www.poverty.org.uk).

Chapter 6
Nationalism and the Welsh language

Charlotte Aull Davies

Contents

1   Introduction

In the late 1960s and 1970s, an upsurge of organised ethnic activity in the developed countries of the West came as a complete surprise to most social commentators, whether from the academic world, journalism or politics. This activity appeared in different guises, depending in large measure on the nature of the state in which it occurred. In the United States, white ethnic groups increasingly sought greater recognition for their distinctive cultural identities in a conscious rejection of the ideology of the 'melting pot'. Elsewhere, French speakers in Quebec and New Brunswick made use of the federal structure of the Canadian state to build movements that campaigned for official support for the French language by means of increased political autonomy.

Most long-established European states, including France, Spain and Great Britain, contain culturally distinct regions, which were absorbed by these states via conquest or other means between the late middle ages and the eighteenth century. Often called stateless nations today, these regions gave rise to movements for cultural and political recognition that waxed and waned from the middle of the nineteenth century onwards. During the 1970s, most of these ethnic nationalist movements – so called because they based their appeal for political autonomy on their cultural distinctiveness – among them the Welsh nationalist movement, also experienced a significant resurgence.

This resurgence is what first brought me – an anthropologist interested in the study of ethnic nationalism, with its intertwining of politics and culture – to Wales, and so began my intellectual and personal involvement with Welsh culture, identity and politics, which has now spanned over three decades. When I first arrived in Wales in 1976, both cultural and political aspects of the nationalist movement were at a high ebb. The campaign for official recognition of the Welsh language, spearheaded by Cymdeithas yr Iaith Gymraeg/the Welsh Language Society, had begun to have an effect with bilingual road signs increasingly to be seen and official forms beginning to be made available in Welsh. Plaid Cymru, the political party with Welsh self-government as its central aim, had three members of parliament elected in 1974, out of 36 Welsh MPs, and had made important advances in local government.

However, by the end of the decade, political nationalism was in a steep decline following a decisive 'No' vote in the 1979 referendum for devolution of political powers to Wales and Scotland, a decline from which it only began to recover toward the end of the 1980s. The Welsh language movement did not follow quite the same trajectory and achieved some important successes in the 1980s and 1990s, in particular the establishment in 1982 of S4C, the Welsh-language television service, and the passage of the 1993 Welsh Language Act.

The Welsh nationalist movement has been transformed because of the remarkable turnaround that produced a 'Yes' vote in the 1997 referenda to establish an elected assembly in Wales and a parliament in Scotland. Plaid Cymru, which continues to provide the main political expression of nationalist ideals, received a much higher percentage of the vote in the first National Assembly election in 1999 than it had ever done before in UK-wide elections and became the second largest party after Labour. As a consequence of the 2007 election results, Plaid Cymru became a party of government in coalition with the Labour Party in a period when the powers of the National Assembly for Wales (NAW) were being extended.

The aims of this chapter are to allow you to:

■ look at the relationship between language, identity and nationalism and at the Welsh language's role in Welsh national identity and in the nationalist movement

■ understand the development of the Welsh nationalist movement, in both its political and its cultural manifestations, since the middle of the twentieth century

■ examine the circumstances that have seen Plaid Cymru evolve from an apparently insignificant, minority cultural and linguistic movement to a mainstream political party and eventually a party of government within a devolved Welsh political structure

■ ask what kind of nationalism is to be found in Wales and how the Welsh nationalist movement fits into the various theories of nationalism that try to analyse its characteristics or to explain why it has been so influential.

But you will begin not with politics in the conventional sense but with culture and especially language. You will look first at the relationship between language, identity and nationalism and then at the role the Welsh language has played in Welsh national identity and in the nationalist movement.

2 Language and identity

I arrived in Wales in 1976 to carry out fieldwork on the Welsh nationalist movement. I was aware that Welsh was the first language of just over one fifth of the people of Wales and the main language of many of its communities. But I had also been assured that learning Welsh was not a formal requirement for my research since virtually the entire adult population also spoke English. Nevertheless, as an anthropologist, I was conscious of the importance of language for understanding other cultures, and so for some months prior to my departure, I tried to teach myself something of the language, including the words of the national anthem, '*Hen Wlad fy Nhadau*'. I also enrolled in a Welsh-language summer course upon arrival. My intention at the outset was to acquire at least a basic competence in Welsh, in order to promote goodwill and facilitate access to certain factions and individuals.

In practice, I did not maintain this detachment for long but quickly became fully committed to acquiring fluency in Welsh. I came to realise that my immersion in the Welsh language was necessary for my research, not in the technical sense that Welsh-speaking informants would be less forthcoming if interviewed in English, but because learning Welsh gave me a deeper understanding and more immediate access to the complex relationships between language and identity.

An illustration of this occurred in an interview with one individual, a nationalist, who, as a product of a non-Welsh-speaking home and area, had for years promoted the perspectives and advancement of non-Welsh speakers in Plaid Cymru. He had been very successful in this regard, but eventually decided to learn Welsh himself. Reflecting on the experience, he remarked, 'I still identify with the non-Welsh-speaking Welshman. But as a speaker you do begin to take on some of the political overtones of the linguistic nationalists'. From his testimony, as well as my own experiences as a Welsh learner, I felt sure that he was not referring to a change in his perception of where his interests lay politically but to a very basic shift in standpoint, an ability to see issues from a different perspective entirely.

2.1 Language and personal identity

Language and identity are tied together at many levels. In an article written in the first half of the twentieth century, the American linguist Edward Sapir discussed this relationship and foresaw much subsequent research on language and identity. As you read the following excerpt from this essay, try to identify the two levels at which language and identity are connected.

Extract 6.1

Language is a great force of socialization, probably the greatest that exists. By this is meant not merely the obvious fact that significant social intercourse is hardly possible without language but that the mere fact of a common speech serves as a peculiarly potent symbol of the social solidarity of those who speak the language. ... [A]t the same time [language is] the most potent single known factor for the growth of individuality. The fundamental quality of one's voice, the phonetic patterns of speech, the speed and relative smoothness of articulation, the length and build of the sentences, the character and range of the vocabulary ... the readiness with which words respond to the requirements of the social environment, in particular the suitability of one's language to the language habits of the persons addressed – all these are so many complex indicators of the personality.

Source: Sapir, 1970 (1933), pp. 15–16, 19

Sapir is telling us in this excerpt that language is an important means by which we establish collective identity and belonging and, at one and the same time, it is a powerful expression of our individuality. Now consider the following illustration of how much we infer about the identities of others from their use of language.

> Imagine, if you will, a group of strangers waiting at a taxi stand. An empty taxi drives past without stopping, and the following remarks ensue:
>
> A   Out*rage*ous.
>
> B   I say.
>
> C   F*ckin hell.
>
> Quite likely, you have pictured in your mind what A, B and C look like. You can probably tell me something about how they are dressed, their background, what they do, what they are like, and whether you would like them or not (Joseph, 2004, p. 4).

The reason you are likely to have formed these surprisingly specific images of the three speakers above from such brief utterances lies in how we are socialised into language use. As we develop our linguistic competence throughout our lives from earliest childhood onwards, we learn to communicate in ways that are appropriate to the various groups with which we are associated. These groups may be as small and personal as a family unit or as large and relatively impersonal as a social class. Sociolinguists have shown that ways of communicating vary with a huge variety of social statuses, including gender, age, ethnicity, 'race', social class, profession and nationality, to name but a few.

Just as we make inferences about others' identities from how they speak, we also use language to establish and project our own identities to others. Our identities have multiple facets, and we are all adept at communicating in ways that emphasise some aspects, or downplay or attempt to hide others, depending on context. That is, we can all speak in different registers, changing our manner of communicating (accent, choice of vocabulary, use of grammar, and so on) to suit the occasion. We do not normally speak to our best friend and our boss in the same way, nor use similar language at a funeral as at a football match.

Activity 6.1

Think about how you communicate in several different contexts, for example, with family, at work, in a single-sex group, in a committee meeting. How does your choice of vocabulary, grammar and speaking style vary? What influences the choices that you make? If you are fluent in more than one language, how do you go about deciding which language to use?

2.2 Language and national identity

Making ourselves more aware of how we use language reveals its powerful role in establishing personal identities and in supporting feelings of solidarity and difference with various social groups. This is the case even among speakers of the same language. When there is a difference of language linked to another social identity, such as nationality, the effect is enhanced greatly. Few sociolinguists believe language difference in itself causes social conflict, but it is often implicated in conflict. As you read this next excerpt from Sapir, consider how and when, according to Sapir, language and national identity came to be so closely linked. What circumstances may lead to language-based conflict?

Extract 6.2

While language differences have always been important symbols of cultural difference, it is only in comparatively recent times, with the exaggerated development of the ideal of the sovereign nation ... that language differences have taken on an implication of antagonism. In ancient Rome and all through mediaeval Europe there were plenty of cultural differences running side by side with linguistic ones, and the political status of Roman citizen or the fact of adherence to the Roman Catholic church was of vastly greater significance as a symbol of the individual's place in the world than the language or dialect he happened to speak. It is probably altogether incorrect to maintain that language differences are responsible for national antagonisms. It would seem to be much more reasonable to suppose that a political and national unit, once definitely formed, uses a prevailing language as a symbol of its identity ...

In earlier times there seems to have been little systematic attempt to impose the language of a conquering people on the subject people ... Definitely repressive attitudes toward the languages and dialects of subject peoples seem to be distinctive only of European political policy in comparatively recent times. The attempt of czarist Russia to stamp out Polish by forbidding its teaching in the schools ... [is an example] of the heightened emphasis on language as a symbol of political allegiance in the modern world.

Source: Sapir, 1970 (1933), pp. 40–2

Here, Sapir maintains that the close association of language and national identity is a product of modern times. We will return to this when we look at the origins of the ideology of nationalism. He also points to the repression of minority languages as a potential source of conflict. Although he was certainly incorrect to suggest – even in the 1930s – that such repression was limited to Europe, it has certainly been a feature of state building there. Indeed, the Welsh language experienced centuries of repression: Henry VIII banned Welsh from all official usage in Wales with the Act of Union in 1536. In subsequent centuries, the language was systematically stigmatised, most famously in the 1847 *Report into the State of Education in Wales*, which pronounced the language a 'great evil', holding it responsible for the supposed economic and moral degeneracy of the Welsh people (Roberts, 1998). This report, also referred to as '*Brad y Llyfrau Gleision*'/'The Treachery of the Blue Books', was prepared by three English barristers, none of whom could speak or understand Welsh. Possibly the most devastating action against the Welsh language was forbidding its use in schools, a prohibition that continued into the early twentieth century.

Although the centralising activities of the English state successfully eliminated virtually all the administrative, legal and other institutional differences between England and Wales, the Welsh language remained the language of the majority of the population of Wales and most of its communities through the nineteenth century. However, as Figure 6.1 shows, the percentage of people speaking Welsh declined steadily through the twentieth century. The reasons for the decline are complex, but can be linked to the economic and social position of Wales within an increasingly powerful British state.

Figure 6.1
Percentage of Welsh
population able to
speak Welsh,
1891–2001

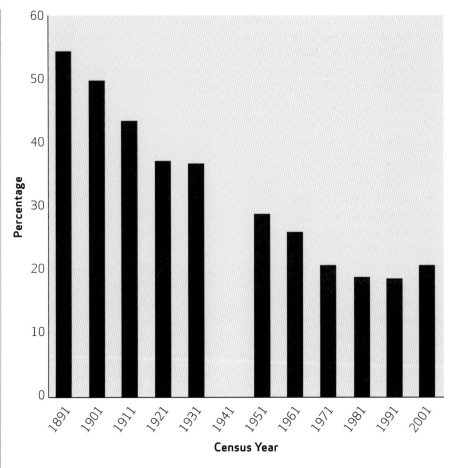

Note: There was no UK Census in 1941

2.3 The Welsh language and political nationalism

Thus, in 1925 when a small group of nationalists – none of whom were
professional politicians – established Plaid Genedlaethol Cymru/the
Welsh Nationalist Party, one of its main aims was the promotion of the
Welsh language and culture. The founders of this new political party
were mainly middle-class professionals – teachers, ministers and
lecturers – and the Welsh language was central to both their personal
and working lives. The party aimed to secure Welsh self-government,
including (by 1932) membership for Wales in the League of Nations, and
to promote Welsh culture and the Welsh language. Although the party
was fully bilingual in its publications from the 1930s onwards, it was
almost entirely Welsh-speaking in its internal organisation and
membership (Davies, 1983, pp. 179–86). Most of the members were
inspired primarily by their concern for the Welsh language and its
preservation in the face of the external factors that were undermining it,
deriving from Wales's lack of autonomy within the British state.

The Welsh Nationalist Party had little electoral impact in its first two decades and could be characterised as more of an intellectual and cultural movement than a political party. However, its character began to alter dramatically from the mid 1940s as Plaid Cymru (the Party of Wales) began its transformation into a political party, contesting both parliamentary and local elections across Wales with the intention of gaining political power as the means to its goal of full Welsh self-government.

As Plaid Cymru became more embedded in mainstream political activity, the promotion of the Welsh language, while remaining a central tenet, became less predominant in party concerns. Nevertheless, the language continued to be a major source of inspiration for many party activists. One individual I interviewed in 1977, a prospective parliamentary candidate for Plaid Cymru and mainly active as a political – rather than a cultural and linguistic – nationalist, told me: 'Without the language, the mainspring would go out of my motivation. Welsh freedom would still be worth working for, but I would not be as passionate about it' (Davies, 1989, p. 44).

The deep connections between language and identity mean that language can be an important source of inspiration and means of recruitment of nationalists if the achievement of political autonomy is seen as necessary for the protection, indeed the survival, of the language. Furthermore, the Welsh case suggests that this is not limited to speakers of the language. Many non-Welsh speakers have also embraced the nationalist cause primarily because of the language issue, arguing that they were deprived of the language themselves as a result of the linguistic oppression of Wales by the British state. They may try to reclaim the language – for themselves, through learning it as adults; for their children, through their support for the Welsh-schools movement; and/or for their nation, through political activism to achieve Welsh self-government.

Activity 6.2

The following two excerpts illuminate what the Welsh language has come to mean to some who are not first-language Welsh speakers. The first is by the Anglo-Welsh poet and Welsh nationalist Harri Webb, who was raised in Swansea and learned Welsh as an adult, adopting the Gwentian dialect he had heard while working as a librarian in Dowlais. The second is from an essay, 'Coming home', by the academic Sylvia Prys Jones, who was born in England and moved with her family to Cardiff when she was ten. Regarding each extract, what are the author's reasons for learning Welsh? How does each of them connect language with personal and national identity?

Extract 6.3

The Old Language

> They called us, shyly at first, those words
>
> That were and were not ours.
>
> They whispered in names whose meaning
>
> We did not know, a strange murmur
>
> Like leaves in a light wind you hardly feel
>
> Stirring the autumn wood of memories
>
> That were and were not ours.
>
> We did not stop to heed, nor pause to wonder.
>
> But we could not escape them, they were always
>
> Around us, whispering. Did they croon
>
> A crazed witless song, a bad spell,
>
> Voices crying out of an old dark wood?
>
> Some shuddered, fled, stumbled.
>
> Others listened.
>
> Suddenly we knew, understood
>
> Whose voices these were, knew
>
> What they had been telling us all the time:
>
> Our true name;
>
> And the dead leaves turned into a shower of gold.

Source: Webb, 1995 [1963], p. 60

Extract 6.4

'Coming home'

At secondary school I studied Welsh, French, Latin and Greek ...

But it was Welsh which captured my interest, for it represented not just a language but an identity. I was a shy, diffident teenager: ... The Welsh language gave me roots and a sense of direction, and also set me apart from the crowd.

I became a fervent Welsh nationalist. ...

The strange aspect of this Welshness was that it was almost entirely an inward experience, a strange romantic notion in my imagination. ...

My Welsh nationalism ... had no political content. I had little grasp of political matters, and even less interest. ...

Looking back at that period of fervent nationalism makes me blush, bearing, as it did, little relation to the Wales of reality. I knew little of the geography of Wales ... I knew less of the people, of their struggle for survival and the preservation of their language. My Welshness was largely 'psychological': less of a response to the real, historical Wales than to a dim unperceived need within myself. ... But even now, as I wince in memory, I wonder whether it was such a bad thing.

... Is it a crime to want to belong, to be a part, to have roots? And if, in the process, we chance upon something of such immeasurable worth and beauty as the Welsh heritage, so much the better.

Source: Jones, 1992, pp. 6–7

Summary

- Language and identity are closely associated. We use language to express individual personal identity and establish collective identities and solidarities.

- A distinctive national language can contribute to a nationalist movement as the main inspiration for activists – even those who choose to concentrate their activities in a more conventional political arena rather than in language campaigns.

3 Welsh language and nationalism

Important as the Welsh language has been as a source of inspiration for nationalists, this is far from being the only contribution the language has made to the nationalist movement. Although the percentage of Welsh speakers declined through most of the twentieth century, the language became an ever more important basis for the movement. The actions of the British state, as it expanded and consolidated its hold over its territory, resulted in Wales entering the modern period with no institutional distinctiveness from England. All administrative, legal, educational and other differences between Wales and England had been eliminated. Welsh identity was based virtually entirely on cultural differences, most obviously the Welsh language.

3.1 Welsh language activism

Beginning in the late 1940s, the Welsh Nationalist Party undertook a gradual transformation from acting primarily as a cultural movement to behaving like a conventional political party. Under the leadership of Gwynfor Evans, Plaid Cymru (as it was known from the 1950s) devoted itself to contesting elections for the Westminster parliament and for local government, with the goal of eventually winning self-government by constitutional means. However, progress was slow and by the early 1960s many members were disillusioned by their lack of success.

Then in February 1962, Saunders Lewis, one of the party's founders and its president from 1926 to 1939, gave a radio address, '*Tynged yr Iaith*' ('The Fate of the Language'), which was to have a profound effect on the nationalist movement. In his lecture, he reversed his earlier position that achieving self-government was the first priority and called for direct action and civil disobedience to win official recognition for the Welsh language in Wales.

This speech was an attempt to move Plaid Cymru away from what seemed at the time to be its completely futile electioneering. However, the effect was not to sway the party but rather to inspire a group of younger members to establish a new campaigning organisation, Cymdeithas yr Iaith Gymraeg (the Welsh Language Society). The Society's first campaign was to establish the right to court summonses in Welsh, and they began their activities in February 1963 with a sit-down demonstration blocking Trefechan bridge leading into Aberystwyth. The intent was to elicit summonses that could be refused for being in English. However, none were forthcoming, and it was not until 1966 that a member was arrested for refusing to display an English-only motor vehicle tax disc.

The Society's major campaign in the late 1960s and 1970s was for bilingual road signs. This campaign, in which Cymdeithas members first painted out English-only signs, then later began to remove them entirely, attracted a great deal of negative publicity and also led to a large number of arrests over many years. Even so, as you will see, if judged either by government response or by its impact on Welsh society, it was a very successful campaign.

Prior to the appearance of this form of language activism – non-violent direct action against property – there had been no response by government to decades of more conventional political activism.

The only significant legislation on the language had been the Welsh Courts Act 1942, which had allowed Welsh speakers to give evidence in Welsh if they considered they were at a disadvantage using English. However, shortly after the Trefechan bridge demonstration, the government appointed the Hughes Parry Committee to enquire into the language's legal status. The committee's report resulted in the passage of the 1967 Welsh Language Act, which provided 'equal validity' for the Welsh language, basically that things done in Welsh in Wales had the same legal status as things done in English.

While it was an important step forward in terms of official recognition of the Welsh language, the Act was limited in its applicability and had no mechanism to compel adherence to the principle of equal validity. Nevertheless, the Bowen Committee, which was set up early in the 1970s to consider the issue of bilingual road signs, cited equal validity as the primary reason for recommending bilingual road signs (with Welsh given priority) throughout Wales. The subsequent appearance of bilingual Welsh/English road signs, albeit gradual and often disputed, gave official recognition, publicly displayed, not only to the Welsh language but also to the existence of a distinctive Welsh identity.

Many non-Welsh speakers also regarded this public display of the Welsh language as an affirmation of their Welsh identity. Recent research into changes in family life in Swansea between the 1960s and the start of the twenty-first century found many instances of a greater self-confidence in assertions of Welsh identity, and two interviewees made explicit references to Welsh road signs (Davies et al., 2006, p. 46). One said: 'When I come over the Severn bridge and I see the signs in Welsh, I'm happy.' And another told us:

> I'm Welsh and I'm proud that I'm Welsh. When I go over to England, because I mean I do travel around the country, when I go across to England, I say uh, that's England, but as soon as I come to it, I say yes I'm home. As soon as you see that Welsh sign you're home. Yeah. Very important that I'm Welsh. I mean I don't speak Welsh.

The focus of Cymdeithas yr Iaith campaigns changed as different issues gained prominence. In the 1970s they concentrated on acquiring a Welsh-language television service using techniques such as climbing television masts to prevent broadcasting. This campaign was the only one in which they were joined officially by Plaid Cymru, which orchestrated a campaign of civil disobedience in 1980 when nearly two thousand people refused to pay their television licence fee and Gwynfor Evans announced his intention to fast to the death unless the fourth channel, which was being set up at that time, was made a Welsh-language channel in Wales.

During the 1980s and into the 1990s, Cymdeithas yr Iaith concentrated on two areas: (i) the perceived threat to Welsh-speaking communities from the conversion of housing stock to holiday homes and second homes; and (ii) the need for a new Welsh Language Act. We will return to the first of these a bit later.

For the quarter of a century following the passage of the 1967 Welsh Language Act campaigners worked to realise the promise of equal validity in a variety of contexts, such as provision of bilingual road signs and official forms in Welsh and recognition of the right of individuals to correspond with public bodies in Welsh. As the Act's shortcomings became all too apparent, demands for a new Act increased. The Act that was eventually forthcoming, the 1993 Welsh Language Act, provided that Welsh and English should be treated 'on a basis of equality' in the judicial system and in public administration, although the meaning of this 'basis of equality' was not fully clarified and was subject to considerations of practicability. The Act did not declare Welsh to be an official language in Wales despite the support for such a measure. But it did establish a mechanism to ensure that its provisions were carried out: the advisory Welsh Language Board became a statutory body with powers to oversee the development by public bodies of required Welsh language schemes to treat Welsh and English on a basis of equality.

3.2 The Welsh language and Welsh institutions

As we think about the activities and accomplishments of Cymdeithas yr Iaith Gymraeg and other language campaigners over the past decades, we can see that the language played a much more extensive role in the nationalist movement than simply as an inspiration for activists, important as this may be. The Welsh language provided an officially sanctioned recognition of Welsh distinctiveness for the first time since the sixteenth century. Furthermore, it became one basis for creating an institutional infrastructure within Wales, again something that had not existed for centuries.

One area in which the language was particularly useful in stimulating the development of distinctive Welsh institutions was education. In the years immediately after the close of the Second World War, parents in several areas in Wales began to pressurise local authorities to set up Welsh-medium primary schools. Initially, these schools were intended to provide for children from Welsh-speaking homes in areas of Wales where the predominant language was English. However, comparatively quickly, parents who did not speak Welsh began to request that their children also be admitted to these Welsh-medium schools. Thus, although at first led by a Welsh-speaking middle class, the movement soon drew support from non-Welsh-speaking and working-class parents. They were attracted by the demonstrated educational successes of the schools, the opportunity to restore to their children the Welsh linguistic heritage of which they felt deprived, and, from the 1980s, the lure of high-status jobs with a Welsh-language requirement in the media and in the constantly expanding government bureaucracy in and around the Welsh Office.

By the early 1980s, many Welsh-medium schools had a majority of pupils from non-Welsh-speaking homes, and the class composition of the intake was representative of the areas in which the schools were located. At the end of the twentieth century, 27 per cent of all primary schools in Wales used Welsh as the main medium of instruction, and about 20 per cent of all pupils were fluent in Welsh at age 11. Since over one third of all children who spoke Welsh came from homes where neither parent spoke Welsh, primary schools have played a major role in maintaining the Welsh language (Welsh Language Board, 1999, p. 2). Census figures for percentages of Welsh speakers in different age groups over the second half of the twentieth century show this clearly.

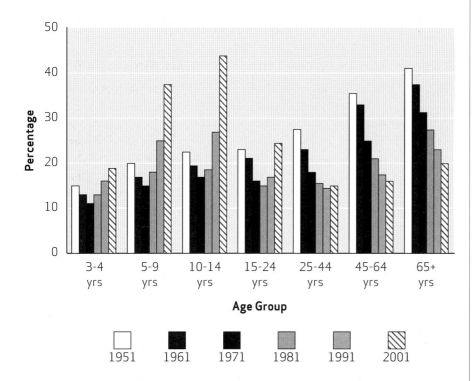

Figure 6.2

Percentage of Welsh population able to speak Welsh in different age groups, 1951–2001

Activity 6.3

Figure 6.2 shows the percentage of Welsh speakers in different age groups from 1951 to 2001. If you look at age group 65+, you will see that the percentage of Welsh speakers has declined steadily from over 40 per cent in 1951 to under 20 per cent in 2001. Now look at each of the other age groups. For which groups has the decline been arrested? For each of these groups, when did the change to increasing percentages occur?

Comment

The three youngest age groups first showed increases over the previous census figure in 1981, the 15–24 age group in 1991, and the percentage of Welsh speakers in the 25–44 age group increased for the first time in 2001 (from 14.5 per cent to 15.1 per cent). The timing of these increases across age groups suggests that the development of Welsh-medium education over the past half-century has changed the demographic profile of the Welsh language, from being concentrated among older age groups to experiencing most growth among younger age groups.

The Welsh Office was given control over primary and secondary education in Wales in 1970, and this enabled the growth of a professional elite of Welsh educationalists. Thus, when the Education Reform Act 1988 was introduced, this Welsh educational infrastructure exerted considerable influence on the new national curriculum being created by the Act. The strongest argument for special treatment for Wales under the Act was the special circumstances of Welsh-medium schools. However, Welsh educationalists had a broader remit than the Welsh-medium sector, and they secured a Welsh dimension to the curriculum in the form of two requirements unique to Wales – the Curriculum Cymreig (Welsh Curriculum), designed to incorporate teaching about the culture of Wales throughout the curriculum; and the study of Welsh as a first or second language in all schools in Wales. Looking again at Figure 6.2, you can observe the particularly large increases between 1991 and 2001 for groups containing individuals of school age (5–19). This is very likely an effect of 'the place given to Welsh in the National Curriculum, especially as a foundation subject in English-medium schools' (Welsh Language Board, 2003, p. 2).

Summary

- A distinctive national language may bolster a sense of national identity and contribute to a nationalist movement by securing public recognition from the state, for example, by mandating its use on official documents and signs, and forcing provision of other services, like public broadcasting, in the national language.

- A distinctive national language can also enable the creation of organisations and institutions specific to the national territory, for example, in the area of education.

- None of the ways in which a national language may contribute to a nationalist movement is limited to speakers of the language. Non-Welsh speakers may be inspired by the language to become involved in various forms of nationalist activity, whether they undertake to learn it as a second language or not. The strengthening of national identity provided by greater public recognition for the language, as well as the creation of new national institutions, affects both Welsh and non-Welsh speakers.

4   Problems and conflicts

However, having a national language that is also a minority language within its own territory presents some serious problems for a nationalist movement. In such circumstances, the political nationalist movement is likely to be seen as primarily concerned with language issues and risks being regarded as irrelevant to the interests of the majority of the electorate. This has been an ongoing concern in Plaid Cymru at least since the 1930s and was an important factor driving its transformation from the 1950s onwards. But as the party moved closer to mainstream politics, some nationalists began to accuse it of losing sight of its commitment to Welsh culture.

As you read above, Cymdeithas yr Iaith was set up by young members of Plaid Cymru, and in its early years, the relationship with Plaid was close. However, as the direct-action campaigns began to attract negative publicity, some Plaid leaders accused the Society of harming their electoral prospects. Relations between the two organisations were most strained around the 1970 general election, when Gwynfor Evans lost his seat, amid claims that negative public reaction to the road signs campaign contributed to his defeat.

On balance, though, Plaid Cymru benefited from the existence and activities of Cymdeithas yr Iaith. Cymdeithas, along with the broader language movement, took the burden of language campaigning from Plaid Cymru and enabled it to concentrate on social and economic issues in the political mainstream. It could thus work to broaden its appeal and relevance to the wider Welsh electorate without too many concerns that it was weakening its fundamental commitment to the Welsh language and culture. Being a little removed from this cultural nationalism was an important factor in the party's gradual acceptance as a viable electoral option – although it took decades of campaigning for the party to differentiate itself from Cymdeithas yr Iaith in the public

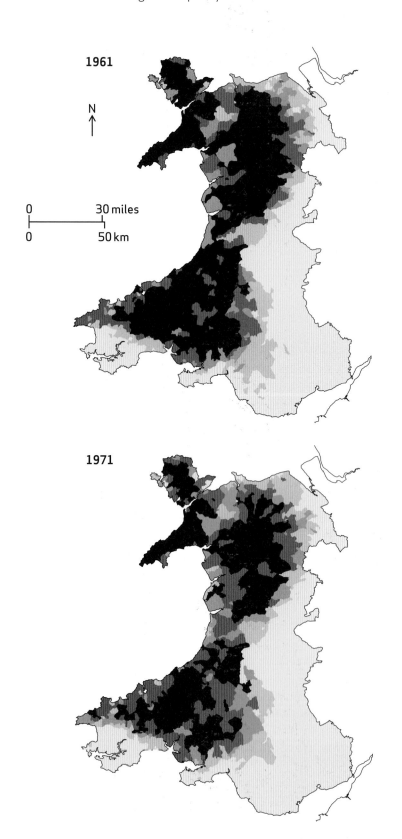

1961

N

0   30 miles

0   50 km

1971

Key   **Percentage**

80-100

65-80

50-65

20-50

0-20

Base 1961

Figure 6.3
Four maps showing
changes in the spatial
distribution of the
Welsh language in
Wales 1961–91.
(Source: adapted from
Aitchison and Carter,
1994)

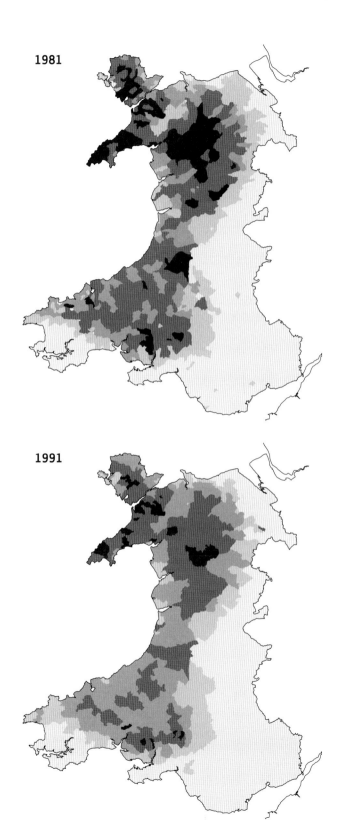

Figure 6.3
(Continued)

eye. A further benefit from the activities of Cymdeithas was its effect on other political parties in Wales, basically forcing them to clarify their position on the language.

4.1 A fragile consensus

By the late 1990s, as the National Assembly for Wales was being established, there was much talk about an emerging cross-party consensus on the Welsh language. All political parties in Wales were officially in favour of securing the future of the language, although differences remained as to how this could best be accomplished. This political consensus was not surprising given that public opinion polls were also finding widespread support for the language. However, a complex set of issues surrounding social and economic trends that had been adversely affecting Welsh-speaking communities for decades continued to fester and this led to open conflict within Plaid Cymru and the nationalist movement early in the twenty-first century.

Activity 6.4

Figure 6.2 paints a fairly optimistic picture for the language in its depiction of the percentages speaking Welsh in different age groups. Now look at Figure 6.3, a series of maps showing changes in the spatial distribution of the language between 1961 and 1991. If you look at the 1961 map, you will see a large contiguous region in the north and west – *Y Fro Gymraeg*, or the Welsh heartland, as discussed in Chapter 2 – where two thirds or more of the population speak Welsh. Looking at the other maps, describe the changes in this area over the next three decades. Thinking back to Activity 6.1 and the influence of context on language use, how do you think these changes affect the use of Welsh in the communities of *Y Fro Gymraeg*?

As early as the 1970s, Cymdeithas yr Iaith had begun to warn against the danger that increasing numbers of holiday homes posed to the small communities of *Y Fro Gymraeg*. It argued that the comparatively large number of such holiday homes – usually owned by people from outside the area and left vacant for most of the year – was undermining community life in many small towns and villages in this Welsh-language heartland. The society adopted non-violent tactics, such as occupying vacant holiday homes and disrupting auctions of these properties. However, in the period of general nationalist despondency and frustration following the 1979 referendum, a number of vacant holiday homes were deliberately set on fire. Both Cymdeithas yr Iaith and Plaid Cymru dissociated themselves publicly from these measures; nevertheless, activists from both organisations came under police suspicion, although neither was ever found to be involved. The fires – about 220 in all – continued to occur sporadically through the 1980s and came to an end in the early 1990s. Responsibility for the incidents was usually claimed by a group calling itself 'Meibion Glyndŵr' (Sons of Glyndŵr), but no perpetrators were ever apprehended.

During the 1980s the holiday homes campaign was overtaken by demographic changes that were to have a much greater impact on Welsh-speaking communities, namely the movement of large numbers of people (retirees, 'good life-ers') from urban areas to smaller rural communities. Most of these incomers to communities in *Y Fro Gymraeg* were from urban areas in England, and were non-Welsh-speaking. Typically, their financial resources were greater than local residents', with the result that their entry into the local housing market brought inflationary pressure. Many had sufficient capital (often from sale of a house in England where house prices were substantially higher) to invest in a local business with the result that the language of shops, post offices and pubs in many communities changed. This reduction of public domains where Welsh was the normal language caused grave concern to language activists. In addition, the increased prices for local housing exacerbated the existing problem of limited job opportunities for young people in their home communities and led to more young people leaving these communities for work elsewhere.

The effect of large numbers of incomers was most immediately apparent in the schools, particularly in small rural schools, where the ratio of Welsh speakers to non-Welsh speakers could shift substantially with a few families moving into an area (see Figure 6.3). Local authorities tried to ensure that Welsh remained the language of primary schooling by providing intensive courses to integrate the children of incomers into the schools. These measures were not without critics on both sides, but some of the other possible responses to the demographic shift proved more controversial. Among these were arguments for greater control over the housing market, so that incomers could not so readily acquire local properties. This latter approach was found in other parts of Britain, for example the Lake District, but in Wales the existence of a language difference between locals and incomers led to proposals for action on housing being branded as racist.

4.2 Cymuned and *Y Fro Gymraeg*

This is what occurred in the aftermath of a BBC radio interview in 2001 when Seimon Glyn, a Gwynedd county councillor and member of Plaid Cymru, stated that the movement of non-Welsh speakers into Welsh-speaking areas was detrimental to the language and needed to be monitored more carefully. His remarks received extremely negative publicity in the English-language press. *The Welsh Mirror* reported it under the headline 'Voice of Hate. "Racist" Plaid councillor's attack on the English' (18 January 2001). And in a column in *The Independent on Sunday*, Janet Street-Porter expressed her hope that 'Mr Glyn is reported under the Race Relations Act' (21 January 2001).

The then head of the Commission on Racial Equality in Wales also criticised Seimon Glyn publicly. This increased the existing distrust of the Commission among many Welsh speakers: relationships had been strained since the 1980s when non-Welsh speakers had used the Race Relations Act on several occasions to challenge Welsh-speaking requirements for some public service jobs in *Y Fro Gymraeg*. The response of the Welsh-language press to the Seimon Glyn affair could be seen on the cover of *Barn*, a journal of current affairs and opinion, which reproduced Street-Porter's article with a superimposed headline '*Pwy sy'n hiliol?*' [Who is racist?] (see Figure 6.4). The accompanying editorial concluded, '*Mae galw "hiliaeth" ar ymdrechion i warchod cadarnleoedd daearyddol olaf cymuned ieithyddol fregus ... yn peri i'r Comisiwn Cydraddoldeb Hiliol ymddangos fel y Ministry of Truth yn nofel George Orwell, 1984*' (Brooks, 2001, p. 6). ['Labelling as "racist" efforts to protect the last geographical strongholds of a fragile linguistic community ... makes the Commission for Racial Equality resemble the Ministry of Truth in George Orwell's novel 1984'].

This incident was the specific stimulus for the formation later in 2001 of Cymuned, an organisation whose primary mission was to oppose what its supporters regarded as the colonisation of Welsh-speaking communities.

Fairly early on, Cymuned began to display a duality in its make-up, 'a ... more practical and organic wing based in the rural areas of north and west Wales and the more intellectual wing based in Aberystwyth' (Jones and Fowler, 2008, p. 176). The first of these informal groupings, which coalesced around Seimon Glyn, engaged in activities such as providing information through estate agents about the linguistic make-up of the area to those considering moving to these communities. The second was more concerned with developing an analysis of the processes under way in *Y Fro Gymraeg*. They contended that they were not opposed to normal in-migration in which 'incomers respect the language, culture and identity of the country to which they migrate, learn the language and integrate into the society and its culture (whilst retaining their own language, culture and identity as well)' (Cymuned, 2003, p. 5).

But they argued that what was occurring in *Y Fro Gymraeg* was colonisation, where 'colonists impose their language, culture and identity on the country, assimilating the indigenous people and/or displacing them' (Cymuned, 2003, p. 6).

Figure 6.4

The response of the Welsh-language press to the Seimon Glyn affair: cover of *Barn* magazine

The leadership of Plaid Cymru was at pains to dissociate the party from Seimon Glyn's comments and from Cymuned. Although Plaid Cymru had been wrestling with the problem of how to deal with distortions to the housing market caused by in-migration, the party had long been committed to an inclusive interpretation of Welsh identity, based in Welsh citizenship, that embraced all the people of Wales, whatever their

Civic nationalism is an inclusive nationalism in which national belonging is based on citizenship and defined in terms of residence in the national territory.

origins or linguistic background. Cymuned opposed Plaid Cymru's adherence to this model of **'civic' nationalism**, arguing that this resulted in Welsh-language issues being given low priority. While Cymuned could not accuse Cymdeithas yr Iaith of disregard for language issues, it regarded Cymdeithas also as advocating civic nationalism and consequently failing to prioritise the situation of the Welsh language in *Y Fro Gymraeg*.

In spite of its use of some inflammatory rhetoric and analogies with colonialism, Cymuned engaged in various practical activities at a community level to encourage incomers to become involved in Welsh culture. It also put forward considered proposals to address the problems of *Y Fro Gymraeg*, many of which had been advanced in one form or another by Cymdeithas yr Iaith and Plaid Cymru over the years. In a presentation to the Local Government and Housing Committee of the National Assembly in 2001, Cymuned representatives suggested:

> [T]he Welsh language should be a material consideration within all planning decisions made within the Welsh heartland; ... the Welsh language should be incorporated more fully into the sustainability appraisals conducted on proposed developments within the Welsh heartland; affordable housing should be designated for local residents; welcome packs should be provided by estate agents to house buyers in order to make them aware of the cultural and linguistic characteristics of the Welsh heartland ...
>
> (Jones and Fowler, 2008, p. 182)

These ideas, along with most of Cymuned's more practical community activities, were acceptable to other nationalist organisations. Nevertheless, Cymuned, and the set of ideas it represented, led to fundamental disagreements within the nationalist movement. Both Plaid Cymru and Cymdeithas yr Iaith opposed Cymuned's concentration on *Y Fro Gymraeg*, arguing that the Welsh language was not confined to these areas and that campaigns to encourage its spread throughout Wales were of equal importance. In particular, they rejected the tendency to divide Wales spatially into Welsh-speaking and non-Welsh-speaking areas. Furthermore, Plaid Cymru was particularly sensitive to accusations of racism called forth by some of Cymuned's rhetoric. To understand this sensitivity, you need to look at theories about **nationalism** and the character of nationalist movements.

Nationalism is an ideology that maintains that each nation should rightly have its own political institutions.

Summary

- The 2001 Census showed increases in the percentage of Welsh speakers in Wales as a whole and in most parts of south and east Wales, but a continuing decline in *Y Fro Gymraeg*.

- Some language activists (Cymuned) blamed the decline on non-Welsh-speaking incomers and advocated measures to control their numbers.

- Although many of Cymuned's recommendations and practical activities were acceptable to both Plaid Cymru and Cymdeithas yr Iaith, their rhetoric about 'colonisation' opposed the civic nationalism of these other nationalist organisations, prompted charges of racism, and undermined the commitment to a fully bilingual Wales, instead dividing Wales into Welsh-speaking and non-Welsh-speaking areas.

5 Nationalism

Nationalism is an ideology whose origins can be found in the processes of state building in Europe from the eighteenth century onwards. This ideology sees the world as naturally and rightly divided into nations, whose members share a national identity by virtue of such attributes as common history, language, religion and other cultural characteristics. Nationalism proclaims the right of every nation to its own political institutions, that is, each state ideally should contain only one national grouping.

Why did nationalism appear when and where it did in human history? And how did national cultures and a consciousness of national identities arise? Most who have tried to answer these questions have seen nations not as something natural about human society, simply waiting to be discovered. Instead, they were created as the response to a specific set of requirements, the needs of emerging industrial capitalism for a homogeneous and mobile labour force. Ernest Gellner (1983) argued that states introduced mass education to produce such a labour force. The content of this education was created by building on an arbitrarily selected local 'folk' culture. This became the national 'high' culture and the basis of national identity, and in the process it displaced the variety of different 'folk' cultures that existed within the state's boundaries. Thus, as Gellner (1983, p. 55) remarked, 'It is nationalism which engenders nations, and not the other way round'.

5.1 Varieties of nationalism

Although nationalism arose at a particular time and place in response to a specific set of historic circumstances, it has proved to be highly adaptable and effective as the basis for popular political mobilisation in many different contexts. Gellner's ideas are better at explaining the origin of nationalism than they are at accounting for the impetus behind the many varieties of nationalism that have since emerged. Thus, his portrayal of national cultures as artificial inventions is contradicted by the perpetuation of a distinctive Welsh identity, which became the basis for a nationalist political movement, centuries after Wales's incorporation into a British state that was hostile to Welsh culture.

Although the many varieties of nationalist movement that have arisen appeal to the same ideology, there are large differences between them, reflecting the different contexts in which these movements developed.

Activity 6.5

Read the following extract by James Kellas about different forms of nationalism. Notice where he places Welsh nationalism in his typology. As you read about the characteristics of different nationalist movements, make a list of them and of the ways in which these movements differ from one another. Does this categorisation help to explain the concern noted earlier of many in Plaid Cymru about Cymuned's rhetoric regarding 'colonisation'?

Extract 6.5

Classical European nationalism

[T]he ideology of nationalism seems to have originated in Europe. ... But this nationalism, even within Europe, was divided into a 'western' and an 'eastern' form. The 'western' nationalism was ethnically 'inclusive' in that it was based on a 'social nation' which could encompass more than one ethnic group. It was essentially about the cultural homogeneity of the state, and the common citizenship of those sharing that culture. 'Eastern' European nationalism, on the other hand, was ethnically 'exclusive' and was focused on the nation as a community of common descent, language, and religion. ...

The forms taken by nationalist movements in Europe set the pattern for nationalisms throughout the world. The inclusive nationalisms were more liberal and democratic, and did not engage in genocide, transfers of population, etc. The exclusive nationalisms were intolerant and often led to authoritarianism. ...

Unification movements

The unification of the German nation and of the Italian nation in the late nineteenth century was accomplished through war and conquest of existing states. ... This type of nationalism is also called

'Risorgimento' (rebirth) nationalism ... and it combined the aim of national unification with liberal ideals of democracy and freedom from oppression ...

National secession movements

In most cases, nationalism led to the break-up of existing states, not their joining together in one large 'nation-state'. So nationalist movements in Ireland, Greece, Poland, Serbia, and Norway, for example, achieved independence for their nations by breaking away from Britain, the Ottoman Empire, the Russian Empire, the Austrian Empire, and Sweden, respectively, Today, national secession movements are still active in Europe: in Scotland, Wales, the Basque country, Corsica ...

Integral nationalism

Integral nationalism differs from 'risorgimento' nationalism in its belief that one's nation is superior to all others, and may even be the result of biological natural selection. ...

Integral nationalism is an absolutist ideology (the absolute loyalty to the nation is demanded), and in politics is clearly linked to totalitarian, Fascist, and Nazi forms of government.

Colonial nationalism

In the European colonial empires ... a nationalism developed among the European settlers, which led to the independence of the colonies from the mother country. ...

Anti-colonial nationalism

... The emergence of indigenous 'national liberation' and anti-colonial movements in the British Empire corresponded with the spread of nationalist ideology from Europe ...

Given the existing colonial state structure at independence, the nationalists of the new 'nation-states' had to preserve boundaries which reflected the boundaries of colonial power rather than cultural or national divisions. Thus 'nation-building', irredentisms [nationalisms that make claims on the territory of other states], and secessions were permanently on the agenda of nearly all these new states. Now nationalism did not usually mean anti-colonialism ... Instead it meant interethnic disputes, communalism, and sometimes genocide.

Source: Kellas, 1991, pp. 73–7

5.2 The nature of Welsh nationalism

Kellas begins by making a distinction between 'western' and 'eastern' forms of nationalism. His 'western' form of nationalism is essentially the same as what we have referred to as 'civic' nationalism, an inclusive social movement with national 'belonging' based in citizenship. Both Plaid Cymru and Cymdeithas yr Iaith advocate this type of nationalism. 'Civic' nationalism can be contrasted with **ethnic nationalism**, in which 'belonging' is understood in terms of some form of common descent, which may be genetic or may simply mean a shared history. Cymuned is usually taken to advocate a form of 'ethnic' nationalism.

Ethnic nationalism is national belonging defined in terms of culture and common descent, although not necessarily genetic descent.

As with all typologies, there is often a degree of overlap between categories. For example, shared culture is important for both civic and ethnic nationalism but is treated differently by them. For Cymuned, the Welsh language is the defining characteristic of the Welsh nation, to the extent that if the Welsh-speaking communities were to disappear, so too would the Welsh people 'cease to exist', an outcome Cymuned regards as 'ethnocide' (Cymuned, 2003, p. 5). Cymuned has rejected charges of racism and welcomed in-migrants, 'who learn Cymraeg [Welsh] and become part of the community ... from all nations (including England) and all races', seeing them as 'enriching a multi-racial Welsh-speaking society' (Cymuned, 2003, p. 7). Nevertheless, there is an exclusivist element in the suggestion that only Welsh speakers can truly claim Welsh identity, and this underlies much of Plaid Cymru's disavowal of the group's position.

In Extract 6.5 you saw that Kellas characterises Welsh nationalism as being a type of 'national secession' movement, an inclusive movement in that 'the existing citizens of a territory were acceptable as members of the nation' (Kellas, 1991, p. 73) and one example of many such movements that have arisen within a liberal democratic tradition. However, other types of nationalism – and in particular what Kellas calls 'integral nationalism' – have different characteristics: illiberal; autocratic; intolerant; racist. Thus, Welsh nationalists have had to face accusations from political opponents of 'narrow nationalism', and even 'racism' and 'fascism', which largely stem from a failure to acknowledge the very broad range of movements coming under the nationalist label.

We now turn to an examination of some aspects of Plaid Cymru's political philosophy and policies in order to characterise more fully the nationalist movement in Wales.

5.2.1 Nationalism and internationalism

Welsh nationalism was a product of the radical politics and socialist ideals that developed in Wales during the early decades of the twentieth century. The political importance of Welsh identity was an integral part of this context – Keir Hardie, the first independent Labour member of parliament from Wales, was a supporter of Welsh national identity and campaigned for Welsh home rule. In the years just prior to the First World War, several prominent members of the Independent Labour Party (ILP) tried to create a separate Welsh ILP, and although unsuccessful, continued to advocate a union of nationalist and decentralist socialist ideals (Davies, 1983). Some of them would become members of the Welsh Nationalist Party after its establishment in 1925.

The distinctiveness of the Welsh Nationalist Party lay in its emphasis on the Welsh language and culture, and in its independence from any British political party. But the party could not be accused of being 'narrow nationalist' in outlook. At the first of their annual summer schools in 1926, party president Saunders Lewis addressed directly the issue of nationalism versus internationalism. In his lecture entitled *Egwyddorion Cenedlaetholdeb*' ('Principles of Nationalism'), he maintained that 'the thing that destroyed the civilization of Wales and ruined Welsh culture, that brought about the dire plight of Wales today, was – nationalism' (Lewis, 1975, p. 5). His argument was that the concept of nationalism that arose during the period of European state formation was materialist and based entirely on force. He advocated that Welsh nationalism should be inspired by an earlier principle, when an acceptance of an international authority, that of the Christian Church, across Europe was combined with respect for a diversity of cultures. Lewis then proceeded to argue that the recently established League of Nations was 'an attempt to loosen the hard chains of material nationalism' (Lewis, 1975, p. 9), and advocated that one of the conditions of Welsh self-government should be a seat in the League of Nations.

5.2.2 Nationalism and socialism

There was a socialist element among Welsh Nationalist Party members from its foundation, although they were less prominent among the leadership. Kate Roberts, a member from 1926 onwards and a close associate of Saunders Lewis, explained her initial refusal to join: 'as I am a Socialist I really cannot reconcile myself with his [Lewis's] ideas. Personally, I see no difference between doffing one's cap to an English merchant and doffing one's cap to our old Welsh princes' (Davies, 1983, p. 124).

At the 1938 party conference, a group of university students from Bangor challenged Saunders Lewis's proposed social programme, arguing that the party's philosophy was in essence socialist and that this should be acknowledged in order to win over Welsh socialists for the goal of Welsh self-government. The rejection of their motion in favour of Lewis's concept of *perchentyaeth* (literally, home ownership-ism) may have been less a rejection of socialism than a reflection of the great personal respect for Lewis among the membership (Davies, 1983, pp. 104–5). Regardless of this rejection of the label 'socialist', the party's primary spokesperson on economics during their first two decades, Dr D.J. Davies, was a former member of the Independent Labour Party and developed party economic policy based on his socialist vision.

Plaid Cymru began to move towards an explicit socialist position in the 1960s when an infusion of a new type of member began to affect the party. These new members were products of the educational opportunities created by the post-Second World War welfare state for working-class people; many were young, non-Welsh-speaking and from the industrial areas of south Wales. Although most came from families and communities that were traditionally loyal to the Labour Party, they rejected Labour for what they regarded as its betrayal of socialism. One party member from a Valleys constituency, interviewed in 1977, said he had joined Plaid Cymru as a teenager in the mid 1960s.

> My generation began to realise that all this tremendous loyalty to Labour had got us nowhere in our area and had got Wales nowhere as a whole ... We suspected Labour not just on practical grounds, that they had not delivered on their promises, but also on ideological grounds that they were not a true socialist party ... We chose nationalism as the best way to pursue socialist ideals.
>
> (Davies, 1989, p. 72)

By the early 1970s the socialist direction, not just of Plaid Cymru but also of the language movement, was beginning to be acknowledged by some intellectuals on the left.

Activity 6.6

Read the following extract by Raymond Williams from his review of Ned Thomas's book *The Welsh Extremist*, on the Welsh language and the language movement, published in 1971. What do you think were Williams's reasons for changing his view of Welsh nationalism as parochial and conservative to seeing it as a part of 'a cause better than national and more than international ... a very general human and social movement' (Williams, 2003 [1971], p. 3)?

Extract 6.6

I used to think that born into a Border country at once physical, economic, and cultural, my own relationship to the idea of Wales was especially problematic. But I now see, from Ned Thomas, among others, that it was characteristic. I remember focusing first on the powerful political culture of industrial South Wales: in the first half of this century one of the major centres of socialist consciousness anywhere in the world. But the necessary movement from that kind of centre was into a larger society. ...

But there was always another idea of Wales: the more enclosed, mainly rural, more Welsh-speaking west and north. For me, in the beginning, that was much more remote. ... In the last decade especially ... another idea of Wales, drawn from its alternative source, has come through in the campaigns of Plaid Cymru and the Welsh Language Society.

The relation between these two phases has been especially difficult. Many English Socialists, and many Welsh Labour Party people, have seen the later phase as a marginal or romantic irrelevance, or as worse. 'Nationalism means Fascism', somebody said to me angrily. He is especially the kind of man who should read Ned Thomas's book. For the strange thing is this: that through its radical emphasis on identity and community, and in its turn to popular campaigning, to demonstrations and to direct action, this new Welsh movement ... has come through as part of the new socialism and the new thinking about culture ...

... [I]t seems to be true that in late capitalist societies some of the most powerful campaigns begin from specific unabsorbed (and therefore necessarily marginal) experiences and situations. Black Power in the United States, civil rights in Ulster, the language in Wales ...

Source: Williams, 2003 (1971), pp. 3–4

Comment

Williams's intellectual journey illustrates the difficulties that Welsh nationalism faced as a consequence of the wide variety of movements that have been labelled 'nationalist'. It also points to changes in the understanding of socialism, in particular a growing acceptance of the importance of 'local' experiences and cultural meanings, which have moved the two ideologies closer together.

In the early 1980s, Plaid Cymru officially incorporated socialism into the party's aims, while still rejecting the state socialism it associated with the Labour Party. A Commission of Inquiry into the future of the party defined its political stance as 'decentralist socialist'. However, some in the party remained concerned about the contradictions between decentralism and socialism and, in a minority report, Phil Williams argued that government functions should be conducted at as low a level as feasible without undermining 'the basic equality of individuals and communities within society'. Thus, socialism and decentralism could be combined, 'but when the two principles contradict it is to socialism that we should give our highest priority' (Plaid Cymru, 1981, p. 111).

5.2.3   Green nationalism

Phil Williams's minority report was grappling with an issue similar to that raised by Raymond Williams – the relationship between different levels of social organisation and their associated cultural meanings. Raymond Williams identified with a new form of socialism, the New Left, composed of broad social movements (the women's movement, Black Power, the Welsh language) yet rooted in the particularities of locality and common interest. Another social movement, the ecological movement, became increasingly prominent from the 1980s, advocating a similar blend of global awareness and local action.

Phil Williams, who had been one of the young 'non-traditional' recruits to nationalism in the early 1960s and whose ideas had a major influence on Plaid policy over four decades, was among the first to press the party for action on green issues. He persuaded the 1983 Conference to establish a working party on ecological and environmental issues. This policy area came to be particularly closely associated with west Wales as a result of the agreement between Plaid Cymru and the Green Party to field a joint candidate for the constituency of Ceredigion and Pembroke North in the 1992 general election. This decision produced a victory for Cynog Dafis, who became the fourth Plaid MP and the first Green MP at Westminster. The agreement with the Green Party held until 1995 and was instrumental in getting some environmental measures through parliament.

After his election to the National Assembly in 1999, Phil Williams continued his work on the problem of climate change, arguing that Wales could contribute significantly to action to reduce global greenhouse gas emissions. In a speech to the National Assembly in May 2000, he described climate change as 'the overriding imperative of global politics and ... the most important single issue since the 1980s'. As a professional physicist, he felt obliged to convey the 'sense of reasoned, responsible panic' of key environmental scientists. At the same time, he detailed actions by the National Assembly for Wales that, he maintained, would make a genuine contribution to addressing the crisis. Speaking as a nationalist, yet recognising the necessity of international cooperation, he concluded:

> [A]lthough no single parliament has the power to solve the problem globally, this Assembly, with the exception of the climate change levy, has all the necessary powers to ensure that Wales plays not only its full role but perhaps a leading role. That is my dream.
>
> (Williams, 2004, p. 62)

5.3 Nationalism under devolution

Plaid Cymru's agreement in the 1990s with the Green Party confirmed the party's ability to appeal to a constituency with a high proportion of incomers and non-Welsh speakers, not regarded as their natural supporters. It also signalled Plaid's willingness to work with other political parties to achieve common goals. Both factors were instrumental in the party's establishing itself as a 'civic' nationalist movement, and contributed to its finally achieving a degree of political power in a Welsh government under devolution.

The establishment of the National Assembly for Wales has had two major effects on the nationalist movement. In the area of political nationalism, Plaid Cymru moved from being a tiny minority at Westminster to the second largest party in the National Assembly in the first elections in 1999. This signified a substantially altered position for nationalism within Welsh political life. And indeed the subsequent decade was marked with the movement of all political parties in Wales toward more 'nationalist' positions, including even the Conservative Party in Wales, which came to support the extension of the powers of the National Assembly to include legislative powers. Furthermore, after the 2007 elections, all other parties engaged in negotiations with Plaid Cymru as a potential coalition partner in government, and a coalition was eventually agreed with the Labour Party. This set of events, legitimising the role of the 'nationalists', demonstrated that Plaid Cymru had finally achieved acceptance within the mainstream of Welsh politics.

In terms of Welsh national identity, the creation of a democratically elected representative body provided a historically new basis for Welsh identity. The National Assembly for Wales strengthened Welsh identity in a number of ways: it became an important focus for lobbying and protest, being more accessible than Westminster and (in spite of the limitations on its powers) more relevant to the concerns of Welsh people. It also encouraged the development of civil society in Wales, making explicit provisions – even setting up umbrella organisations – to

Figure 6.5
Cymdeithas yr Iaith poster, showing then First Minister Rhodri Morgan. It is promoting a 2005 rally for a new language act ('Language Act Rally – This is the Opportunity'), which was convened outside the Welsh Assembly Government headquarters in Cathays Park, Cardiff

establish channels of communication with Third Sector (i.e. non-profit, voluntary and non-governmental) organisations.

These considerations bring us back to the relationship of language and national identity with which we began. What effect has the establishment of the National Assembly had on the Welsh language as a marker of Welsh identity? In 2003 the Welsh Assembly Government published its detailed Welsh language policy, *Iaith Pawb: A National Action Plan for a Bilingual Wales*. This was the strongest commitment ever by government to the Welsh language with the ultimate goal of creating 'a truly bilingual nation ... where people can choose to live their lives through the medium of either Welsh or English and where the presence of the two languages is a visible and audible source of pride and strength to us all' (Welsh Assembly Government, 2003, p. 11). However, the practical implications for the language remained disputed as serious reservations were expressed about the adequacy of provision for specific mechanisms and additional resources to enable implementation.

Summary

■ Nationalist movements vary widely from liberal democratic to intolerant autocratic. Most Welsh nationalist organisations (Plaid Cymru, Cymdeithas yr Iaith) advocate an inclusive 'civic' nationalism.

- A few organisations (e.g. Cymuned) reject civic nationalism, while still maintaining an anti-racist position.

- Plaid Cymru's political philosophy has incorporated internationalism, socialism, and green nationalism.

- Post-devolution, Plaid Cymru became a mainstream political party and eventually a party of government. Other Welsh political parties moved closer to a 'nationalist' perspective. National identity was strengthened and legitimised, and the Welsh Assembly Government made a strong commitment to the Welsh language, but doubts remained about practical provisions for implementation.

6 Conclusion

Language is intimately connected with the processes by which we establish and maintain our personal identities, as well as collective identities. National identity is one such collective identity for which language and language differences are important.

The Welsh language has been important for Welsh national identity and for the Welsh nationalist movement in many ways. It has provided an inspiration for activists in the movement. Welsh has also been used to win official recognition for the Welsh nation by means of its public display (e.g. on signs) and use (e.g. by public services). And the language has been a basis for the establishment of specifically Welsh institutions (e.g. Welsh-medium schools).

However, the Welsh language is under pressure from a range of social and economic processes, and disagreements about the appropriate way to respond to these pressures have led to conflict within the nationalist movement and to attacks from outside.

Although there are many varieties of nationalism, and some of them are autocratic and intolerant, Welsh nationalism derives from a radical democratic socialist tradition within Wales and displays the concern with liberal democracy and egalitarianism characteristic of this tradition. The Welsh nationalist movement can be characterised as a democratic and inclusive form of 'civic' nationalism with a political stance that encompasses internationalism, socialism, and environmentalism.

References

Aitchison, J. and Carter, H. (1994) *A Geography of the Welsh Language 1961–1991*, Cardiff, University of Wales Press.

Brooks, S. (2001) 'Golygyddol: Seimon Glyn' [Editorial: Seimon Glyn], *Barn*, no. 457, Chwefror [February], pp. 6–9.

Cymuned (2003) *In-migration, Yes, Colonisation, No!* Aberystwyth, Cymuned.

Davies, C.A. (1989) *Welsh Nationalism in the Twentieth Century: The Ethnic Option and the Modern State*, New York, Praeger.

Davies, C.A., Charles, N. and Harris, C. (2006) 'Welsh identity and language in Swansea (1960–2002)', *Contemporary Wales*, vol. 18, pp. 28–53.

Davies, D.H. (1983) *The Welsh Nationalist Party 1925–1945: A Call to Nationhood*, Cardiff, University of Wales Press.

Gellner, E. (1983) *Nations and Nationalism*, Oxford, Blackwell.

Jones, R. and Fowler, C. (2008) *Placing the Nation: Aberystwyth and the Reproduction of Welsh Nationalism*, Cardiff, University of Wales Press.

Jones, S.P. (1992) 'Coming home' in Bowie, F. and Davies, O. (eds) *Discovering Welshness*, Llandysul, Gomer.

Joseph, J.E. (2004) *Language and Identity: National, Ethnic, Religious*, Houndmills, Basingstoke, Hampshire, Palgrave Macmillan.

Kellas, J.G. (1991) *The Politics of Nationalism and Ethnicity*, Houndmills, Basingstoke, Hampshire, Macmillan.

Lewis, S. (1975 [1926]) *Egwyddorion Cenedlaetholdeb/Principles of Nationalism*, Cardiff, Plaid Cymru.

Plaid Cymru (1981) *Report of the Plaid Cymru Commission of Inquiry*, Cardiff, Plaid Cymru.

Roberts, G.T. (1998) *The Language of the Blue Books: The Perfect Instrument of Empire*, Cardiff, University of Wales Press.

Sapir, E. (1970 [1933]) 'Language' in Mandelbaum, D. G. (ed.) *Edward Sapir: Culture, Language and Personality*, Berkeley and Los Angeles, University of California Press.

Webb, H. (1995 [1963]) 'The old language' in Stephens, M. (ed.) *Harri Webb: Collected Poems*, Llandysul, Gomer.

Welsh Assembly Government (2003) *Iaith Pawb: A National Plan for a Bilingual Wales/Iaith Pawb: Cynllun Gweithredu Cenedlaethol ar Gyfer Cymru Ddwyieithog*, Cardiff, Welsh Assembly Government.

Welsh Language Board (1999) *Continuity in Welsh Language Education*, Cardiff, Welsh Language Board.

Welsh Language Board (2003) *Census 2001: Main statistics about Welsh*, Cardiff, Welsh Language Board, available at: www.byig-wlb.org.uk/english/publications/publications/332.doc

Williams, P. (2004) *Phil Williams: the Assembly Years 1999–2003*, Cardiff, Plaid Cymru.

Williams, R. (2003 [1971]) 'Who speaks for Wales?' in Williams, D. (ed.) *Who Speaks for Wales? Nation, Culture, Identity: Raymond Williams*, Cardiff, University of Wales Press.

Further reading

Davies, J. (1993) *The Welsh Language*, Cardiff, University of Wales Press, provides a good introduction to the development of the Welsh language and to Welsh-language culture.

An accessible introduction to theoretical discussions about nationalism is Guiberneau, M. (1996) *Nationalisms: The Nation-State and Nationalism in the Twentieth Century*, Cambridge, Polity Press.

McAllister, L. (2001) *Plaid Cymru: The Emergence of a Political Party*, Bridgend, Wales, Seren, is a study of the party in the second half of the twentieth century.

The following two books provide perspectives from within the language movement and political nationalism:

Thomas, N. (1991 [1971]) *The Welsh Extremist*, Talybont, Wales, Y Lolfa.
Williams, P. (1981) *Voice from the Valleys*, Aberystwyth, Wales, Plaid Cymru.

Chapter 7
Labour traditions

Andrew Edwards

Contents

1 Introduction

Very little that happens in Wales is predictable – certainly not the weather, the fortunes of the national sports teams or the economy. However, over the past hundred years or so, there has been one exception. If you were born any time after the First World War, you might not be able to plan a barbeque, place a safe bet on the outcome of a Welsh football match, or make predictions over the prospects of the Welsh economy, but you could, with some confidence, predict that Labour would win the majority of Welsh seats in any general election.

From the 1920s onwards, the Labour Party dominated Welsh politics, winning the majority of parliamentary seats for the first time in 1923 and thumping its rivals with consummate ease on numerous other occasions (especially, as we shall see, in 1966 when the party won 32 out of 36 seats and again in 1997 when it won 34 out of 40).

Unsurprisingly, historians, political commentators and sociologists, from inside and outside Wales, have become used to seeing Welsh politics through the red lens of 'Labour Wales'. In popular discourse, 'Labour Wales' is associated with industrial south Wales, chapels, coal mines, terraced houses, working-men's clubs, male voice choirs and the proud traditions of an industrial working class. The fact that many people in Wales did not vote Labour – around a fifth of Welsh voters regularly voted Conservative after 1918 – escapes the attention of many. So too has the fact that the image of 'Labour Wales' outlined above is misleading: Labour, and the Labour tradition, did exist (and enjoyed success) away from south Wales, in rural areas, and in 'Welsh-speaking' Wales.

However, in 2009, 'Labour Wales' no longer seems secure. Election results and public opinion suggest that the Labour tradition is on the wane. In the 2009 European elections, Labour captured just 20 per cent of the vote, following a disappointing performance in the 2007 Welsh Assembly elections when it captured only 32 per cent of the vote. In 2009, an opinion poll suggested that Labour could be on course to receive just 26 per cent of the Welsh vote in a general election, trailing behind the Conservatives (30 per cent) for the first time in the democratic era (Kettle, 2009).

The problems facing Labour were summed up by the journalist Martin Kettle in the *Guardian*:

> Let's not mince words. If those figures are even approximately right, Wales would experience a political and existential earthquake ... it would massively challenge aspects of the way that many in Wales see themselves and their nation ... in the twentieth century, the electoral geography of Wales was predictable. Labour held the heavily

populated old industrial south from Newport across to Llanelli and through the mining valleys ... but it is all to change now...

(Kettle, 2009)

As Kettle argues, if the polls were right, Labour faces a crisis, and a tradition that has become central to the lives of many people in Wales could be on the point of expiry.

The aims of this chapter are to:

- explore the Labour tradition in Wales, by examining its origin, and then its development between, and after, the two world wars

- look at the personalities who helped develop and sustain the Labour tradition

- examine the often close, but equally complex, relationship between Labour and 'Welshness'

- discuss the impact of devolution on the Labour tradition, and examine the direction of the Labour tradition as we enter the second decade of Welsh Assembly governance.

2 The origins of the radical and Labour traditions

Although I want to focus on the period after 1945, we have to go a bit further back to understand the origins of the radical tradition in Welsh politics. I'm trying to avoid using the term 'Labour tradition' for now because it took some time for Labour to establish itself as the main, radical force in Welsh politics and the tradition that many now see as 'Labour' started out as a tradition that was attached to other political parties and movements. It is difficult to pick a precise point when the 'Labour tradition' started, but we can safely locate its origin in the 1920s, when Labour became the dominant radical force in Welsh politics.

However, we need to remember that Labour does not have exclusivity rights to the 'radical tradition'. Plaid Cymru and the Liberal Democrats could both be seen as radical political parties and both could justifiably claim to represent many elements of a tradition that has been dominant in Welsh politics for over a century. Other smaller parties (for example, the Green Party and many of the 'splinter' socialist parties that have emerged over recent years) may say the same. What you should note is that other groups and movements have also been part of that radical tradition. Although many of these had close connections to political parties (for example, the trade union and cooperative movements) and were thus part of a Welsh labour tradition (note the small-case 'l' denoting the wider labour movement, rather than the political party), they were part of a much wider history, tradition and political culture.

What ended up as a tradition linked to political parties and political movements started out as a form of popular protest in the nineteenth century – the 'Rebecca' riots of the late 1830s and early 1840s (a radical campaign which opposed the exploitation of the agricultural community by wealthy landowners); the Chartist movement of the 1840s (a radical movement for political and social reform); the formation of Wales's first trade unions and the election of its first 'radical' MPs. But that's for another day. A good place to start would be to point out that it was the Liberal Party that (following the extension of the franchise to ordinary people) first represented Welsh political radicalism (as we now recognise it) in the late nineteenth and early twentieth centuries.

The Liberal Party's radical identity was linked with a number of important social, cultural and political issues in Wales, including disestablishment of the church (the Liberals, like Labour later on, were closely linked with the Welsh Nonconformist chapels), temperance, land reform, concern for the Welsh language and Welsh culture, and the question of Welsh home rule (self-government). Welsh radicalism was also linked to many other radical causes that were evident across Britain and Europe at the time, including better healthcare for the working classes, better education and better working conditions (including representation by trade unions).

However, Labour began to 'inherit' the radical tradition before, and especially after, the First World War. There were several reasons for this – not least, the gradual movement of the trade unions away from the Liberal Party and towards Labour, the negative association of the Liberal Party with the war, and the changed social conditions brought about by war which meant that many of the 'old' Liberal concerns (see above) no longer held the same importance in the 'new' post-war world.

In the inter-war period Labour had established a strong foothold in Welsh politics, although the party's strength was largely confined to the working-class communities and industrial valleys of south Wales. At this time also, Labour's relationship with powerful trade unions had made it a formidable political force in industrial Wales. A classic example of these trade unions was the South Wales Miners Federation, affectionately known as '**the Fed**'.

'**The Fed**' or the South Wales Miners Federation was formed in 1898. At its peak in 1923, the south Wales coalfield employed 252,617. The vast majority were members of 'The Fed'. The union was at the centre of working-class life in the coalfield.

Labour MPs were returned for every parliamentary seat with a substantial mining vote after 1918. In the coalfield, Labour built on deep social and industrial loyalties, blurring the distinctions between the union, Labour, the local councils, the working class, the community and even the chapel (Tanner, 2000). Being 'Labour' became a fact of many people's lives. Table 7.1 shows how Labour dominated mining and semi-mining areas in the inter-war years.

Table 7.1 Seats contested by Labour, 1918–1945: mining and semi-mining constituencies, south Wales (% votes won) (Source: Tanner et al., 1999, p. 119)

	1918	1922	1923	1924	1929	1931	1935	1945
Caerphilly	54.8	57.2	58.7	59.0	57.9	67.6	76.3	80.2
Gower	54.8	54.2	59.1	57.2	54.0	53.4	66.8	68.5
Neath	35.2	59.5	62.3	unop	60.2	64.0	unop	79.2
Ogmore	unop	55.8	unop	unop	56.7	61.0	unop	76.4
Pontypridd	42.8	47.2	54.9	55.9	53.1	58.3	unop	68.6
Aberdare	21.4	57.2	58.2	61.6	64.6	unop	unop	84.3
Merthyr Tydfil	47.3	53.0	60.1	59.8	59.6	69.4	68.0	81.4
Rhondda East	unop	55.0	71.9	unop	50.2	68.1	67.8	48.4
Rhondda West	unop	62.1	65.4	unop	65.1	84.3	unop	unop
Abertillery	unop	unop	unop	unop	64.5	unop	unop	86.6
Bedwellty	53.6	63.0	67.6	unop	79.0	unop	unop	82.1
Ebbw Vale	unop	65.4	65.6	unop	60.3	unop	77.8	80.1
Pontypool	39.0	40.6	50.6	52.6	51.5	56.3	67.9	77.3

Note: Bold type represents Labour victories. 'Unop' represents 'unopposed'.

Labour's popularity in the coalfield constituencies in south Wales meant that the party's candidates were often unopposed (presumably because Labour's rivals saw this as a waste of time and money). Even when there was opposition, Labour still established a sizeable vote. Huge majorities became the norm for Labour MPs.

In the coalfield areas of south Wales, Labour's radicalism was manifest in the revolutionary sentiment and political doctrine of Marxism, which enjoyed some support in the early 1920s. Such sentiments became an integral part of a Labour tradition, informing a myth and stereotype that has influenced popular understandings of 'Labour Wales' in the twentieth century. However, the 'radical tradition' and the Labour tradition were often far more moderate than some acknowledge (discussed in greater length below).

Labour's strength in Wales in the inter-war period is best demonstrated by the general election of 1931. Across Britain, this was a disastrous election for the Labour Party following the collapse of the 1929 Labour government. Having won 288 seats in 1929, the party won only 52 in

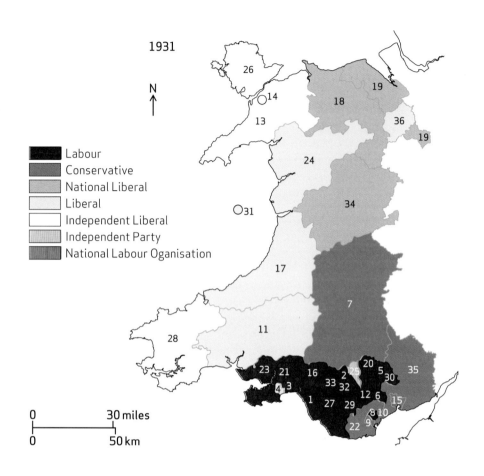

1931

N
↑

Labour
Conservative
National Liberal
Liberal
Independent Liberal
Independent Party
National Labour Oganisation

0   30 miles
0   50 km

Figure 7.1
Electoral map of Wales, 1931 (Source: Jones, 1999, p. 174)

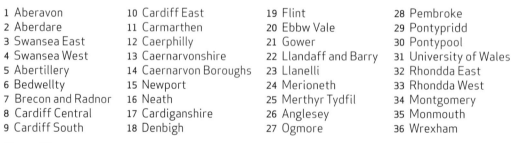

1 Aberavon	10 Cardiff East	19 Flint	28 Pembroke
2 Aberdare	11 Carmarthen	20 Ebbw Vale	29 Pontypridd
3 Swansea East	12 Caerphilly	21 Gower	30 Pontypool
4 Swansea West	13 Caernarvonshire	22 Llandaff and Barry	31 University of Wales
5 Abertillery	14 Caernarvon Boroughs	23 Llanelli	32 Rhondda East
6 Bedwellty	15 Newport	24 Merioneth	33 Rhondda West
7 Brecon and Radnor	16 Neath	25 Merthyr Tydfil	34 Montgomery
8 Cardiff Central	17 Cardiganshire	26 Anglesey	35 Monmouth
9 Cardiff South	18 Denbigh	27 Ogmore	36 Wrexham

1931. However, as Figure 7.1 shows, 16 of these were in Wales; Wales was among the very few parts of Britain to stay loyal to Labour.

The south Wales industrial heartland remained loyal to Labour despite severe economic difficulties and mass unemployment. In the 1930s, Wales was ravaged by the effects of the economic depression that swept the world in the aftermath of the 1929 Wall Street crash. The bonds that formed the Labour tradition were stretched to breaking point by unemployment and poverty on an unparalleled scale. In industrial south Wales, unemployment reached 32 per cent by 1930; in 1935, 70 per cent of coal miners in Merthyr and Dowlais were out of work. However, these harsh social conditions also helped reinforce the bonds of working-class solidarity and attachment to Labour, providing fertile ground for Labour propaganda on issues such as health, housing and workers' rights. Although some of the difficulties of the early 1930s had been addressed by 1939, it took a second world war to alleviate many of the problems of the 1930s. After 1945, radical politicians in Labour's ranks were determined that the miseries of the inter-war period would not be repeated. The next section explores how the Labour tradition was developed immediately after 1945.

Summary

- Radicalism is a long-established political tradition in Wales, with roots dating back to the nineteenth century.

- The Labour Party became the main representative of that tradition from the early 1920s onwards.

- Labour's popularity in industrial south Wales was based on a combination of social, cultural, religious and economic factors.

3   The development of the Labour tradition after 1945

In popular discourse, the Labour Party in Wales is often associated with the working class, industrial militancy and powerful trade unions. But there was much more to the Labour tradition after 1945 than this. I shall start by looking at the personalities who represented the Labour Party in Wales and who helped mould the Welsh Labour tradition in south Wales.

3.1 Personalities and the Labour tradition

To start to understand different Labour traditions, I shall look briefly at the backgrounds and beliefs of two Labour MPs who became powerful figures in the party (at British as well as Welsh level) after 1945: James Griffiths, Labour MP for Llanelli from 1936–1970; and Aneurin Bevan, Labour MP for Ebbw Vale from 1929–1960. These two politicians are often used to highlight the different traditions in the Labour Party. The following is an extract from a lecture delivered by the Welsh historian K.O. Morgan in which he used the analogy of 'red dragon' to describe Griffiths (denoting his 'Welshness') and 'red flag' for Bevan (denoting his left-wing, socialist views). In the first extract, Morgan discusses the backgrounds of both men.

Activity 7.1

Read Extract 7.1 and notice the differences in their social, religious and linguistic backgrounds. Consider as you read how this may have influenced the political ideas and styles of these two men in later years.

Extract 7.1

As regards their origins, James (or, to give him his proper Christian name, Jeremiah) grew up in an intensely Welsh-speaking community, the Amman valley at the turn of the century. His brother 'Amanwy' was a noted local eisteddfodic bard. Jim Griffiths was much affected by the 1904 religious revival (when he was fourteen) and also by the preaching of Rev. John 'Gwili' Jenkins who preached a powerful brand of humanitarian, ethical Christian socialism ... Griffiths moved on to the Independent Labour Party ... he attended the White House at Ammanford, a workers' forum for the discussion of socialist and radical ideas ... the First World War and Griffiths's entry into the Marxist Central Labour College in 1919 did not really alter this inheritance.

Nye Bevan came from a notably different background – Tredegar in Gwent ... the radicalism of the eastern valleys (of south Wales). Bevan, unlike his father, was not Welsh-speaking; in religious terms he was an agnostic, a devotee of 'the religion of socialism'. His reading was much more eclectic than that of Griffiths. It fortified his claim to have been a nineteenth-century romantic ... although seven years younger than Griffiths, Bevan seems to have been influenced by the Cambrian Colliery strike of 1910–11, the riots at Tonypandy and the neo-syndicalist pamphlet, *The Miners Next Step*, with its call for industrial action ... he thus derived a very different lesson from the Central Labour College which he attended at the same time as Griffiths.

Source: Morgan, 1988, pp. 2–3

Comment

So, although both emanating from south Wales, and with links to the coal-mining communities, Bevan and Griffiths came from quite different backgrounds, with Griffiths's background much more moderate and religious than Bevan's more militant roots.

The second extract deals with Griffiths's and Bevan's attitudes towards Wales. Again, read and note the differences, especially on the question of Welsh self-government:

Extract 7.2

Griffiths was, without doubt, strongly sympathetic to the national heritage. He spoke Welsh freely. During the war, he had advocated Welsh devolution during his time on the Welsh Reconstruction Committee. In the Attlee Cabinet after 1945, he urged that Wales should be treated as a distinct administrative unit in the nationalization of electricity. He also pressed in vain for the Council of Wales to be given more powers in 1949 ... Griffiths was also instrumental, while party deputy leader in 1956–9, in getting a Welsh Secretaryship of State put on Labour's manifesto ... Appropriately, in his last years Griffiths was a staunch supporter of devolution for Wales.

Bevan was, apparently, a strong critic of Welsh separateness, by contrast. In the first 'Welsh Day' debate in the Commons in 1944, he asked ironically how Welsh sheep differed from English sheep, and claimed that the whole idea of a Welsh debate was a waste of time. He was unsympathetic to supporters of the Welsh language ... Bevan often gave the impression of being somewhat bored by Wales, by the Puritanism of the chapels, by the parochialism of village life. He seldom dined at the 'Welsh table' at the House of Commons. His intimates were altogether more colourful and cosmopolitan ... yet Bevan's antipathy to Welshness can be overdone ... Bevan, after all, grew up in the South Wales industrial world ... Bevan grew up in a homogenous Welsh working-class society, the pit, the working-men's club ...

Source: Morgan, 1988, pp. 11–12

Comment

So Griffiths was much more sympathetic to the concept of self-government than Bevan. We could describe Griffiths as a de-centralist and Bevan as a centralist.

Bevan and Griffiths were politicians who were as much part of a British Labour tradition and history as they were Welsh. Both played a formative role in the development of the welfare state developed by the 1945–51 Labour governments under Clement Attlee. Bevan is best remembered for his role in establishing the National Health Service (NHS) in 1947 and his resignation from the government in April 1951 over the abolition of free prescriptions. The implementation of socialism during this formative period in Welsh and British politics provides one example of why people like Bevan saw a safer future for Wales wrapped in the red flag, rather than trusted to an unproven Welsh dragon.

Through the creation of the welfare state and the nationalisation of key industries, the 1945–50 Labour government was responsible for ensuring the betterment in the quality of lives of ordinary people living in industrial south Wales. But Labour was also responsible for ensuring a better quality of life in the north too.

3.2 The Labour tradition outside the heartland: a case study of north-west Wales

When looking at Bevan and Griffiths as politicians who represented two different strands of the Labour tradition, we are still looking at two individuals who came from the south, and represented south Wales constituencies. But what about the Labour Party in the north? What about Wales outside the industrial areas? I have already mentioned that Labour's progress in the north was slower than in the south. If you look again at the map for the 1931 election (Figure 7.1 above) you'll see that the Liberal Party was still popular in the north in the inter-war period. But this changed after 1945. Figure 7.2 is an electoral map of Wales following the 1951 general election.

You can now see that the red of Labour has become established in the north, with the party gaining seats in north-west Wales and consolidating its position in the north-east.

During a period that could be described as disastrous for the party in Britain as a whole (Labour lost the 1951, 1955 and 1959 general elections), the party in fact improved its position in Wales. This not only indicates the depth of anti-Conservatism among the majority of the Welsh population, but also the extent to which Labour's appeal transcended social and cultural divisions in Wales. In a decade when many areas of the UK enjoyed the benefits of the 'affluent society', Labour, not the Conservative party, was seen as the party most likely to deliver affluence in Wales.

Perhaps unsurprisingly, given the party's implantation and success in the south, much less has been written on the Labour Party in the north, and in Welsh-speaking as opposed to anglicised areas of Wales. However, there was more to the Labour Party in Wales during the twentieth century than the politics of the coalfield.

A message that Labour-led economic modernisation and planning could serve north Wales did not translate 'naturally' into electoral support in these semi-rural, and oddly urbanised, seats (oddly in that the seats were

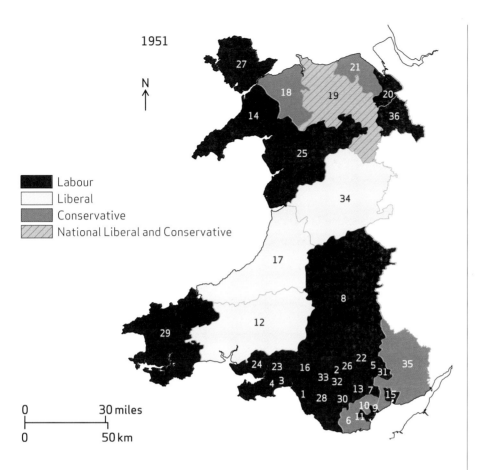

1951

N

Labour
Liberal
Conservative
National Liberal and Conservative

0   30 miles
0   50 km

Figure 7.2
Electoral map of Wales,
1951 (Source: Jones,
1999, p. 174)

1 Aberavon
2 Aberdare
3 Swansea East
4 Swansea West
5 Abertillery
6 Barry
7 Bedwellty
8 Brecon and Radnor
9 Cardiff South-East
10 Cardiff North
11 Cardiff West
12 Carmarthen
13 Caerphilly
14 Caernarvonshire
15 Newport
16 Neath
17 Cardiganshire
18 Conway
19 Denbigh
20 Flint East
21 Flint West
22 Ebbw Vale
23 Gower
24 Llanelli
25 Merioneth
26 Merthyr Tydfil
27 Anglesey
28 Ogmore
29 Pembroke
30 Pontypridd
31 Pontypool
32 Rhondda East
33 Rhondda West
34 Montgomery
35 Monmouth
36 Wrexham

predominantly rural, but with slate-quarrying, industrial 'pockets').
Labour's proposals did not have quite the same resonance as in other
Welsh constituencies. They worked only when economic modernisation
went hand in hand with Labour's defence of local interests and values –
when it became the party of the **gwerin**.

Labour is typically portrayed as a party of the working class and trade
unions, but its appeal in north Wales was also based on its support of a
local society where the Welsh language, Welsh culture and the local
chapels formed the backbone of local communities. The protection of

Gwerin, a term
commonly attached to
Welsh radicalism and
political discourse, refers
either to the people in
general or else the
common people (in
contrast to the gentry). It
also denotes a 'positive',
'good' and 'warm'
concept, in a way that
'working class' does not
today.

the *gwerin* was far removed from the proletarian, industrial politics of the south Wales valleys. This had been an important, but not entirely successful, feature of the strategy adopted by some Labour figures in Wales since the turn of the century.

Labour argued that it could deliver economic prosperity and defend Welsh cultural, social and linguistic aspirations – arguing that the first could only help the second. Labour would support and sustain the best aspects of local values and culture. The politics of Labour's candidates and MPs after 1945 were a crucial component in this process (as I'll explain shortly). Significantly, the Labour Party was not averse to placing the needs of the local community above party loyalty in order to create the right 'blend' of appeals.

The second side of Labour's appeal in north-west Wales after 1945 was its role as guardian of local interests and of a particular form of 'Welshness', and of the values and social institutions which had previously been safeguarded by the Liberal Party.

The new generation of Labour candidates in north-west Wales after the Second World War shared the values outlined above and could represent them with conviction. They were sympathetic to Welsh, 'nationalist', issues but they favoured socialism not political nationalism. Unlike many prominent 'cultural' nationalists of the day, they sought to preserve Wales through modernisation, by allowing it to retain its people and gain the employment and opportunities that were essential to preserving Welsh life and the language and culture of Welsh-speaking Wales. All three Labour MPs in north-west from 1945–59, Goronwy Roberts, T.W. Jones and Cledwyn Hughes were local, Welsh-speaking, patriots. All three supported the Parliament for Wales campaign in the early 1950s and were strong advocates of a Secretary of State for Wales as a prerequisite to some form of Welsh devolution. These were candidates who a generation earlier may conceivably have been Liberals. Let's look at Hughes and Roberts as examples.

Cledwyn Hughes, Anglesey's Labour MP from 1951, was a Welsh-speaking radical from the professional classes. Hughes's father had been a prominent and respected Holyhead Liberal. His status as a Welsh radical and his ability to arouse support for the Labour Party in working-class Holyhead – a town which had posed problems for the Labour Party in the 1920s – were crucial to his success. Hughes's personal papers include letters from Madoc Jones, Secretary of the Welsh Liberal party, affectionately addressed to 'the virtually Liberal member for my native county of Anglesey'. At the time, Jones was attempting to convince Hughes of the political benefits to be gained from creating a new 'Radical' party in north Wales, a fusion of the radically minded elements from Labour, the Liberals and Plaid Cymru. Even by 1967, when he was Secretary of State for Wales, Hughes was still treated with some suspicion within Labour circles, where he was regarded as one of a select band of Labour MPs who were 'nationalists first and socialist second'. Even for some of those actively involved in Labour politics in the north, Hughes was seen as dabbed with a 'little too much green paint' (a reference to his nationalist sympathies) to be trusted completely.

In Caernarvonshire, Labour's MP from 1945 to 1974 was Goronwy Roberts. During the 1930s Roberts had helped found the Grwp Gwerin movement at the University College of North Wales in Bangor. A left-wing, patriotic group, it was firmly committed to establishing the Labour Party as the 'national' party of Wales and espousing a truly balanced and legitimate view of 'national socialism' or 'Labour nationalism'. The movement's strong support for a Welsh parliament reflected Roberts's own views. Roberts's status as a patriot was unquestionable. As an aspiring Labour MP in the run-up to the 1945 election, he had campaigned on two fronts: 'as a Labour candidate, but also as a Welsh candidate'. At the heart of this vision was the belief that Labour was out to protect and extend the cultural and industrial well-being of the nation (Edwards, 2004).

So, after 1945, Labour enhanced its reputation in north and south Wales. In the next section we will look at the development of that reputation and the Labour tradition.

Activity 7.2

1   Summarise and note the main differences between 'northern' and 'southern' dimensions of the Labour tradition.

2   Refer back to Chapter 6, Section 5.2 and summarise and note the differences between Labour politicians with 'nationalist' sympathies and nationalists who were members of Plaid Cymru.

Summary

- Labour was represented by individuals from very different social, cultural and political backgrounds.

- After 1945, Labour also became popular in north Wales.

- In north, Welsh-speaking, Wales, Labour's values were often quite different from those in the south and included support for a number of 'nationalist' concerns.

4   Labour's status as 'the party of Wales'

4.1 An overview of developments

After an absence of thirteen years, Labour returned to power in 1964. The party's popularity in Wales was confirmed in the 1966 general election when it won 32 out of 36 constituencies. Figure 7.3 highlights that Labour dominance spread across north and south Wales, across rural and industrial areas, and into anglicised and Welsh-speaking regions.

Figure 7.3
Electoral map of Wales, 1966 (Source: Jones, 1999, p. 175)

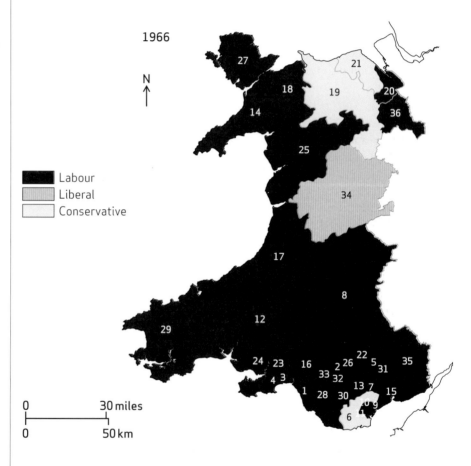

1 Aberavon	10 Cardiff North	19 Denbigh	28 Ogmore
2 Aberdare	11 Cardiff West	20 Flint East	29 Pembroke
3 Swansea East	12 Carmarthen	21 Flint West	30 Pontypridd
4 Swansea West	13 Caerphilly	22 Ebbw Vale	31 Pontypool
5 Abertillery	14 Caernarvonshire	23 Gower	32 Rhondda East
6 Barry	15 Newport	24 Llanelli	33 Rhondda West
7 Bedwellty	16 Neath	25 Merioneth	34 Montgomery
8 Brecon and Radnor	17 Cardiganshire	26 Merthyr Tydfil	35 Monmouth
9 Cardiff South-East	18 Conway	27 Anglesey	36 Wrexham

By the mid 1960s, Labour could claim with some justification to be 'the party of Wales'. The establishment of a Secretary of State for Wales (a post many saw as the first logical step to devolution) and a Welsh Office were two manifesto commitments delivered in 1964, a Welsh Language Act was passed in 1967 and, around the same time, the party also considered devolution for Scotland and Wales. Many prominent nationalists from Plaid Cymru 'defected' to Labour in the 1960s, believing that only Labour could deliver self-government for Wales. Among those who won one of the 32 Labour seats in 1966 was Elystan Morgan, Labour's MP for Cardigan from 1966–1974 and a former prominent member of Plaid Cymru.

The following is an extract from a lecture given by Elystan Morgan in 2008. Read the extract, and note the variety of reasons behind Morgan's decision to join the Labour Party.

Extract 7.3

When I joined Plaid Cymru I believed ... that a coalition of nationalists of every political colour could one day win majority support in Wales [and] force the government of the day ... to grant Wales an Assembly. By the 1960s, it was clear that this would not happen in our lifetime. I had underestimated the traditional strengths of the old political parties. Although the Parliament for Wales campaign had won some support, it was very limited. Later, of course, there was the failure of the campaign to save Cwm Tryweryn ... in addition, the 1964 general election proved a failure for me and other Plaid Cymru candidates. Our vote fell from 77,571 in 1959 to 69,507 five years later ... when the Labour government ... after the 1964 general election ... established the post of Secretary of State for Wales, I felt a strong desire to join the Labour Party. After all, establishing the Secretaryship was recognition of Wales's existence as a country and as a nation. That was the first major constitutional change since the Act of Union in 1536. For me, the whole situation had changed. Before establishing the Secretaryship, there was no way of winning constitutional ground. After ... there was hardly nothing that was not within Wales's reach ... I didn't doubt that if I had been born in England, I would have been Labour from very early in my life. Therefore ... I decided that the right thing for me to do was to leave Plaid Cymru and join Labour.

Source: Morgan, 2008, pp. 4–5 (author's translation)

Tryweryn was a controversial UK government-sanctioned scheme in 1957 to 'drown' a Welsh-speaking north Wales village, Capel Celyn, in order to build the Tryweryn reservoir to supply water to Liverpool. It has been mythologised by nationalists.

So, Morgan's reasons for joining Labour were largely based on the party's capacity to deliver more autonomy to Wales and to prevent controversial schemes like **Tryweryn** from reoccurring.

In reality, however, the advances after 1966 were slow to materialise. The 1966 general election disguised many underlying problems for Labour. Only a couple of months after the general election, Labour lost a famous by-election in Carmarthen to Plaid Cymru. In 1967 and 1968, Plaid Cymru came close to capturing two more Labour seats in by-elections in Rhondda West and Caerphilly, both 'safe' Labour seats. Of course, the pressure to preserve success in the north and south, and the differences of opinion between many of the party's representatives could, and did, lead to conflict, especially on the question of devolution. Ironically, perhaps, the 'rise of nationalism' in the 1960s undermined the position of pro-devolutionists in Labour's ranks because devolution was seen by opponents and sceptics as an appeasement of nationalism, and the first 'slippery step' on the road to separatism. When the Labour government appointed a Royal Commission on the Constitution (the Kilbrandon Commission) to examine the question of devolution in the UK in 1968, it could be argued that this was more an effort to bury the issue in a mountain of red tape, rather than a desire to see its implementation.

By the time the Royal Commission reported positively on the need for devolution in 1973, Labour was already facing a crisis. The economic problems of the 1960s meant that there were serious problems facing many areas of Wales. In the north-west, for example, this meant that Labour was vulnerable to the challenge posed by a reinvigorated, dynamic and 'radical' nationalist party. In the general election of February 1974, two seats in the north-west were lost to Plaid Cymru. These, together with further defeats at the hands of the Scottish National Party in Scotland, forced Labour's hand on devolution. When another general election took place in October 1974, Labour's manifesto contained a commitment to devolution in both Scotland and Wales. But this was the start of a hugely problematic period for the party.

4.2 Labour and devolution

Between 1975 and 1979, Labour's image as the 'party of Wales' was torn to shreds as it became embroiled in a civil war between supporters and opponents of devolution. As these divisions were exposed, the party in Wales seemed divided between those of a 'centralist' and those of a 'de-centralist' political disposition, as well as on geographic, linguistic and cultural grounds. As you read in Chapter 6, the crushing defeat of devolution in the referendum of March 1979 – when not a single Welsh county voted in favour of the proposal – was an embarrassment for the Labour government and exposed differences that ran through the party at both Welsh and British levels.

In some popular accounts, the battle for devolution is presented as a conflict between good Welshmen and -women (the pro-devolutionists in the 'yes' camp in 1979) and the British Welsh (the 'no' campaigners). All political parties in Wales engaged in that battle in some shape or form. But for Labour, devolution presented a particular problem. Although it was a Labour manifesto commitment in 1974, many members of the Welsh Labour Party remained fundamentally opposed to self-government. This was less an issue of being pro-Welsh or anti-Welsh and, to return to a point I made earlier, it was more a battle between two different interpretations of what would be best for Wales. While pro-devolutionists believed that Wales would be better served by having its own elected body, making decisions that best met Welsh needs, anti-devolutionists believed that Wales would be better off by remaining part of the centralised British state, enjoying the benefits of British wealth and of policies administered at an all-British level.

You have already seen how Bevan and Griffiths represented the two sides of this divide. In the 1970s, opponents of devolution came from a wide range of social, cultural and political institutions and from across the political spectrum (not just the Labour Party). However, it was the opposition from Labour's 'gang of six' (Leo Abse, Neil Kinnock, Donald Anderson, Ioan Evans, Fred Evans and Ifor Davies) that captured most attention. Their objections to devolution were wide-ranging and all-encompassing, ranging from the cultural and linguistic to the social and economic. It is this opposition – remembered as 'betrayal' by some – that has generated so much antagonism between supporters and critics of devolution since the 1970s.

The referendum defeat followed a dirty battle. Some anti-devolutionists developed their own version of the 'domino theory', portraying devolution as the next step (following the creation of a Welsh Office in 1964) toward Welsh independence. This view was shared by many in Westminster. Plaid Cymru vilified Kinnock in particular, arguing that those who opposed devolution had their hearts (and their homes) in England. He and others were accused of betraying Wales, sacrificing their own Welshness in the interests of a British political career (the fact that Kinnock became leader of the Labour Party a few years later adds value to this in popular mythology). Acid was poured on his car and there was a good deal of personal abuse. The Wales Labour Party exerted less personal, but equally forceful, pressure on those who rebelled.

Some 'No' campaigners exploited north–south rivalries, jealousies and animosities. The Assembly was portrayed as potentially an elitist, antiquated, talking shop, refusing to accept the realities of a changing world and placing greater emphasis on the culture and language of a minority than the on 'real' economic problems of the majority. Sensationalism and xenophobia permeated debate. Reference was made to border checkpoints staffed by Welsh nationalists and restrictions on the movements of English 'aliens' into post-devolution Wales. It was suggested that nationalists had conspired to aid the Nazi war effort during the Second World War (a reference to the Penyberth incident in 1936 when prominent members of the Welsh Nationalist Party burned an RAF bombing school). A Welsh Assembly, according to Abse, would offer as much to Wales as would 'Brains brewery to the treatment of alcoholics'. Some Labour opponents of devolution questioned the calibre and quality of potential Assembly members, likening them to 'glorified county councillors' (Tanner and Edwards, 2004, p. 63).

This story is embellished from time to time in the accounts of some of the main protagonists, but the reality is that the campaigns of Labour opponents should be just one factor in explaining the defeat of devolution in 1979. Others, for example the failure of the pro-devolution political parties (Labour, Plaid Cymru and the Liberals) to work together effectively, the failure of the Labour government to promote devolution to a sceptical public, and the tarnished reputation of the 1976–79 Labour government (especially on the back of the 'winter of discontent' of 1978–79), also need to be considered.

The devolution debate was a battle not just over which form of governance was best for Wales. It also exposed differences over different forms of 'Welshness' and Welsh identity. In the next section you will move on to look at the relationship between Labour values and Welsh values.

Summary

- By the mid 1960s, Labour could justifiably claim to be 'the party of Wales'.

- However, devolution was a problematic issue for the party from the late 1960s onwards.

- The 1979 referendum campaign exposed fundamental social, geographic and linguistic tensions within the labour movement in Wales.

5   Labour's 'Welsh' values

5.1 Labour values and Welsh values

A consequence of Labour's domination of Welsh politics over the twentieth century and beyond is that, in popular political discourse, Wales is considered to be 'Labour-land'. In attempting to explain Labour's popularity, some have suggested that the Welsh have 'Labour' in their DNA. A great deal of Labour propaganda over the years has alluded to the 'fact' that the Welsh were, in some way, inherently socialist and had a particular set of values that made them receptive to Labour's message and appeal, and to socialism. It is often assumed that the Welsh are more democratic, more liberal, more tolerant and more classless than people from many other areas of Britain.

Activity 7.3

Pause a moment to think about 'Labour' values and different forms of Welsh identity and what some consider to be 'Welsh' values. Write down the answers to the following questions:

■ Are there elements of the Welsh national character that help us to understand attachment in Wales to Labour and 'Labour' values?

■ Is the Labour tradition better explained by understanding Wales's social and economic experience?

■ What are 'Labour values'?

Comment

If I were answering Question 3, I'd start with the easy ones – that Labour stands for radicalism, collectivism and equality. If I was answering thirty years ago, I would probably have said socialism, but I'm not so sure that I would today. So, we need to think of values that are not necessarily static.

5.2 The Labour tradition in the 1980s and 1990s

The conditions that had helped mould the Labour tradition in Wales in the 1920s and 1930s almost disappeared in the last three decades of the twentieth century. The old Welsh industries which had helped sustain that tradition started to disappear. In the north, the slate industry fell into terminal decline in the late 1960s, devastating many local communities. As you read in Chapter 3, in the south, coal mines and steel mills closed down with equally catastrophic social and economic consequences in the 1970s and 1980s. Unemployment in Wales reached 10 per cent in 1989 and peaked at 14 per cent in 1986. Of course, these are averages, with the picture much worse in many towns. Clearly, major political events in the 1980s – notably the 1984–1985 miners' strike – had a devastating impact on 'Labour' communities but, ironically, these were not the constituencies that deserted Labour in the early 1980s.

Steel and mining areas, as we have seen, were symbols of Labour strength and values. The occupations that once supported the Labour Party in vast numbers all but vanished. Economic change was matched by challenges to old ideas and social structures and by the appearance of new injustices and inequalities, as well as new expectations. In many parts of Wales, the Labour tradition was threatened by competition from a cultural and political nationalism and from a popular brand of conservatism. At British level, the party was torn apart by bitter disagreements over policy.

Figure 7.4

Electoral map of Wales, 1983 (Source: Jones, 1999, p. 176)

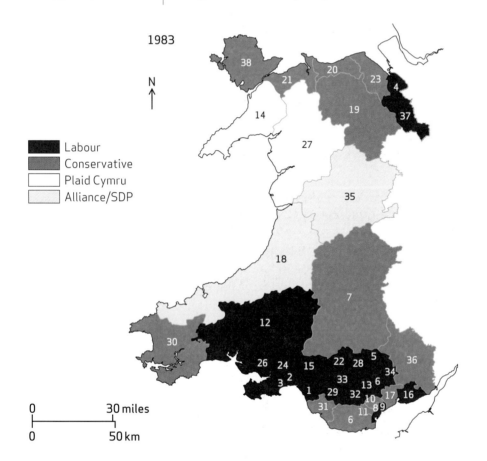

1983

N

Labour
Conservative
Plaid Cymru
Alliance/SDP

0   30 miles
0   50 km

1 Aberavon	10 Cardiff North	19 Clwyd South-West	29 Ogmore
2 Swansea East	11 Cardiff West	20 Clwyd North-East	30 Pembroke
3 Swansea West	12 Carmarthen	21 Conway	31 Bridgend
4 Alun and Deeside	13 Caerphilly	22 Cynon Valley	32 Pontypridd
5 Blaenau Gwent	14 Caernarvonshire	23 Delyn	33 Rhondda
6 Glamorgan	15 Neath	24 Gower	34 Torfaen
7 Brecon and Radnor	16 Newport East	25 Islwyn	35 Montgomery
8 Cardiff Central	17 Newport West	26 Llanelli	36 Monmouth
9 Cardiff South and	18 Cardigan and	27 Meirionnydd Nant Conwy	37 Wrexham
Penarth	North Pembroke	28 Merthyr Tydfil and Rhymney	38 Ynys Mon (Anglesey)

The crisis facing Labour in Wales was highlighted in the 1983 general election when the party's Welsh vote fell to under 40 per cent for the first time in a generation. Figure 7.4 is a map of Wales following the 1983 general election.

Activity 7.4

Compare Figure 7.4 above with Figure 7.3 showing Wales after the 1966 general election. Consider the reasons for the erosion of Labour's support.

By 1987, Labour had lost three general elections in a row (1979, 1983 and 1987) and the social and economic problems facing Wales (outlined above) were forcing many pro- and anti-devolutionists to think again. 'Thatcherism' had three negative consequences for Welsh democracy: (i) centralisation of power at Westminster; (ii) emasculation of local government by stripping powers away from many democratically elected (often Labour-controlled) councils; (iii) an increase in the number of (undemocratic) quasi-autonomous, non-governmental organisations (quangos).

Equally powerful in highlighting the crisis of a 'democratic deficit' in Wales was the Conservative Party's performance in Wales during its years in power at Westminster (1979–1997). In the 1979 general election, the Conservative Party won 11 seats in Wales. In 1983, its best performance for more than a generation, it won 16. However, in 1987 and 1992, it won eight and six seats respectively. In 1997, it failed to win a single seat, a 'feat' which the party also repeated in 2001.

So, the Conservatives ruled Wales on the back of English (and to a lesser extent) Scottish votes: the party did not enjoy majority support for Wales. This was one reason that some of those who opposed devolution in 1979 changed their minds in the 1990s. The realisation that the people of Wales consistently voted Labour, but were governed by the Conservative Party, started to sink in by the early 1990s. One convert to devolution was Ron Davies, Labour MP for Caerphilly and later Secretary of State for Wales in the 1997 New Labour government. Read Extract 7.4, which is from Davies's evidence to the Richard Commission in 2002. This will help you understand why Davies saw the form of government that was operating before devolution as unsatisfactory.

Extract 7.4

I think that the point is worth making that the form of government we have now is infinitely better than we had before 1997 and in that sense I am proud of it. But that doesn't mean it couldn't be better. So the question is in what ways? I think we have improved governance in Wales ... there are a number of reasons why we had devolution, one of those clearly was the idea of the democratic deficit. There were others relating to the performance of public services and indeed the national question: identity and image and nation building. But the question that really resonated with the public during the 1990s was the question of the democratic deficit, the issue of the quangos, the issue of the Secretary of State, the issue of legislation going through Parliament. I think we have done that, I think that we do have a form of government now that, despite its imperfections, despite the sense of isolation that comes from its distant geography, I think we have opened up Wales.

Source: Davies, 2002, p. 3

It is important to stress that Davies was not alone in being won over to the positives of devolution.

A commitment to devolution had been included in Labour's 1992 election manifesto. When New Labour under Tony Blair won a landslide election victory in May 1997, devolution was again a manifesto commitment. Later in the same year Welsh voters were given the opportunity to claim devolution. In the referendum of September 1997, 50.3 per cent voted in favour. The margin of victory was hardly a ringing endorsement of the executive form of devolution on offer, but it was a substantial increase in the 'Yes' vote compared to 1979. The 1997 referendum campaign took place in a very different political atmosphere from that of 1979. While there were still many anti-devolutionists in Labour's ranks in Wales, few spoke out against the measure, not least because they did not want to undermine the status and reputation of the first Labour government for eighteen years and to risk the wrath of those who had suffered during this long period of Conservative rule.

You read in Chapter 6 some of the debates on what changed between 1979 and 1997, but clearly the transformation in opinions over devolution were not due to a single reason, but to a variety of social, economic, cultural and political concerns. In the next section you will look at the development of the Labour tradition following the arrival of devolution.

Summary

- Some believe that symmetry exists between 'Labour' and 'Welsh' values.

- The harsh economic conditions of the 1980s, and the prolonged period of Conservative rule, rekindled the devolution debate.

- Some politicians who had opposed devolution in the 1970s changed their minds over the issue around this time.

- Following Labour's return to power in 1997, devolution was approved, but by a very small majority.

6   Labour and devolution

6.1 The Labour tradition and devolution

The arrival of devolution in 1999 opened a new chapter in the history of Welsh Labour. Contrary to the fears of many nationalists, Labour has not ended up dominating the Welsh Assembly. The Assembly has 60 seats, some of which are allocated on a traditional 'first past the post' constituency basis, and others on a regional, 'proportional representation' basis (see Chapter 8). In the first three elections for the Welsh Assembly in 1999, 2003 and 2007, Labour won 27, 30 and 24 seats respectively. Labour has thus failed, to date, to establish an overall majority in Cardiff. One of the defining features of the Welsh Assembly has been the advent of coalition government. In 2000 Labour secured joint control of the Assembly through coalition with the Liberal Democrats and, in 2007, a most unlikely (given the antipathy between the parties for most of the previous century) coalition with Plaid Cymru. As results for the first three Assembly elections demonstrate, other 'radical' parties have also performed well and, for the first time in over a century, the Conservative Party is responding to the challenges of contemporary Wales with a voice and a mandate which has a distinctively Welsh feel and with an agenda that is not unsympathetic to some 'radical' concerns (especially the need to preserve, and even extend, Welsh self-government).

It is clear that devolution and coalition government have posed challenges for Labour. Among the positives for Labour (and, indeed, the other parties) in the first ten years of devolution has been the attempt to address the gender imbalance in Welsh politics. As a result of a policy that some call 'positive discrimination', Labour selection processes included all-women shortlists in many constituencies prior to the 1999 Assembly election. Partly as a consequence of this, in the first Welsh Assembly, 46 per cent of the seats were held by women; in 2003, this rose to 50 per cent. Before the 2007 election, the Welsh Assembly had 29 male Assembly members (AMs) and 31 female. In 2003, the Welsh Assembly cabinet also had a female majority (five out of nine ministers). Since May 2007, 47 per cent of AMs are women. At Westminster 19.5 per cent of MPs are women and 20 per cent of Welsh MPs are women.

Another benefit has been the continuance of a Welsh Labour tradition in attempts to construct a Labour agenda that is distinctively Welsh. When I think back to Morgan's analogy of 'red dragons' and 'red flags' (the division of Labour Wales into decentralist and centralist camps), I think it's safe to say that the spirit of both has been awakened in Cardiff Bay. In the first couple of years of devolution, Welsh Labour struggled to break free from the shackles of the party's London leaders. This was highlighted by the controversy surrounding Alun Michael's term as First Minister between 1999 and 2001, when Michael was seen by media commentators, the party's opponents and even some Welsh Labour members like Paul Flynn as Tony Blair's 'groupie', or 'poodle' in Cardiff (Flynn, 1999, p. 44). Michael was also unpopular among many pro-devolutionists because he had a record of being, at best, lukewarm on the question of devolution. However, after Michael's resignation in 2001, his successor, Rhodri Morgan, attempted to mould a Labour agenda for Wales that is different to that in London. The whole point of devolution was that Wales could, if it wanted, develop policies that were different from those in other parts of the UK. The need for this approach was famously summed up by Morgan in December 2002 in what has since become known as the 'clear red water' speech. This highlighted a desire not only for Wales to be different, but also for Labour to draw on strands of its heritage and tradition. Extract 7.5 is an excerpt on the subject from a speech delivered in Cardiff in March 2003.

Extract 7.5

The key point is that we organise ourselves and the values that we hold are shaped by this experience of living in relatively small settlements and medium sized villages, towns, valley agglomerates and cities. The consumerist approach to choice in public services that stresses differentiation may fit best the practicalities and the experience of those metropolitan settlements of a million or several million people that are a feature of counties that are urbanised in a different way to Wales. As an Assembly Government, we have given higher priority to the provision of high quality, community based, comprehensive secondary schools than we have to the development of a choice of specialist schools. This does not mean we are against choice and diversity ... it seems to me that our values and our geography lead us to stress the community basis of our schools ... involving parents, families and community groups in the life of the schools.

Source: Morgan, March 2003

The 'clear red water' speech focused on hospitals. Here, Morgan focuses on schooling as an area in which policy divergence is desirable.

Activity 7.5

Consider and note other areas of policy where the difference between English needs and values may be different to traditional Labour and Welsh values. For example, you could consider how policies on tourism in the rest of the UK may not always be conducive to Welsh needs.

So we have red dragons, red flags, and now red water as a means of defining what the Labour tradition is all about. We could actually portray Rhodri Morgan as a red dragon, someone who comes from the same sort of political tradition as James Griffiths, a Welsh speaker, with sympathies for the culture and language of Wales, but also with clear socialist beliefs and tendencies and an unequivocal supporter of Welsh self-government.

6.2 The Labour tradition in twenty-first-century Wales

Earlier I talked about Labour identities and Welsh identities. One consequence of the Welsh Assembly is that discussions of 'Welsh' values and 'Welsh' political priorities have blossomed. In numerous political statements and speeches, the NHS and the assumed principles behind it have been ascribed a prominent role in an apparently distinct 'Welsh way'. This assumed trajectory includes commitment to more communitarian and collective policies than in many other parts of the UK (Tanner and Michael, 2007, p. 38). Read Extract 7.6, from an article written by Duncan Tanner and Pam Michael, which builds on Activity 7.4 on Labour values and Welsh values. Consider how this extract corresponds with your own ideas.

Extract 7.6

Few people can detect a neat transition from 'English' to 'Welsh' values upon entering Wales. Nevertheless, references to 'Welsh values' within policy circles and political debate are now common. During the campaign for devolution and since the establishment of the National Assembly for Wales, politicians have frequently appealed to 'Welsh values' as a distinctive marker and as a justification for policy deviation. Indeed, an appeal to 'Welsh values' has almost become a hallmark of true 'Welshness'. It is much used by politicians seeking to establish their credentials as representatives of Welsh opinion and by central government ministers charged with managing Welsh affairs – perhaps especially where their own policies are not particularly distinctive or are tied by the policies of a UK-wide party. Thus on 26 November 2002 Peter Hain, newly appointed Secretary of State for Wales in the Labour government, duly assessed the National Assembly for Wales, declaring the need to protect 'our very own and very special values in Wales ... Welsh values of community. Welsh values of caring. Welsh values of family life. Welsh values of mutual co-operation and mutual respect. Welsh values of democracy. Welsh values of internationalism. Welsh values of multi-racialism' ... The innumerable references to Aneurin Bevan in political speeches ... and to the NHS, is part of a process through which populist history has become a powerful contemporary influence. For example, in 1998, Alun Michael, then Secretary of State for Wales, enunciated Wales' special commitment to the principles of the NHS and adherence to the values articulated in the NHS in the preface to the policy document *Putting Patients First*: 'None of the values enshrined in the NHS when Aneurin Bevan created it will be lost. The NHS in Wales will continue to be a truly national service available to all on the basis of need'... Swearing allegiance to Bevan's legacy is an important political gesture in Wales. In an online opinion poll in 2005 to find the top 100 Welsh heroes, Aneurin Bevan beat all-comers, ahead of the charismatic 15th-century hero of Welsh resistance to English rule, Owain Glyndwr, the singer Tom Jones, and the 'Welsh wizard' and architect of state pensions, David Lloyd George.

Tanner and Michael, 2007, pp. 39–40

So, reference to tradition and history is an important mechanism for allowing the current crop of Labour politicians to develop a message that has resonance, allowing them to communicate ideas and values that ordinary people can engage with and understand.

Labour has tapped into its heritage and traditions in other ways. Under the coalition agreement with the Liberal Democrats in 2000, policy priorities included the abolition of prescription charges and dental charges for over-60s, free school milk, free travel for pensioners and educational reforms. It is no exaggeration to suggest that these policies are not far removed from the priorities of radical political parties in Wales a hundred years ago. When Wales became the first and only country in the UK to have free prescriptions in 2007, this was another example of radical attempts to pursue a distinctive socialist agenda in Wales and one with longstanding resonance.

Of course, developing policies around devolution has presented numerous problems and challenges. As has always been the case, the merits and demerits of devolution have continued to divide opinion in

Labour's ranks. As I suggested earlier, the establishment of a Labour/ Plaid Cymru coalition government, marked by the publication of the *One Wales* policy document in 2007, was a major achievement and a landmark in the history of the radical/Labour tradition in Wales (especially as this was an alliance unthinkable in the 1970s and unlikely in the 1980s and 1990s). Across the political spectrum in Wales there are people determined to see devolution succeed, and determined that it does so in a way that does justice to the history, traditions and cultures of Wales. But there are still those who (like Bevan sixty years ago and Kinnock in the 1970s) see devolution as a waste of time and a waste of money. When, in 2003, the Richard Commission was looking into the possibility of extending the powers of the Welsh Assembly, it took evidence from a number of individuals and bodies in Wales. Among the individuals was the Labour MP Llew Smith, one of the few 'No'-campaigners in 1997 to receive significant media attention. Extract 7.7 comes from Smith's evidence to the Commission. Read the extract and note why Smith remained reticient about the value of the Welsh Assembly.

Extract 7.7

Are we, for example, to accept that the NHS in Wales is run more efficiently than in England, since many of the powers have been devolved to Cardiff. Do we accept that Wales is any less a quango state since the establishment of the Welsh Assembly? No. Is there anything fair about an Assembly continuing to subsidise one of the richest areas in Wales, in Cardiff Bay, at the expense of some of the poorest communities? Has the Assembly benefitted those deprived communities in a way which a Labour government would have failed to do so? No ... To save any further embarrassment for the Welsh Assembly, I will refrain from providing any other examples, but there are many ... other than a 'bonfire of the quangos', the other claim made by Ron Davies and supported by the 'Yes' campaign was (that) £20 million would amply fund a democratically elected and accountable Welsh Assembly and with a lot to spare. This money ... will obviously not be sufficient ... the ridiculous claim that £20 million would fund the Welsh Assembly was highlighted by Jim Pickard in the *Financial Times* (8/3/02) when he revealed that 'government officials have admitted that the annual running costs of the Welsh Assembly are now £148 million, more than double the £72 million spent in the last year of the Welsh Office ... The revelation makes a mockery of New Labour's claim in 1997 that Welsh devolution would only cost an extra £15 – £20 million each year'.

Smith, 2003, pp. 4–5

As had been the case in the 1970s, the costs of running an Assembly and its alleged failure in bringing democratic accountability are at the forefront of Smith's concerns.

For many, Labour's disappointing performance in the 2007 Assembly elections has been used as a rallying point to awaken Labour to the importance of its history and traditions. The emergence of movements and focus groups such as the newly formed 'Wales 20:20' (a 'think tank' intended to prompt socialist debate) are intended to renew the Labour movement across Wales, remould Labour as a policy-driven organisation and help facilitate a wide-ranging and inclusive debate under what it calls the 'democratic socialist' banner in Wales. Among the most prominent activities of Wales 20:20 has been the campaign to eradicate child poverty in Wales.

Through such groups and movements, new Labour figures are emerging who see the Welsh Assembly as a mechanism for improving the lives of ordinary people living in Wales. One who fits this category is Huw Lewis, Labour's Assembly member for Merthyr. Lewis was active in Wales 20:20, reviewed the Welsh Assembly Government's flagship anti-poverty programme 'Communities First', and wrote the Welsh Assembly Government's plan to eliminate child poverty. Making what many saw as a bid for the leadership of Welsh Labour in 2009, Lewis talked of the need to rekindle the bonds that have always been part of the radical Welsh Labour tradition. Extract 7.8 is from a pamphlet published by Lewis and Wales 20:20 in 2009.

Extract 7.8

The Labour Party was created to represent the interests of progressive people organised in the workplace. In this respect little has changed – it is that group of people for whom we try to effect most change and who make up our most valuable resource in terms of members, thinkers and supporters. However, a growing dislocation between different branches of the Labour movement in Wales risks not just a weakening of these ties, but schism. There is something profoundly disturbing about the current relationship between the Labour Party in Wales and what should be its most natural of brethren – the Trade Unions and the co-operative movement. The latter have become the undervalued pair in the progressive triumvirate needed to drive Wales forward. Elsewhere in Europe, Trade Unions are the vanguard of policy creation in areas like health and safety and work/life balance – we need the same action and support in Wales. Genuine social partnership must be the cornerstone of a renewed Welsh Labour. Historically, co-operatives and the Unions have not just helped, or followed Labour in Wales, they have led on the policy agenda, and quietly through successful stand alone projects they continue to do fantastic work, but we have stopped recognising that and no longer progress common values from a common platform. This goes for all affiliates who make up the Labour family – Young Labour and Labour Students in Wales for example should be, as it once was, the training ground for new leaders and great Trade Unionists of the future – these organisations are now undervalued, underused and underfunded.

Lewis, 2009, pp. 14–15

You will probably have noted that the key feature of this extract is that Lewis sees a future for the traditional Labour Party/trade union alliance. You may also have made note of the way that he refers to the existence of a 'Labour family' in Wales.

Other prominent Welsh Labour figures have been making similar calls for a revival of a Labour tradition that seemed to have disappeared. Among these has been Peter Hain, Labour's MP for Neath, who was Secretary of State for Wales from 2002 to 2008. Extract 7.9 is from a paper written by Hain. As you read, you will note how he views the Labour tradition, its values, and the changes that have occurred since the 1980s.

Extract 7.9

Wales is a very different place compared with when I first came to live here 18 years ago, and has developed at a pace since Labour came to office in 1997, accelerating even further since the assembly began work in 1999 ...

The communities in which the roots of Labour's support and bases of activism were bred and sustained for generations are disappearing, increasingly fragmented with neighbours more strangers than family friends. The caring values which have for generations epitomised many Welsh neighbourhoods – especially in the valleys – can no longer be taken for granted. The large workplaces that were the heart of the old labour movement in Wales as elsewhere have all but disappeared. Trade unions – the bedrock of the old Welsh Labour – have steadily declined. Even under Labour, trade union membership in the workforce fell sharply by 13 per cent between 1998 and 2006 ... significantly greater than almost every part of Britain: four times greater than Scotland and three times the north-east. While public sector membership is high (68 per cent), private sector membership is very low (22 per cent). Just a third of all Welsh workers are trade union members today – though high by European standards, sharply down on the past. Solidarity and class have been eroded as the key voting determinants. The Labour vote traditionally passed down from parents and grandparents to children and grandchildren is no longer the binding glue of the Labour Party's electorate. Typically, young people encountered on the doorstep 'don't know' or 'don't care' or 'won't vote'.

In traditional Labour areas in Wales where the older vote can be rock solid, the younger people are less likely to vote Labour or to vote at all. In the 2007 Assembly elections fully 80 per cent of registered 18–34-year-olds did not vote; half of 18–24-year-olds knew nothing about the Assembly.

Hain, 2008

The challenges Labour faces as it seeks to rekindle its traditional appeal in Wales are numerous. In the following extract, also from Hain's paper, he notes that Labour's traditional appeal will need to be remoulded to fit contemporary needs and aspirations.

Extract 7.10

Alongside party renewal there are four ideological challenges facing Welsh Labour. First and above all, Welsh Labour must be the party for an aspirational Wales, and this means appealing both to 'middle Wales' as well as motivating our 'traditional Welsh Wales' vote to turn out in a way it has been increasingly reluctant to do. These constituencies are not at all incompatible: on the contrary, appealing to both simultaneously holds the key to a Labour revival, as was the case in 1997. Second, we have to win the argument for deepening devolution within Britain rather than as a bridgehead to separatism outside Britain. Third, we must not allow the nationalists to claim the Welsh language as their fiefdom: we must advance a positive vision for the language with a distinctive global perspective rather than the parochial one of Plaid and too many of their fellow travellers in Welsh public life. Where their instinct is to make Welsh speaking almost obligatory, ours is to ensure choice for all, Welsh and non-Welsh speakers alike. Fourth, we must claim authorship of a proud Welsh patriotism that is simultaneously British, European and internationalist, rather than separatist. Devolution for Labour was never about creating an inward-looking, parochial Wales, or about satisfying that strand in Welsh society which is basically so insecure that it seeks to huddle with its back to the outside world ... Our citizens have quite different aspirations from 1997. The issues are no longer mass unemployment and collapsing public services. The modern Wales majority has different aspirations and different pressures. People now rightly expect to have not just any job, but a decent job with opportunity to progress; not just any school for their children but a high-achieving one; not just low hospital waiting times but high-quality personalised care; not just a roof over their heads but affordable housing to buy or rent; not just more police but better neighbourhood policing; not just reduced crime but reduced violence, reduced antisocial behaviour and more respect. And they are right to demand this of Welsh Labour.

Hain, 2008

In the wake of Rhodri Morgan's decision to step down as Welsh Labour leader and First Minister in 2009, the battle for the leadership of the party encapsulated the need for Labour to reignite and rediscover its traditional appeal in Wales. The eventual victor of that contest was Carwyn Jones, Labour's AM for Bridgend. He promised that Labour would fight back to restore its electoral fortunes in Wales, renewing its traditional appeal in Wales through a commitment to public services and to 'putting ordinary working people first' (Jones, 2009).

So, the challenges facing Labour in Wales are numerous. As Hain acknowledged, Wales has changed considerably from the one identified with the Labour tradition in the 1920s and 1930s. It is different, even, from the one that existed before devolution a decade ago. Labour needs to respond to the new challenges and new aspirations if the tradition is to survive.

Summary

- In Welsh Assembly elections, Labour's domination of Welsh politics has been secure.

- Since 2001, Labour has attempted to redefine its values, to meet distinctive Welsh needs.

- It is widely accepted that the Labour tradition has to adapt and change to meet the aspirations of twenty-first-century Wales.

7   Conclusion

In the course of this chapter, we have looked at the origins and development of a political tradition that has shaped Welsh politics and society for nearly a century. As we have seen, there was much more to the Labour tradition than simply the politics of the coalfield. The Labour tradition – a radical tradition – cut deep into the Welsh psyche, representing social, cultural, linguistic and political aspirations that often cut across boundaries based on social class. At times, as we have seen, Labour values and Welsh values were indistinguishable from one another, blurring contested notions of identity in different parts of Wales.

I want to finish where we started, with the Martin Kettle article in the *Guardian* in September 2009. Kettle concluded his article by arguing:

> Maybe this scenario is cast too dramatically ... any claim that Wales is a Conservative nation now – especially based on the support of fewer than one voter in three – is ridiculous. But the idea that it is still a Labour nation is increasingly ridiculous too. As Labour prepares to choose a successor to Rhodri Morgan, its admirable Welsh leader who is 70 this month, Welsh politics is changing fast. Land of my fathers no more.
>
> (Kettle, 2009)

The scenario need not seem so pessimistic. As we saw in the last section of the chapter, Labour representatives are alive to the challenges ahead. The party needs the personalities and the policies to reinvent or reshape the tradition, to rekindle its relevance to ordinary people living in north and south, Welsh-speaking and anglicised, Wales. If it can do this, as optimists suggest, we may still be debating the merits of the Labour tradition in another half-century.

References

Anderson, D. (2003) Transcript of Oral Testimony given to the Richard Commission, www.richardcommission.gov.uk/content/evidence/oral/andersond/index-e.htm (Accessed 20 November 2009).

Davies, R. (2002) Transcript of oral testimony given to the Richard Commission, www.richardcommission.gov.uk/content/evidence/oral/rdavies/index.htm (Accessed 20 November 2009).

Edwards, A. (2004) 'Answering the challenge of nationalism: Goronwy Roberts and the appeal of the Labour party in north-west Wales during the 1950s', *Welsh History Review*, vol. 22, no. 1.

Evans, J.G. (2006) Devolution in Wales: Claims and Responses, 1937–1979, Cardiff, University of Wales Press.

Flynn, P. (1999) *Dragons Led by Poodles: the Inside Story of a New Labour Stitch-Up*, London, Politicos.

Francis, H. and Smith, D. (1980) *The Fed: a History of the South Wales Miners in the Twentieth Century*, London, Lawrence and Wishart.

Greer, S.L. and Rowland, D. (eds) (2007) *Diverging Policy, Diverging Values? The Values of the United Kingdom's National Health Services,* London, Nuffield Trust.

Hain, P. (2008) 'Changing Wales: changing Welsh Labour', www.peterhain.org (Accessed 18 November 2009).

Jones, B. (1999) *Etholiadau'r Ganrif/Welsh Elections, 1885–1997,* Talybont, Y Lolfa.

Jones, C. (2004) *The Future of Welsh Labour,* Cardiff, Institute for Welsh Affairs.

Jones, C. (2009) 'Leader for the whole of Wales', www.welshlabourleadership.org. uk/uploads/ed233b87-90b7-27a4-1d24-265903f2f0f4.pdf (Accessed 14 January 2010).

Kettle, M. (2009), 'Wales: a land lost to Labour?', www.guardian.co.uk/ commentisfree/2009/sep/15/wales-tories-cameron-labour, (Accessed 20 November 2009).

Lewis, H. (2009) *Winning for Wales: Remaking the Welsh Labour Movement for Government,* Wales 20:20.

Morgan, E. (2008) National Library of Wales 2008, Political Archive Lecture, www.llgc.org.uk/fileadmin/documents/pdf/darlith_archif_wleidyddol_2008.pdf (Accessed 18 November 2009).

Morgan, K.O. (1981) *Rebirth of a Nation: Wales 1880–1980,* Oxford, Oxford University Press.

Morgan, K.O. (1988) *The Red Dragon and the Red Flag: The Cases of James Griffiths and Aneurin Bevan,* Aberystwyth, National Library of Wales.

Morgan, P. (1968) *Background to Wales,* Llandybie, C. Davies.

Morgan, R. (2003) 'Delivering for Wales: The implementation of public policy in a small country', Annual Lecture, Welsh Governance Centre, Cardiff.

Osmond, J. and Jones, J.B. (2003) *Birth of Welsh Democracy: the First Term of the National Assembly for Wales,* Cardiff, Institute for Welsh Affairs.

Smith, L. (2003) Transcript of oral testimony given to the Richard Commission, www.richardcommission.gov.uk/content/evidence/oral/smithl/index-e.htm (Accessed 18 November 2009).

Stephens, M. (1986) *The Oxford Companion to the Literature of Wales,* Oxford, Oxford University Press.

Tanner, D., Williams, C. and Hopkin, D. (eds) (2000) *The Labour Party in Wales, 1900–2000,* Cardiff, University of Wales Press.

Tanner, D. and Edwards, A. (2004) 'Slippery slope', *Agenda,* Summer 2004, Cardiff, Institute of Welsh Affairs.

Tanner, D. and Michael, P. (2003) 'Values vs policy in NHS Wales' in Hazel, R. (ed.) *The State of the Nations 2003: the Third Year of Devolution in the United Kingdom*, Exeter, Imprint Academic.

Trench, A. (ed.) (2004) *Has Devolution made a Difference? The State of the Nations 2004*, Exeter, Imprint Academic.

Williams, G.A. (1985) *When was Wales?* London, Penguin.

Further reading

For more on why Labour was so popular in industrial south Wales in the 1920s and 1930s, an excellent starting point is Chapter 9 ('The frontier years') of Williams, G.A. (1985) *When was Wales?*, London, Penguin.

Both Chapter 8, 'Wales's locust years', of Morgan, K.O. (1981) *Wales: Rebirth of a Nation, 1880–1980*, Oxford, Oxford University Press, and Chapter 5, 'The pattern of Labour politics, 1918–1939', in Tanner, D., Williams, C. and Hopkin, D. (2000) *The Labour Party in Wales, 1900–2000*, Cardiff, provide more material on establishment in the 1920s and 1930s.

For more on the formative 1951–64 period, Chapter 8, 'The structure of power in Labour Wales, 1951–1964', in Tanner et al., *Labour Party in Wales*, provides an excellent overview of developments in north and south Wales.

Chapter 10, 'Labour and the nation', in Tanner, D. et al., *Labour Party in Wales*, pp. 241-64 provides an evaluation of Labour's dilemmas over devolution.

Finally, for an in-depth view of Labour and devolution, some of Evans, J.G. (2008) *Devolution in Wales*, Cardiff, University of Wales Press, is useful.

Chapter 8
Political representation

Anwen Elias

Contents

1   Introduction

The word **democracy** comes from the Greek demos (the people) and kratos (rule).

Political representation is a core feature of any modern **democratic** system, organised around the core principle of *rule by the people*. This is because we periodically elect representatives who take political decisions, and implement policies, on our behalf. But political representation is also a very contentious issue. Political scientists and politicians disagree on key questions relating to the basic notion of political representation, such as *who* should be represented, who should *do* the representing, and *what kind* of representation is desirable.

This chapter examines how some of these questions about political representation have been addressed in Wales. In particular, it will examine how concerns with the *quality* of political representation in Wales by the mid 1990s led to a major programme of constitutional reform – **devolution** – and the creation of a new democratically elected body, the National Assembly for Wales (NAW). Champions of devolution during the mid 1990s saw this as a process that would bring about a new form of politics in Wales, one that would be characterised first and foremost by its inclusivity. This chapter examines whether Welsh politics has in fact become more inclusive since then, and the degree to which devolution has enhanced the quality of political representation in Wales.

Devolution is a process whereby political authority is transferred from central government to a lower (regional) level of government.

The aims of this chapter are to:

■ provide an overview of how Wales has been represented historically within the British political system

■ examine the factors that led the British Labour Party to embrace a far-reaching programme of constitutional change by the mid 1990s, of which devolution was a central component

■ outline the main features of the Welsh devolution settlement, as well as what the National Assembly does and how it works

■ examine how inclusive Welsh politics has become since 1999 – from the perspective of formal representation within the National Assembly, and, in the broader sense, the inclusion of all kinds of social groups that have hitherto been marginalised from the political process

■ discuss the 'output' of devolution by looking at the kinds of policies that the National Assembly has passed and the impact these have had on Wales, as well as levels of public support for devolution as a system of governing Wales

■ assess the degree to which devolution has indeed improved the quality of political representation in Wales.

2 A history of political representation in Wales

In this section, you will begin by looking at how Wales has been historically represented within British politics, and why such a system of political representation was considered to be unacceptable by some people and organisations in Wales. This will lead on to an examination of the growing demand for devolution for Wales during the 1960s and 1970s, and then again in the mid 1990s. The section concludes by examining the devolution plans put forward by New Labour in 1997, and the structure and powers of the NAW created soon after.

2.1 Political representation in pre-devolution Wales

Historical overviews of political representation in Wales often make reference to an entry in the index of an early edition of the *Encyclopaedia Britannica*, where it was stated 'for Wales, see England'. That Wales was referred to in such terms reflected the country's thorough incorporation into the institutional, legal and administrative apparatus of the English state through legislation in 1536 and 1543 (the Acts of Union). The Wales and Berwick Act of 1546 stated that 'in all cases where the Kingdom of England, or that part of Great Britain called England, hath been or shall be mentioned in any Act of Parliament, the same has been and shall henceforth be deemed and taken to comprehend and include the Dominion of Wales' (Bogdanor, 1999, p. 144). This Act remained in force until 1967.

In practice, however, Welsh interests have not been as completely subsumed under 'England' as is sometimes asserted. Of course, Wales has always sent representatives to sit in the House of Commons. But, in addition to this, since the beginning of the twentieth century successive governments in Westminster have recognised the necessity of treating Wales differently in certain policy areas. In areas including education, the Welsh language and agriculture, several Wales-specific bodies were established to tailor policies to specific Welsh needs, and to oversee their implementation in Wales. This amounted to a process of administrative devolution. By the 1950s no fewer than seventeen government departments had established administrative units in Wales. Henry Brooke was appointed the first Minister for Welsh Affairs in 1957, and a Welsh Office (headed by the first Secretary of State for Wales, James Griffiths) was established in 1964 in order to 'express the voice of Wales' in central government policy making (Bogdanor, 1999, p. 160).

However, **administrative devolution** did not satisfy everyone. Since the late nineteenth century, certain groups and political parties have argued that this form of political representation is inadequate and insufficient.

Administrative devolution refers to a transfer of responsibility for policy areas with a specific Welsh dimension from Whitehall to Wales-specific bodies.

Let's look in more detail at some of these concerns with the quality of political representation in Wales.

2.2 Contesting political representation in Wales

Historically, several different groups have contested the system of political representation in Wales. For example, and as you know from Chapter 6, in 1925, Plaid Genedlaethol Cymru (the Welsh National

Figure 8.1
'Why you should vote NO in the referendum': the 1979 pamphlet

Why you should VOTE NO

1 By voting 'NO' you will be stopping the start of the slide down the slippery slope to the break-up of the United Kingdom .... *Your Country!*

2 Full independence is Plaid Cymru's main aim .... *Your Country!*

3 At present Government expenditure is over £167 per head higher in Wales than in England – do you want to lose this advantage ... *Your Money!*

4 The Assembly would cost £6½ million to set up *Your Money!*

5 The Assembly would cost £12½ million, and possibly more, to run .... *Your Money!*

6 The Assemblymen would be able to fix their own salaries, pensions and gratuities .... *Your Money!*

7 The Assemblymen would be able to appoint as many officers as they like .... *Your Money!*

8 The Assemblymen would need at least another 1,150 Civil Servants .... *Your Money!*

9 The Assembly would mean yet another tier of Government – more money .... *Your Money!*

10 Welsh M.P.s will no longer have the power to decide on matters of education, housing and health .... *Your Interests!*

Keep Britain united by voting 'NO' on Thursday 1st March.

Printed by Qualitex Printing Ltd, Cardiff and published by A. J. Mackay, 9 Cowbridge Road East, Cardiff.

Party, later to be known as Plaid Cymru, the Party of Wales) was established in defence of the Welsh language and to demand 'freedom' for Wales to decide on its own political affairs. Plaid Cymru, along with its Scottish counterpart, the Scottish National Party (SNP), played an important role in putting the issue of devolution onto the UK political agenda in the 1960s and 1970s. Partly in response to the growing electoral threat of Welsh and Scottish nationalism, the British Labour Party committed itself to a programme of devolution for new democratically elected bodies in Scotland and Wales. These plans were presented to Scottish and Welsh voters in a referendum in 1979.

Activity 8.1

Figure 8.1 is a facsimile of a pamphlet summarising some of the main arguments put forward by opponents to devolution in the 1979 referendum on Welsh devolution. As you read it, consider how persuasive these arguments are, and what kind of arguments supporters of devolution might have made in response to these claims.

Comment

You may agree or disagree with these arguments against devolution to Wales. But in 1979, as you read in Chapter 7, those plans were firmly defeated. These results, and the election of a new Conservative government in 1979 which had little interest in such issues, meant the issue of devolution was off the British political agenda for several years. And yet, as you read in Chapter 7, it was during the eighteen-year reign of the Conservative Party – from 1979 to 1997 – that concerns about the *legitimacy* of political representation in Wales grew to such levels that, by the mid 1990s, there were renewed demands for devolving power to a democratically elected Welsh Assembly.

The concept of legitimacy is an extremely important term in politics, but it can be difficult to agree on a single definition of the term. One way of thinking about it is in terms of 'rightfulness' (Heywood, 2000, p. 29). So, for example, if we wanted to assess the legitimacy of a political system, we would want to know to what extent people living under that system think that the ways in which political decisions are taken are 'right'. If a political system produces *fair* policy outcomes that are accepted and (in the case of laws) obeyed by the people living under the system, then we would say that this is a legitimate political system. This is because the members of the political community agree to be governed in a particular way, and obey the political decisions made by those who govern. A political system that lacks legitimacy would be one where there is a feeling that those in power *do not have a right* to take political decisions on behalf of people living in that community.

In order to help you think about the legitimacy of a system of political representation, it is useful to think in terms of the 'inputs' and 'outputs' of any process of political representation (Judge, 1999, p. 21).

- The 'inputs' refer to elections, and here we are interested in the 'rightfulness' of the way in which representatives are elected (e.g. are the elections fair, open and transparent?), the degree to which representatives reflect the policy preferences of voters, and who the representatives are.

- The 'outputs' refer to what representatives do once they have been elected; here we are interested in whether or not our representatives have acted responsibly and in a way that corresponds to our preferences.

In Wales by the mid 1990s, it is arguable that political representation suffered from problems of both *input* and *output* legitimacy. With regard to input legitimacy, there were two main issues of concern. The first related to the political preferences of Welsh voters, and how these were reflected (or not) in the government that ruled in Westminster.

Table 8.1 provides the general election results for Wales between 1979 and 1997. If you look in particular at the row for 'Conservatives', you will notice what happens to the party's electoral results between 1979 and 1997. Compare this, then, to the row for 'Labour' and you will notice that the biggest difference in the electoral performance of these two parties is that the Conservative Party has never had an electoral majority in Wales.

Table 8.1 General election results in Wales, 1979–1997

	1979		1983		1987		1992		1997	
Party	%	Seats	%	Seats	%	Seats	%	Seats	%	Seats
Labour	48.6	22	37.5	20	45.1	24	49.5	27	54.7	34
Conservative	32.2	11	31.0	14	29.5	8	28.6	6	19.6	0
Liberal Democrats	10.6	1	23.2	2	17.9	3	12.4	1	12.4	2
Plaid Cymru	8.1	2	7.8	2	7.3	3	8.8	4	9.9	4
Others	0.5	0	0.5	0	0.2	0	0.7	0	3.4	0
Total	100	36	100	38	100	38	100	38	100	40

Source: Thrasher and Rallings, 2007, p. 223

The Conservative Party's levels of electoral support declined from the mid 1980s onwards. This is in contrast to the Labour Party, which strengthened its dominant position in Welsh politics over the same period of time. So, as noted above in Chapter 7, Wales was being governed by a political party that did not enjoy the support of most Welsh voters. The growing frustration caused by this situation was expressed clearly by Ron Davies, Labour Party MP for Caerphilly and one of the main architects of Welsh devolution:

> In 1987 and again in 1992 I clearly remember the sense of despair not only at the return of a Conservative government but the consequences of Wales having so clearly turned its face against the Tories yet still facing the prospect of a Tory government, a Tory Secretary of State and Tory policies imposed on us in Wales. I vividly recall the anguish expressed by an eloquent graffiti artist who painted on a prominent bridge in my constituency, overnight after the 1987 defeat, the slogan 'we voted Labour and we got Thatcher'.
>
> (Davies, 1999, pp. 4–5)

This feeling of being governed by an 'unelected' political party was aggravated by the fact that many secretaries of state appointed to the Welsh Office – and therefore affecting the substance and style of policy making affecting Wales – were MPs from English constituencies. Only one of the six Conservative Welsh Secretaries between 1979 and 1997 held a seat in Wales.

As far as output legitimacy is concerned, the Conservative Party's policy decisions were frequently felt to be imposed on Wales against the will of most Welsh voters. This was aggravated by the fact that the Welsh Office was at times under the leadership of individuals – notably John Redwood – with pronounced Thatcherite views that were manifestly at odds with Welsh political values. Other policy decisions taken by the central government – including the poll tax and the privatisation of heavy industries such as coal – were also deeply unpopular. Conservative Party rule also oversaw the growth of so-called 'quangos' in Wales (quasi-autonomous non-governmental organisations). These are independent bodies under the leadership of government appointees and responsible for regulating newly privatised industries, overseeing cultural and scientific activities, and advising the government on policy. In Wales, this included bodies such as the Welsh Development Agency, the Welsh Language Board, the Welsh Tourist Board, and various regional health authorities. The growth of the quangos exacerbated the feeling that Wales was increasingly being governed by an 'unelected state' (Morgan and Mungham, 2000, pp. 45–67).

Add to these concerns about input and output legitimacy the fact that the Labour Party had been in opposition in the House of Commons for almost two decades, and it is not difficult to understand why this party committed itself to a programme of devolution if it were elected to power. This happened in 1997. Once in office, Tony Blair's New Labour began a significant and wide-ranging programme of constitutional change, one outcome of which was the creation of the National Assembly for Wales in 1999. The next section outlines how these changes came about, and provides an overview of the main powers of the National Assembly for Wales.

2.3 New Labour and the Welsh devolution settlement

New Labour, under the leadership of Tony Blair, promoted devolution on the grounds that 'it will bring government closer to the people, make our politics more *inclusive* and put power in the hands of the people where it belongs' (quoted in Chaney and Fevre, 2001,

Figure 8.2
How the 1997
devolution vote divided
Wales

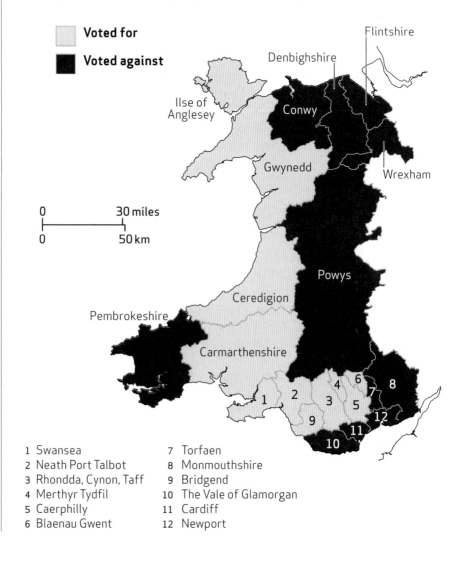

Voted for

Voted against

1 Swansea
2 Neath Port Talbot
3 Rhondda, Cynon, Taff
4 Merthyr Tydfil
5 Caerphilly
6 Blaenau Gwent
7 Torfaen
8 Monmouthshire
9 Bridgend
10 The Vale of Glamorgan
11 Cardiff
12 Newport

pp. 22–3; *emphasis added*). These ambitious plans to create a new inclusive politics were put to the Welsh electorate in a referendum on 18 September 1997.

A week previously, Scottish voters had voted to establish a Scottish parliament, with 74.3 per cent in favour compared to 25.7 per cent against. In Wales, only half of the Welsh electorate – 50.1 per cent to be precise – turned out to vote in the referendum. The result could not have been closer: asked whether they agreed that there should be a Welsh Assembly or not, 50.3 per cent of voters said 'Yes', with 49.7 per cent saying 'No'. Figure 8.2 shows how support and opposition to devolution was geographically distributed across Wales the predominantly Welsh-speaking rural areas of north-west and south-west Wales voted in favour of devolution along with the Valleys, while the more anglicised industrial communities of north-east and south-east Wales voted to reject these proposals.

So, by a mere 6,721 votes, the Welsh electorate said 'Yes' to devolution. This was hardly a ringing endorsement of the devolution project. The closeness of the result could be seen as a sign that the new National Assembly *lacked legitimacy*, given that less than half of Welsh voters voted at all, and that half of those that did didn't want such a body to be established. This is ironic, given that devolution was meant to resolve a perceived lack of legitimacy in Welsh politics.

Activity 8.2

Despite the closeness of the referendum result in 1997, it was nevertheless a result which showed that attitudes towards devolution had changed in important ways since the 1979 referendum. As you read the following, note five important factors that help explain why such a change in opinion had taken place.

Extract 8.1

Why was 1997 different?

The timing of the Welsh referendum of 1997 could not have been better in terms of securing a 'yes' vote. The new Labour government was still enjoying its honeymoon period, little opportunity had existed for left-wing discontent to grow, and the Scots had already a week earlier voted resoundingly for the establishment of a parliament in Edinburgh. Furthermore, the speedy pre-legislative referendum ensured that there was little time for the deficiencies of the government's devolution proposals to be examined. The 'no' campaign was a damp squib. In contrast, the political context of the referendum in 1979 was hostile indeed for the then Labour government. It had lost its majority during 1976 and was reliant on the Liberals and other smaller parties to ensure success for its legislative programme. The referendum took place shortly after the 'winter of discontent' and amidst the resurgence of the Conservative Party under Margaret Thatcher ... These different political contexts in 1979 and 1997 can be seen to have influenced electors' behaviour; to have changed the pattern of support and opposition to devolution; and in the final instance, to have undermined the turnout among 'no' voters sufficiently for a 'yes' result to have crept in under the wire ...

This is not to deny that, although the increase in the proportion of the population of Wales affirming a Welsh identity between 1979 and 1997 was small, Welsh national identity increased in political salience ... [T]wo notable developments have occurred. People with a Welsh national identity have become more pro-devolution. And Plaid Cymru, the nationalist party, has become markedly more acceptable to the mass of the population in Wales ... As there was no marked social change that might account for why a Welsh identity became more politically salient, it is likely to be a political creation. Perhaps the Labour government should thank Plaid Cymru for its work in this area, for without the politicisation of Welsh identity, the swing from 1979 to 1997 would not have been enough.

Source: Evans and Trystan, 1999, pp. 113–14

Comment

Some of the factors that you might have identified as having contributed to a 'Yes' vote in the referendum are:

- the popularity of the newly elected Labour government

- the 'yes' vote in Scotland a week previously

- the speed at which the legislation for holding a referendum was passed through the Houses of Parliament

- a badly organised 'no' campaign

- the increased salience of Welsh identity.

The result of the referendum led to the creation of a National Assembly for Wales. According to the Government of Wales Act 1998, this new body would be characterised as follows:

- Sixty Assembly Members (AMs), elected by an alternative member system (see Box 8.1).

■ The National Assembly would take over the powers previously exercised by the Secretary of State for Wales and the Welsh Office. These areas of responsibility include agriculture; culture; economic development; education and training; the environment; health; sport; economic development; the environment; health; local government and housing; sport; social services; transport and the Welsh language.

■ In these policy areas, the National Assembly would have secondary legislative powers. This meant that all laws (primary legislation) would still be made in Westminster; however, the National Assembly would be able to specify rules and regulations that adapt the legislation to the specific Welsh context.

■ The National Assembly was designed as a 'corporate' body; this meant that, in contrast to the distinction made in most political systems between the executive (the government) and the legislature (the parliament), the National Assembly as a whole would be responsible for proposing, passing and scrutinising policy decisions. This model of governance was designed to promote consensus and cooperation between political parties.

The first National Assembly elections were held on 6 May 1999. Table 8.2 shows the results from these and subsequent elections in 2003 and 2007. The difference between 1st and 2nd votes in these elections is explained in Box 8.1.

Figure 8.3
Inside the National Assembly for Wales

Table 8.2 National Assembly for Wales election results, 1999–2007

Party	1999			2003			2007		
	1st vote (%)	2nd vote (%)	Total seats	1st vote (%)	2nd vote (%)	Total seats	1st vote (%)	2nd vote (%)	Total seats
Labour	37.6	35.5	28	40.0	36.6	30	32.2	29.6	26
Conservative	15.8	16.5	9	19.9	19.2	11	22.4	21.5	12
Liberal Democrat	13.5	12.5	6	14.1	12.7	6	14.8	11.7	6
Plaid Cymru	28.4	30.6	17	21.2	19.7	12	22.4	21.0	15
Others	4.7	4.9	0	4.8	11.8	1	8.3	16.3	1
Total	100.0	100.0	60	100.0	100.0	60	100.0	100.0	60

Sources: Wyn Jones and Scully (2004), p. 194; Scully and Elias (2008), p. 105

Box 8.1   The basics: first-past-the-post versus proportional representation electoral systems

In the United Kingdom, representatives to the House of Commons are elected using the 'first-past-the-post' (FPTP) electoral system. In each constituency, voters are presented with a list of candidates representing different political parties. The voter votes for the candidate he or she prefers, and the candidate with the most votes in the constituency wins. The 'winner takes all' in FPTP elections; there's no reward for candidates that come in second or third place. So, for example, if Candidate A wins 40 per cent of the vote, and Candidate B wins 39 per cent of the vote, Candidate A will be elected because he/she has won most of the votes. FPTP electoral systems are also used in Canada, the USA and India.

'Proportional representation' (PR) electoral systems are different because they try to achieve as close a match as possible between a party's share of the vote and its share of the parliamentary seats. Let's imagine that a PR system was used to elect representatives to the House of Commons. In principle, if party A wins 40 per cent of all votes cast in the United Kingdom, it will have 40 per cent of the representatives in the House of Commons; Party B, which wins 30 per cent of all votes cast, will get 30 per cent of seats, and so on. So we can say that a party's number of representatives is *proportional* to the number of votes it has. Examples of PR systems can be found in Germany and Australia (although several different forms of PR systems exist).

The electoral system used for electing representatives to the National Assembly for Wales can best be described as being *semi-proportional*, since it combines elements of both the FPTP and PR systems. In what is known as the 'additional member system', 40 of the National Assembly's members are elected using FPTP, while the remaining 20 are elected using PR. This means that in National Assembly elections each voter will have two votes. The *first vote* is cast for a single candidate representing a specific constituency, in the same way that representatives are elected to the House of Commons (by putting an X next to the name of the candidate that he/she prefers on the ballot sheet). The *second vote* is used to elect the *additional* members that represent one of five regions within Wales. Instead of voting for an individual candidate, the vote will be cast for a political party; these *additional seats* will be allocated in such a way that corrects for any unfairness in the allocation of the FPTP constituency seats (there is a very complex formula that calculates how many alternative seats each political party should be allocated!). Alternative member systems have also been used widely around the world, including in New Zealand.

It was always expected by prominent Labour Party politicians that devolution to Wales would be a 'process not an event' (Davies, 1999), and that there was scope for change and adaptation over the years. However, the need for change and adaptation arose much sooner than had originally been anticipated. It didn't take long for the drawbacks of this constitutional settlement to become apparent: within a year of its creation, there were calls for the National Assembly's institutional set-up and powers to be revisited. As Chapter 7 noted, the Richard Commission, chaired by the Labour peer Lord Ivor Richard, began its deliberations in 2002 and gathered extensive evidence on how different groups and interests perceived the National Assembly to be working. The Commission's final report, delivered in March 2004, proposed a radical revision of the original devolution settlement. Some of these recommendations were included in a new Government of Wales Act 2006, which contained the following key provisions:

■ the abandonment of the idea of the 'corporate body', with a clearer separation being made instead between the role of the executive (i.e. the Assembly government, responsible for proposing and implementing policy) and the legislature (the Assembly as a whole, responsible for scrutinising the activities of the Assembly government)

■ new powers for the Assembly to request the right for primary legislation to be delegated from Westminster.

Further debate about the future of devolution in Wales was initiated with the creation of an All Wales Convention in 2008 to consider the prospect of further expanding the powers of the National Assembly. The setting-up of such a convention was one of the commitments made by Labour and Plaid Cymru in June 2007 when they agreed to enter into government together in the National Assembly. One of the main objectives of the All Wales Convention was to assess the extent of public support for moving towards full law-making powers for the National Assembly. This would give the institution primary legislative powers in the full range of devolved policy areas, although a new referendum would be required in order for this to happen. As part of its work, the All Wales Convention held a series of public meetings across Wales in order to gather the views of the Welsh public on the issue of further powers for the Welsh Assembly. The Convention's recommendations were presented to the Welsh Assembly Government in November 2009. The evidence gathered suggested that if a referendum on further powers were to be held, a 'Yes' vote was deemed to be possible although not guaranteed (All Wales Convention, 2009).

Figure 8.4

A *Question-Time* style event organised by the All Wales Convention, Cardiff 2009

Summary

- While Wales was thoroughly incorporated into England in the sixteenth century, from the early twentieth century onwards new administrative bodies were established to make and implement Wales-specific policies.

- Demands for a fairer system of political representation for Wales led to an unsuccessful referendum on devolution in 1979, but dissatisfaction with the legitimacy of administrative devolution grew throughout the 1980s and early 1990s.

- A successful referendum on devolution in 1997 led to the creation of a National Assembly for Wales, amid promises of the emergence of a new inclusive politics in Wales.

- Devolution has been a process rather than an event. Thus, since 1999 there have been important changes in the way in which the National Assembly works and its powers; these debates are ongoing.

3 Representation within the National Assembly for Wales

You now have a clear outline of the key developments in the creation of a devolved level of government in Wales: now you will examine the progress that has been made since 1999 in terms of improving the quality of political representation in Wales. You will begin by looking at the impact of devolution on the *input legitimacy* of political representation in Wales, with a particular focus on the inclusivity of Welsh politics. You will already know that this was a key ambition linked to devolution in its early years. Turning the rhetoric of inclusive politics into reality would be crucial if the National Assembly was going to succeed in creating a more legitimate system of political representation in Wales.

In this section and the next, you will examine the extent to which devolution has enhanced the inclusivity of Welsh politics. Let's begin by considering formal representation within the Assembly, and think about the extent to which the different social groups in Wales have succeeded in gaining entry to this new democratic arena.

3.1 Electoral systems as a means of 'engineering' better representation

I've already noted that elections are crucial for any system of political representation. It is through elections that we choose those who represent our interests in the political sphere; elections also give us the opportunity to control our representatives. If we're happy with the decisions that they have taken on our behalf, then we will vote for them again; however, if we are unhappy with these decisions, we can show this by voting for a different representative. In other words, elections are a key mechanism in the organisation of political representation.

So elections provide a crucial link between the members of any given political community, and those that represent them in the political sphere (for example, in parliament or in government). But the nature of this link varies, depending on the type of electoral system used. Different **electoral systems** can help to 'engineer' specific outcomes, such as encouraging cooperation between political parties in a divided society.

Electoral systems are the rules and procedures through which votes cast in an election are translated into seats won, for example in parliament or government.

In Wales, a new electoral system was adopted for elections to the National Assembly with the aim of *producing an elected body that better represented the society that elected it.* It is generally accepted that a certain type of electoral system – PR systems, which you came across in Box 8.1 above – can lead to a more inclusive form of political representation, by making it easier for smaller political parties and groups (including those representing women, ethnic and religious minorities, disabled people and so on) to be elected. The word 'inclusiveness' was first used by the advocates of Welsh devolution in the mid 1990s to refer to the potential positive benefits of a PR electoral system (Davies, 1999, p. 5). The aim was to reduce the dominance of one political party and create a group of political representatives that looked more like the people that actually elected them.

3.2 Political parties as agents of representation

But has this happened? One way of answering this question is to examine the different groups that have been represented in the National Assembly since its creation in 1999. Table 8.2 above gives you the election results for the three Assembly elections that have taken place since 1999.

Activity 8.3

Examine the election results in Table 8.2. Compare these with the general election results provided in Table 8.1. (You can find both of these tables in Section 2.2 of this chapter.) Look in particular at which political parties win seats in each election; these are listed in the first column of each table. Are the same political parties elected in both general and devolved elections? Or have different political parties won seats in devolved elections?

Comment

You will see from these tables that representation within the National Assembly has been dominated by the four main party groups (Labour, Conservative, Liberal Democrat and Plaid Cymru); these are the same four major political parties that have contested elections in Wales since

1945. Very few 'others' have succeeded in being elected. 'Others' is a category that contains a range of political actors; it includes some political parties that you will recognise, such as the Green Party and the British National Party. It also contains other, more localised groups – such as the Blaenau Gwent People's Voice, which contested the 2007 election – as well as independent candidates who are not affiliated to any political party. One independent candidate (John Marek for the Wrexham constituency) was elected to the National Assembly in the 2003 elections, and another in the 2007 elections (Trish Law, for Blaenau Gwent).

So there have been no major changes in which political parties represent Welsh voters in the National Assembly for Wales, in spite of the use of a partially proportional electoral system. No new minority groups have succeeded in gaining seats within this elected body since 1999. This does not mean that there haven't been important changes in party politics in post-devolution Wales. A partially proportional electoral system has contributed to two major changes.

The first relates to the dominance of different political parties in Wales. While the Labour Party dominated Welsh politics from the 1920s up until 1997 (winning 54.7 per cent of the vote in the general election held in that year), it has seen a dramatic decline in its electoral fortunes in elections to the National Assembly since 1999. At the same time, the level of electoral support enjoyed by Plaid Cymru has been notably higher in devolved elections than in elections for Westminster. One explanation for this is that voters tend to focus to a greater extent on Wales-specific issues when making their electoral choice in devolved elections; this translates into greater electoral support for Plaid Cymru than the other UK-wide political parties (since Plaid Cymru is seen as being the most focused on Wales of all the political parties competing in Assembly elections). It's also worth noting that the Conservative Party, which has historically been weaker in Wales than in England, has experienced a period of electoral growth since 1999, with the party commanding 21.5 per cent of votes in the 2007 election to the National Assembly. This is due in part to the party's serious and sustained efforts to rebrand itself to be more appealing to Welsh voters.

Second, and as a result of the changing fortunes of the major political parties along the lines just described, it's become more difficult for a single political party to secure a majority of seats in the National Assembly and form a government on its own. Instead, coalition governments have been formed between different parties. This happened for the first time in October 2000, when Labour and the Liberal Democrats formed a government together which lasted until the second round of Assembly elections in May 2003. A second coalition government was formed in June 2007 between Labour and Plaid Cymru. Coalition government is considered to be normal politics in a great proportion of the democratic world, but it is relatively unfamiliar in UK politics (which is more accustomed to governments formed by a single political party). Coalitions can have important implications for the kinds of policies that are pursued by governments, because participating parties must negotiate and compromise on the coalition government's agenda. For example, Labour had to make important concessions to Plaid Cymru in order to agree a coalition government in 2007. These included a commitment to new legislation on the Welsh language and a referendum on further powers for the National Assembly for Wales before the next Assembly elections in 2011.

So the electoral system has had an important impact on party politics in post-devolution Wales, which in turn also has implications for the kinds of policies pursued by governing parties within the National Assembly.

3.3 Representing minority groups within the National Assembly for Wales

Section 3.2 showed that just looking at patterns of electoral support for political parties suggests that advances have not been made towards a more inclusive politics. A very different picture emerges, however, when we look not at the political parties, but at the individual members of political parties who have been elected to the National Assembly. Looking at the gender of representatives within the National Assembly is particularly striking, because one of the biggest successes of the National Assembly has been to end the marginalisation of women within Welsh politics. In 2006, the National Assembly became the first elected body in the world to have more women than men (31 women to 29 men). To fully appreciate the significance of this achievement, it is useful to compare this situation with how women have been represented in Welsh politics historically. While the representation of women in the UK has traditionally been low, it has been lower still in Wales:

> There have only ever been seven women elected to represent Welsh constituencies at Westminster; until 1970 there had been only three. From 1970 onwards there were none, until Labour's Ann Clwyd won the Cynon Valley by-election in 1984. It was not until 1997 that another three women were elected. Even then, these were all selected under Labour's compulsory 'all-women shortlist' [see Case Study 8.1] ... This brought women's representation to four seats out of 40 in Wales – just 10 per cent, compared with 20 per cent in England. The Welsh nationalist party, Plaid Cymru, has never elected a woman MP

and neither have the Conservatives in Wales (although both parties' representation at Westminster has historically been small). In 1997, women's representation in local government was also low: 20.4 per cent, compared to 27.8 per cent in England.

(Russell et al., 2002, p. 51)

How can this success in boosting the number of women elected as political representatives in Wales be explained? Norris and Lovenduski (1995) identify three sets of factors that have an impact on women's representation in elected political office:

- Systemic factors relate to the formal legal framework, total number of seats in the legislature, the electoral system, party system and general structure of political opportunities.

- Political factors relate to party ideologies and rules, including the selection process and wider culture and organisation of parties that may tend to exclude women.

- Social factors relate to the individual's ability to compete in the system (for example, generally lower incomes, different employment patterns and family responsibilities).

When thinking about these factors in the specific context of the National Assembly for Wales, we have already discussed how specific structural factors – in particular, the adoption of a semi-proportional electoral system – created an opportunity for previously excluded minorities to be included in the devolved political process.

There were also important *political* factors that contributed to increasing the number of elected women representatives (Chaney, 2006). For example, promoting gender equality was identified as a key goal of devolution right at the outset of the devolution process. In a paper outlining its plans for devolution in Wales, the UK government stated its belief that 'greater participation by women is essential to the health of our democracy. The Government also urges all political parties offering candidates for election to the Assembly to have this in mind in their internal selection processes' (Welsh Office, 1998, p. 24). Two political parties in Wales responded to this challenge by adopting new procedures for selecting electoral candidates that would boost the numbers of women representatives being elected to the National Assembly; Case Study 8.1 summarises these. The institutional design of the National Assembly was also aimed at creating a political environment that would encourage women to participate in politics. This included limiting the institution's working hours in order to promote a work–life balance, and adopting gender-neutral titles for all official positions.

Case Study 8.1
Improving the representation of women in the National Assembly

Before the first elections to the National Assembly in May 1999, three of the four main political parties in Wales adopted special candidate-selection processes in order to increase the number of women being elected:

The Welsh Labour Party adopted a 'twinning' strategy, whereby two constituencies were twinned with each other, with one woman and one man being selected as candidates between them. This meant that the party contested the election with equal numbers of male and female constituency candidates. As a result of this policy, 54 per cent of Labour representatives elected in 1999 were women.

Plaid Cymru preferred to use the regional lists to counterbalance any under-representation of women in constituency seats (expected to be male-dominated). Women were guaranteed first and third places on these lists. Following the election, Plaid Cymru's Assembly group comprised six women and eleven men.

Although the Welsh Liberal Democrats didn't adopt any formal positive action strategy, they offered training to encourage women to stand for election. Three of the six Liberal Democrats eventually elected to the National Assembly were women.

Activity 8.4

Social factors can also affect the number of elected women representatives. Consider how things like a woman's income, employment and family responsibilities might affect her ability to participate in elected politics. It might help if you think of these things either in relation to your own life circumstances (if you're a woman) or in relation to a woman you know well (if you are a man).

Having a significant proportion of elected women can have a substantial effect on what issues are discussed by politicians, and the way in which these discussions take place. After examining the contributions made by women to general debates and committee discussions within the National Assembly, Chaney concludes that:

> [W]omen parliamentarians have a greater propensity than their male colleagues to both engage in – and initiate – political debate on 'women's issues' in order to further the substantive representation of

women. It has also been shown that women representatives draw directly upon gendered life experiences to inform debate and that they act to promote women's interests across a broader range of policy areas than their male counterparts.

(Chaney, 2006, p. 709)

The presence of female representatives also has an impact on the tone and nature of political debates within the National Assembly. These debates are often less 'macho' and confrontational than if they were conducted exclusively by male representatives. One female Labour AM commented on the working environment of the National Assembly in the following terms: 'I think on the whole the women that I know have got a different way of working and think things through, and aren't sort of overly aggressive' (Jones et al., 2009, p. 7). Another female (Liberal Democrat) AM agreed, 'because women do things in a different way, do debate in a more consensual style ... our natural way of working is probably more practical and more low key' (Jones et al., 2009, p. 8).

However, no comparable successes have been achieved in improving the representation of other minority groups. By 2009 – ten years after the creation of the National Assembly – there was only one ethnic minority representative within the National Assembly; Mohammad Asghar was elected as a Plaid Cymru AM for South Wales East in 2007. In the words of one scholar, 'as one measure of active citizenship the profile is clearly wanting' (Williams, 2004, p. 158). There is also a chronic under-representation of other minority groups, such as those with disabilities and groups defined by faith, sexual orientation or any other significant markers of identity.

This raises important (and controversial) questions about whether or not steps should be taken to increase the representation of such minority groups, in a similar way as has been done with regard to the representation of women. Supporters of such steps argue that this is the only way of meeting the goal of **descriptive representation** (also sometimes referred to as 'microcosmic representation'). However, descriptive representation is not a solution favoured by everyone. Extract 8.2 summarises some of the problems with such a system of representation.

> **Descriptive representation** is where elected representatives are typical of the people that they represent; this can be on the basis of gender, ethnicity, religion and so on.

Extract 8.2

The problems of descriptive representation

There are three main grounds upon which opposition to microcosmic [i.e. descriptive] representation has traditionally been centred: it is impractical, it is undesirable, and, ultimately, it is impossible. First, it is maintained that it is impossible to represent every social group in proportion to the wider social structure. Even before strict proportionality could be attempted it would be necessary to decide which groups of people warrant representation in their own right: fat people, short people, deaf, blind, disabled, lesbians/gays, unemployed, Catholics, Jews and so on ...

Even if agreement could be reached upon which groups should have more proportional representation, critics proceed to argue that it would be impractical to secure greater representativeness through established electoral procedures. In this manner Birch argues that, 'there is no country in which competitive elections based upon manhood suffrage have produced an assembly which could fairly be described as a social microcosm of the nation' ... He later maintains that 'unless the House of Commons comes to be composed of conscripts chosen by computer, it will never be fully representative in the microcosmic [or descriptive] sense of the word' (Birch, 1975, p. 57).

Even if the practical difficulties could be overcome, the final argument of critics is that proportionality is undesirable. Phillips Griffiths (1960, p. 190) regarded some deviations from proportionality to be positively beneficial: 'we would not want to complain that the large class of stupid or maleficient people have too few representatives in Parliament: quite the contrary'. If representation constitutes a social division of labour, in which some people develop and exercise special political skills on behalf of society at large, then the benefits of this specialisation would be reduced by 'proportionality'.

References

Birch, A.H. (1971) Representation. *London: Macmillan.*

Phillips Griffiths, A. (1960) 'How can one person represent another?' Proceedings of the Aristotelian Society, 34.

Source: Judge, 1999, pp. 44–5

Summary

■ In spite of the adoption of a semi-proportional electoral system, traditional political parties still dominate formal political representation within the National Assembly for Wales. However, the levels of support enjoyed by different political parties have altered in important ways; coalition government has also become a feature of Welsh politics.

■ Welsh political parties have taken important steps to increase the number of women representatives within the National Assembly; however, other minority groups remain chronically under-represented.

- This raises the important, but contentious, question of whether (and if so, what) specific steps should be taken to address the lack of inclusivity among elected representatives in Wales.

4 Broadening engagement and participation in Welsh politics

The term 'inclusive' acquired a second meaning in debates leading up to, and during the earliest years of, devolution, namely 'a concern for fostering wider citizen participation in government and engagement with different social groupings' (Chaney and Fevre, 2001, p. 26). In this sense, inclusive politics means empowering and involving groups of people that have previously been marginalised or excluded from the political process.

In Scotland, devolution was, in part, a response to demands from such disempowered groups for a greater participation in government. In contrast, there were few such demands in Wales. Given the lack of enthusiasm for such a broadening of democratic involvement, the challenge for the National Assembly was to create new opportunities for mass engagement and participation in the political process. We consider the extent to which this has been achieved in the rest of this section. The focus in particular is on the extent to which devolution has created a vibrant civil society in Wales where one did not previously exist. Let's begin by defining this key term.

4.1 Defining civil society

The notion of civil society is much talked about and debated in politics and it is often used by academics and politicians to mean very different things. I use civil society to mean the following:

- Civil society represents a distinct sphere that is separate from the 'state' (political institutions, political parties and other political organisations) and the 'market' (organisations of production and distribution, such as firms and businesses).

- Civil society provides a space for individuals and organisations to discuss, exchange views, and form opinions on matters that are important for society as a whole. Civil society is composed of organisations such as charities, non-governmental organisations, community and environmental groups, women's organisations, faith-based and consumer organisations, professional associations, trade unions, self-help groups, business associations and advocacy groups.

■ Most importantly, these voices and opinions emerging from civil society scrutinise, critique and counterbalance the otherwise overbearing influence of political society (the state) and economic society (the market). Civil society is thus a check – a form of control – on state power. For this reason, a vibrant civil society is often considered to be a vital element for a democratic society.

4.2 Inclusive politics through a vibrant civil society

There is broad agreement among scholars of Welsh politics that devolution has created new opportunities for civil society actors to interact with government structures in Wales, and to influence policy decisions made by the National Assembly. The legal framework of the newly devolved administration required the National Assembly to place the principle of equality of opportunity for all of Wales's citizens at the heart of its political agenda. The National Assembly responded to this duty by implementing a range of initiatives in order to establish new relationships with marginalised and minority groups in Wales. The 'equality' networks that have been set up, for example, comprise voluntary organisations that represent the interests of marginalised groups. These include Disability Wales, Wales Women's National Coalition (since renamed Women's Voice), the All Wales Ethnic Minority Association (AWEMA) and Lesbian, Gay and Bisexual (LGB) Forum Cymru. These networks have been given funding by the National Assembly to pay for new staff to support and expand their activities, expand their membership, and feed into discussions on different policies being developed by the Assembly. The Equality Unit within the Assembly is responsible for giving advice and support to the Assembly in the development of policies, for maintaining dialogue with minority communities, and for disseminating best practice.

The creation of a new sphere of political decision making in Wales has also prompted some civil society groups to develop new organisational structures and strategies in order to maximise their political influence. Oxfam, for example, has rebranded itself as 'Oxfam Cymru' and has dedicated new staffing and financial resources to lobbying the Assembly government and civil service (Royles, 2007, pp. 109–10). In addition, civil society groups and individuals have tried to make the most of the opportunities to interact with AMs and civil servants. One group that has been highly effective in influencing policy making within the National Assembly has been Friends of the Earth Cymru; the various ways in which this has been achieved are summarised in Case Study 8.2. Other groups have been just as active in trying to influence policy making in post-devolution Wales:

Women's and disabled people's groups have submitted written responses to key policy initiatives covering the breadth of the

Assembly's work. They have presented papers to Assembly committees that have formed the basis of discussions between the group's representatives, AMs, committee advisors and officials [and] have been invited to join task groups to develop policies and implement strategies.

(Betts et al., 2001, p. 70)

The evidence considered so far suggests that devolution has indeed succeeded in creating a new form of inclusive politics in Wales. Equality issues are more central to policy making in Wales, and there is more active involvement by minority groups and other civil society actors in the political process.

However, studies of civil society in post-devolution Wales also reveal less positive developments. Some civil society organisations enjoy closer and more exclusive relations with the National Assembly than others. This is due, in part, to the differences between civil society organisations themselves. While some groups, such as Oxfam Cymru and Friends of the Earth Cymru, are well resourced, others are not, and therefore find it considerably more difficult to engage with the National Assembly. As far as the relationship between the National Assembly and groups representing women and minority ethnic groups are concerned, these have been dominated by a narrow elite of middle-class professionals. Most of the members of these organisations are for the large part ignorant of the concerns and activities of the National Assembly (Betts and Chaney, 2004; Williams, 2004). Faith groups outside the Christian mainstream have also found it difficult to get a fair hearing from those in the Assembly and the Assembly government (Day, 2006, p. 650). All of these examples point to major inequalities in power and influence between civil society organisations. Smaller, less experienced and more marginal groups find themselves excluded from interactions between civil society and the National Assembly.

Case Study 8.2
Friends of the Earth Cymru

Friends of the Earth is a large international organisation that works to mobilise people to resist socially and environmentally damaging projects and policies. It is composed of a network of organisations that are active in different national and regional contexts. In the UK, Friends of the Earth is a very visible and influential environmental campaign group.

Friends of the Earth Cymru was set up in 1984 to campaign on environmental issues in Wales. The establishment of the National Assembly for Wales in 1999 provided a new focus for the organisation's activities, especially because this new body would be responsible for developing Wales-specific policies in key areas of interest to Friends of the Earth (such as the environment, economic development, agriculture and transport). Since 1999, the organisation has been highly efficient in feeding into, and influencing, devolved policy making in Wales in several ways:

- preparing policy papers on various issues (such as renewable energy and climate change)

- submitting reports and evidence to the different policy committees within the National Assembly (for example, on carbon reduction in transport)

- presenting draft policies to the National Assembly for discussion (for example, a policy restricting the planting of genetically modified [GM] crops in Wales passed in 2000 was based on an original proposal submitted by Friends of the Earth)

- writing directly to, and meeting with, relevant government ministers in order to put their case forward

- mobilising broad coalitions in public support of different campaigns (such as an open letter signed by a wide range of prominent individuals and AMs from all parties in support of a no-GM policy for Wales)

- commissioning highly visible publicity campaigns to mobilise support for particular issues (see Figure 8.5).

It could also be argued that the National Assembly and the Welsh Assembly Government have made existing inequalities worse by developing more exclusive relations with some organisations and not others. For example, some people within the National Assembly deemed Cymdeithas yr Iaith – a pressure group for the Welsh language that you came across in Chapter 6 – to be too controversial, and therefore unacceptable, as a partner in policy discussions; as a result, the group had only very limited access to key decision makers within the Welsh Assembly Government (Royles, 2007, p. 95, p. 149).

There is also evidence of stronger ties between the National Assembly and civil society organisations that receive funding from the Assembly; these organisations have been shown to have closer contacts with the

Keep our meat and veg GM free
Cadwch ein cig a'n llysiau'n rhydd o GM

Cadwch Gymru'n rhydd o GM.
Chi sydd â'r grym.

Keep Wales GM free. You have the power.

Friends of the Earth Cymru
Cyfeillion y Ddaear Cymru

www.cyddcymru.co.uk
www.foecymru.co.uk

Figure 8.5
Friends of the Earth Cymru poster outside the National Assembly

Assembly's government ministers and civil servants (Royles, 2007). Such relationships have been described as 'neo-corporatist' by Royles. **Neo-corporatism** is not good for democracy, for several reasons. First, a group with privileged contacts with politicians may not be representative of wider civil society. Second, the exclusivity of the neo-corporatist relationship can lead to the further marginalisation and exclusion of other civil society groups. This has been experienced by minority ethnic groups, as is shown in the statement from AWEMA in Extract 8.3 below. Third, the fact that privileged organisations do not want to endanger their relationship with those in power means they may hold back from scrutinising, and being critical of, the actions of the government and elected representatives. This may be especially true for organisations or networks that are funded by the National Assembly, and which do not want to risk losing out financially. As was noted in Section 4.1, this scrutiny function is a core requirement for a well-functioning democracy.

Neo-corporatism refers to a privileged relationship between political actors (especially those in government) and a narrow group of actors representing a specific set of interests.

Activity 8.5

We have already seen that there have been some problems in ensuring the full participation of civil society groups in the Welsh political process. The experiences of one particular group, AWEMA, are summarised in Extract 8.3. This is an extract from the evidence presented by AWEMA to the Richard Commission's investigation into the powers and functioning of the National Assembly. As you read it, make note of the ways in which AWEMA has sought to interact with the National Assembly and how effective it has been in shaping policy making.

Extract 8.3

AWEMA evidence to the Richard Commission

... The Size of the Assembly – With the Acquisition of Further Powers.

1   ...

It is AWEMA's view that its current engagement with the WAG/ NAfW's consultation documents is producing little or no change in the overall strategic approach of policy initiatives. Effective change as such in the overall scheme is not evident. There is no recognition in policy documents that Wales is a multi-cultural and a multi-lingual country.

It is our view that this may be due to the fact that powers on issues of race, religion, language, culture, international development (issues of specific concern to the [black and minority ethnic (BME)] communities) and asylum seekers are not devolved.

It is further our view that due to devolution, Parliamentary Government Departments have tended to ignore Wales in the last four years. Representations by AWEMA have started to reverse this trend, but the fact remains that the Welsh BME communities are being further marginalized from issues of significant concern to them.

2   AWEMA has been engaged in responding to consultation documents in the field of Health, Housing, Education, Citizenship, Economic Development, Social Care, and Culture and the Arts. We have also responded to consultation documents on Languages, European Structural Funds, [Education and Learning Wales (ELWA)] and [Community Consortia for Education and Training (CCETS)].

With the exception of Housing and to a limited extent Social Care, we have made little impact with the WAG with our responses to documents. We see little evidence of our recommendations making it into strategy and policy with attendant attachment of necessary resources or an identified delivery mechanism.

This may well be due to the fact that the aspirations we express are beyond the powers of the Assembly. We have not tested this premise.

3 AWEMA accepts that the acquisition of further powers will necessarily involve a substantial increase in the work of Members not only in analysing, debating and consulting but also examining new laws on committees …

… We would argue, however, that it is much more important to establish relevance and need for the people of Wales … [C]onsideration could be given in ensuring that the considerable expertise of the Voluntary Sector is also used to support the consultation processes so that legislation can be passed, ensuring the delivery of real difference in our communities' lives.

Source: AWEMA 2003

4.3 New opportunities for civil society participation post-2006?

Thus far in this section, most of the evidence for inclusivity in civil society–National Assembly relations we've considered focuses on the early years of devolution. However, as you already know, dissatisfaction with the functioning of devolution led to a new Government of Wales Act in 2006; this saw the Assembly's mode of operation being modified, and an extension of its powers to make laws in new policy areas (subject to the agreement of the Houses of Parliament in Westminster).

This Act created new opportunities for civil society organisations to interact with, and influence, politics in Wales in two important ways. First, the Act contained a provision for a new petitions procedure to be created. This gives members of the public the right to petition the National Assembly – either in writing or using an online e-petitions system – and ask for action to be taken in those areas of policy for which the Assembly is responsible. The first group to submit such a petition was the Kidney Wales Foundation; it asked the National Assembly to fund an organ-donor campaign and an inquiry into presumed consent for organ donation. This petition was successful in securing money for an organ-donation campaign, and prompted the National Assembly to undertake a review of organ-transplantation procedures in Wales. This is a good example of how the new petitions system can enable a civil society group to draw attention to, and prompt political action on, specific issues.

Second, the fact that the National Assembly has the chance to make its own laws creates further opportunities for civil society actors to lobby elected representatives in order to legislate in different policy areas. For example, the National Assembly has considered requesting new powers to make laws in areas such as mental health and the rights of carers. These are clearly policy areas where there is scope for civil society groups to try and influence the nature and scope of the new powers requested. In order to make the most of these new decision-shaping opportunities, new initiatives have been established, such as the Voices for Change Wales project. Financed by a grant from the National Lottery and sponsored by the Wales Council for Voluntary Action (WVCA), Voices for Change Wales aims to help voluntary organisations understand how decision-making processes work in Wales, develop skills and confidence to influence policies and legislation, and share and learn about best practice in developing relationships with the National Assembly.

And yet there remain important limitations in meeting the goal of inclusivity. A 2009 survey of civil society organisations by Voices for Change Wales revealed that while there is a consensus that devolution has increased access to Welsh decision makers, the majority of those questioned still do not have a thorough knowledge of how to engage with the National Assembly successfully or efficiently. For example, fewer than 50 per cent of organisations were aware of the petitions process, with a similar number unclear about how to submit evidence to the National Assembly when proposals for new legislative powers are being drafted (Bradbury and Matheron, 2009). So there is still a long way to go before there is a truly inclusive partnership between civil society and the National Assembly for Wales.

Summary

- Devolution has had some positive democratic effects in Wales. The National Assembly has created new structures for bringing previously marginalised groups into the political process. The Government of Wales Act 2006 contributed to further developing such opportunities for civil society involvement in decision making.

- Civil society groups have also developed new lobbying strategies in order to influence policy making within the National Assembly.

- However, devolution has also had some potentially negative democratic implications. Some civil society groups are better resourced, while others have enjoyed a privileged relationship with the National Assembly.

- These patterns of interaction risk reinforcing exclusion and marginalisation within civil society, jeopardise the inclusiveness of politics in post-devolution Wales, and risk undermining the scrutiny function of civil society vis-à-vis the National Assembly.

5   Output legitimacy in post-devolution Wales

So far, you have looked at how devolution has impacted upon who represents Welsh voters in the National Assembly, and the extent to which civil society groups have been able to participate in policy making in Wales since devolution. These aspects relate to the input legitimacy of political representation in Wales (see Section 2.2). But how has devolution influenced the output legitimacy of political representation in Wales? In other words, to what extent has devolution had good or desirable effects on Welsh politics, economy and society?

There are two ways in which the output legitimacy of devolution can be assessed. The first involves looking at the policies that have been formulated and implemented by the National Assembly, and whether these have been perceived by Welsh citizens as positive or negative. There have certainly been several examples of policy divergence as a result of devolution, where the National Assembly has passed policies that have been very different from those in other parts of the United Kingdom. For example, as you saw in Chapter 7, while people in England still have to pay prescription charges, the National Assembly has abolished such charges in Wales. University students in Wales (and in Scotland) have also paid lower tuition fees than their counterparts in England. But public evaluations of these and other policies have been mixed. A series of regular public opinion surveys conducted since 1999 (Welsh Assembly Election Survey [1999], Welsh Election Study [2001], Welsh Life and Times Studies [2003, 2007]) have asked respondents to state the extent to which the National Assembly has made an impact on their daily lives. In their answers, the majority declare that the National Assembly has not made much of a difference in areas such as healthcare, education and economic standard of living.

On the basis of these public assessments of policy delivery, it may be tempting to conclude that the National Assembly does not enjoy much output legitimacy. However, a different picture is painted when we look at more general attitudes to devolution as a model for governing Wales. Respondents in the same public opinion surveys were also asked to state which level of government they believe should have most influence over Welsh politics. The results are shown in Figure 8.6. A growing proportion believe the National Assembly to be the level of government that should have most influence over Welsh politics; this increases from 56.2 per cent in 2001 to 74.3 per cent in 2007. This is especially significant if you recall that, in the devolution referendum held in 1997, only half of those that voted supported the creation of a National Assembly for Wales.

Figure 8.6
Which level of
government should
have most influence
over Welsh politics?
(Source: adapted from
opinion-poll results
[details on p.261])

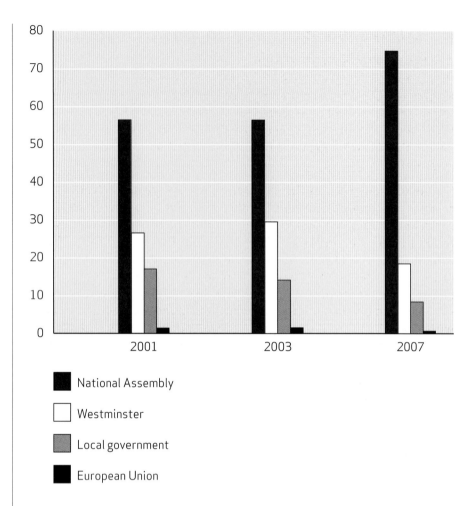

National Assembly

Westminster

Local government

European Union

These findings suggest that, even though the people of Wales feel that
there is more scope for the National Assembly to make an impact on
their everyday lives through its policies, there is nevertheless a general
acceptance that devolution has improved the way in which Wales is
governed. Devolution thus enjoys a substantial degree of legitimacy
because it represents a system of political representation that is more
attuned to the political preferences of Welsh voters.

Summary

■ Although devolution has led to policy divergence between Wales and
the rest of the United Kingdom, these policies have been perceived to
have led to very limited improvements in areas such as health,
education and standards of living.

■ Devolution as a system of governance, in contrast, enjoys increasing
levels of support among Welsh voters.

6   Conclusion

Any legitimate system of political representation should try to ensure that the voices of all citizens – regardless of their age, skin colour, gender, sexual preferences or language – are heard equally, and are listened to by elected representatives that take political decisions on their behalf. A legitimate system of political representation should also be one that leads to good decisions with desirable effects on a political community.

But, as you have seen in this chapter, achieving good political representation can be extremely difficult. In Wales, concerns about the exclusion of certain voices from the political process led to demands for devolution in the 1960s and 1970s, and again by the mid 1990s. Such demands were also based on the perception that the needs and interests of the Welsh people were largely being overlooked by successive London-based governments. In contrast, New Labour's devolution plans were justified on the grounds that they would replace political exclusion with a new inclusive form of politics, where previously marginalised individuals and groups would be given new opportunities to participate in, and inform, the political process in Wales. The creation of the National Assembly for Wales in 1999 provided the framework for creating such an inclusive politics, and for establishing a system of good governance.

Sections 3 and 4 of this chapter examined to what extent devolution has been successful in meeting this goal. On the one hand, positive action by Welsh political parties means that Wales is a world leader in terms of the representation of women. The National Assembly has also taken its commitment to 'equality of opportunity' seriously and has created new structures to make it easier for civil society organisations to feed into debates on policy and legislation. Civil society organisations have responded to these new opportunities by developing strategies for influencing the National Assembly's government and elected members.

On the other hand, less has been done to ensure that other minority groups are represented within the National Assembly, and a partially PR electoral system has not resulted in a broader spectrum of political groups being elected. In this respect, devolution has fallen far short of creating a system of descriptive representation. The involvement of civil society in post-devolution policy making has also been unequal; less-well-resourced groups have found it harder to be effective policy lobbyists, while Welsh policy makers have also been more ready to listen to some groups than to others. The policy-making process in Wales also remains highly complex.

Section 5 examined the legitimacy of the devolution settlement from the perspective of output legitimacy. Here again we see a mixed picture emerging. In spite of the fact that policy making in Wales has differed in significant ways from other parts of the UK as a result of decisions taken by the National Assembly, there is a widespread perception that these policies have not made a major impact on the economy and society in Wales. At the same time as Welsh voters remain unimpressed with what the National Assembly does, they nevertheless support devolution as a better system of governance for Wales.

Some might conclude from these observations that devolution has not resulted in a better system of political representation in Wales. They could argue, in support of this position, that the National Assembly has fallen short of creating a truly inclusive politics and of improving the economic and social well-being of Welsh voters. My own conclusions would be less negative. Like devolution, the task of ensuring a better and more legitimate system of political representation is a process not an event. Important steps have already been taken to broaden and deepen participation in the democratic process in Wales, while devolution has also come to be widely accepted as the appropriate political expression of how people in Wales wish to be governed. There is still work to be done to further enhance the inclusiveness and impact of the National Assembly's 'made in Wales' policies. But devolution has set Wales on the right path towards achieving a more legitimate system of political representation.

References

All Wales Convention (2009) *Report*, www.allwalesconvention.org (Accessed 18 November 2009).

AWEMA (2003) Evidence to the Richard Commission, 11 April 2003 (Accessed 13 January 2010) www.richardcommission.gov.uk/content/template.asp?ID=/content/evidence/written/awema/index.asp (Accessed 17 December 2009).

Betts, S. and Chaney, P. (2004) 'Inclusive and participatory governance? The view from the grass roots of women's organisations in Wales', *Wales Journal of Law and Policy*, vol. 3, no. 2, pp. 173–87.

Betts, S., Borland, J. and Chaney, P. (2001) 'Inclusive government for excluded groups: women and disabled people' in Chaney, P., Hall, T. and Pithouse, A. (eds) *New Governance – New Democracy? Post-devolution Wales*, Cardiff, University of Wales Press.

Bogdanor, V. (1999) *Devolution in the United Kingdom*, Oxford, Oxford University Press.

Bradbury, J. and Matheron, M. (2009) 'The view from the voluntary sector', presentation made to the conference The New National Assembly for Wales: Building on Experience, Llandudno, 13 July 2009, www.tomorrow-wales.co.uk/conference (Accessed 1 October 2009).

Chaney, P. (2006) 'Critical mass, deliberation and the substantive representation of women: Evidence from the UK's devolution programme', *Political Studies*, vol. 54, no. 4, pp. 671–91.

Chaney, P. and Fevre, R. (2001) 'Ron Davies and the cult of "inclusiveness": devolution and participation in Wales', *Contemporary Wales*, vol. 14, pp. 21–49.

Davies, R. (1999) *Devolution: a process Not an Event*, Cardiff, Institute for Welsh Affairs.

Day, G. (2006) 'Chasing the dragon? The ambiguities of civil society in Wales', *Critical Social Policy*, vol. 26, no. 3, pp. 642–55.

Evans, G. and Trystan, D. (1999) 'Why was 1997 different?' in Taylor, B. and Thompson, K. (eds) *Scotland and Wales: Nations Again?*, Cardiff, University of Wales Press.

Heywood, A. (2000) *Key Concepts in Politics*, London, Palgrave Macmillan.

Jones, S., Charles, N. and Davies, C.A. (2009) 'Transforming masculinist political cultures? Doing politics in new political institutions', *Sociological Research Online*, 14, pp. 2/3.

Judge, D. (1999) *Representation: Theory and Practice in Britain*, London, Routledge.

Morgan, K. and Mungham, G. (2000) *Redesigning Democracy: the Making of the Welsh Assembly*, Bridgend, Seren.

Norris, P. and Lovenduski, J. (1995) *Political Recruitment*, Cambridge, Cambridge University Press.

Royles, E. (2007) *Revitalising Democracy? Devolution and Civil Society in Wales*, Cardiff, University of Wales Press.

Russell, M., Mackay, F. and McAllister, L. (2002) 'Women's representation in the Scottish Parliament and National Assembly for Wales: Party dynamics for achieving critical mass', *The Journal of Legislative Studies*, vol. 8, no. 2, pp. 49–76.

Scully, R. and Elias, A. (2008) 'The 2007 Welsh Assembly election', *Regional and Federal Studies*, vol. 18, no. 1, pp. 103–9.

Thrasher, M. and Rallings, C. (2007) *British Electoral Facts 1832–2006*, Aldershot, Ashgate.

Welsh Office (1998) *Llais Dros Gymru – A Voice for Wales*, Cardiff, Welsh Office.

Williams, C. (2004) 'Passions and pathologies in the politics of minority ethnic participation in governance', *Wales Journal of Law and Policy*, vol. 3, no. 2, pp. 157–72.

Wyn Jones, R. and Scully, R. (2004) 'Minor tremor but several casualties: the 2003 Welsh election', *British Elections and Parties Review*, vol. 14, pp. 191–207.

Further reading

Bogdanor, V. (1999) *Devolution in the United Kingdom*, Oxford University Press, Oxford, provides an excellent historical account of devolution debates in the United Kingdom. It also considers Welsh devolution as part of a broader programme of constitutional change.

For an analysis and explanation of changes in party politics in post-devolution Wales, especially the decline of the once dominant Labour Party, see Wyn Jones, R. and Scully, R. 'The end of one-partyism? Party politics in Wales in the second decade of devolution', *Contemporary Wales*, vol. 21, pp. 207–17.

The best study of how devolution has impacted on civil society in Wales, drawing on detailed case studies of different civil society organisations, is Royles, E. (2007) *Revitalising Democracy? Devolution and Civil Society in Wales*, University of Wales Press, Cardiff.

Chapter 9
Cultural representation

Steve Blandford

Contents

1 Introduction – the idea of 'imagining' a nation

In this chapter we examine some of the important ways that Wales has been represented or portrayed, in museums, in the theatre, in cinema and on television, in recent times. We look at the impact that this has had on the life of the country and the way that Wales is 'imagined', both within and outside Wales.

The aims of this chapter are to:

- discuss some of the significant ways in which representations of Wales are constructed

- consider the idea that for most of us our national identity is felt through the ordinary things in life, 'shared cultural practices' – such as the food we eat or the television that we watch

- discuss three of the significant cultural forms that have been influential in the ways that they have represented Wales to the world and to the people of Wales themselves: theatre and performance, cinema and television drama

- draw some of these ideas together by considering the overall importance of representation to Welsh society and the different ways that representations of Wales have circulated and gained currency, particularly in the period since devolution.

Representation is the construction, commonly through words and images, of one particular view of an aspect of reality.

Imagined community is the idea that a community or nation is best understood as constructed through ideas rather than defined by physical and geographical boundaries.

As a starting point, one way of thinking about the **representation** of any nation is through the idea of 'imagining' a nation into being, a notion that you came across in Chapter 1. Benedict Anderson's **Imagined Communities** (1983) is a book that has played a key role in efforts to explain the idea of 'nationalism' in general and the role of culture in making a nation in particular. Anderson's ideas are of central importance to the way that we look at the representation of Wales in this chapter.

This idea of 'imagining' a community is of particular interest for people in places where the nation or state is either new or, as with devolution, is experiencing substantial transformation in its significance. Under these circumstances the 'idea' of a nation has existed for a long while and has shaped the lives of those that live there in profound ways, but now there are new possibilities for national expression.

Activity 9.1

List the specific 'shared cultural practices' that are most important to you when you consider the nation to which you belong.

If you can, ask someone else to construct such a list and try to consider why their list might include different things from your list.

Comment

This personal consideration of what, for you and those known to you, are the small markers of the way that you experience national identity will be of help to you as we consider representations of identity in the rest of the chapter.

Arising from this idea that communities or nations such as Wales are, at least partly, 'imagined' by the people who live in them are a number of other ideas that are relevant to us here:

- If communities are imagined, they can change and they inevitably will change over time as people invent new ways of thinking about themselves and the way that they live.

- Some ideas about the nations and communities in which we live circulate more widely than others (for instance, through television and other forms of mass media). These ideas then come to dominate the way that those both inside and outside the community think of the nation or community.

- The question of who controls the images of and ideas about a community or nation that circulate widely is therefore very important because of how these impact on the way that people see themselves and how they are viewed by the wider world.

We will be looking at the above ideas in various ways throughout this chapter.

2 Banal nationalism

The term '**banal nationalism**' was coined by the social psychologist Michael Billig, in a book with exactly this title (Billig, 2005). Billig was interested in drawing attention to the way that nationalism does not just exist through openly political acts and ideas, but through many of the 'banal', seemingly insignificant acts and conversations of our everyday lives. Later you will read how one cultural commentator lists some slightly old-fashioned and clichéd ideas of 'banal Welshness', but emphasises that on the other hand some other very ordinary, everyday ways of identifying as Welsh endure and remain important to people.

Banal nationalism is the idea that, for most people, nationalism is mainly something that they experience in small ways on a day-to-day basis, often unconsciously.

These might include, for some people at least, eating particular kinds of food that thrive in Wales, such as lamb, or taking part in the *eisteddfodau* that are common in schools in Wales.

In 1997, as the idea of a devolved Wales once again became a possibility after the election of a Labour government, the *Observer* asked Welsh playwright Ed Thomas to comment on the possibilities that this might bring to the people of Wales. Thomas's reply has much to do with both the idea of 'banal nationalism' and 'imagining' a nation:

> Old Wales is dead. The Wales of stereotype, leeks, daffodils, look-you-now boyo rugby supporters singing Max Boyce songs in three-part harmony while phoning mam to tell her they'll be home for tea and Welsh cakes has gone ... So where does it leave us? Free to make up, re-invent, redefine our own versions of Wales, all three million definitions if necessary ...
>
> (Quoted in Roms, 1998, p. 186)

Whether you agree with Thomas's 'hit list' of things that have defined an 'old' Wales or not, you can see that he has understood the way that outsiders have traditionally come to form ideas about what Wales is like. This generally doesn't involve a detailed knowledge of Welsh history and politics, but a sense of what people have seen or heard (often through second-hand images) of Welsh life and culture.

So Michael Billig's idea of 'banal nationalism' is very useful in trying to think about the ways that Wales is represented, both to its own inhabitants and to people outside the country. One of the literal ways in which 'banality' is used and collected is in museums and when a museum defines itself as 'national', as does the National Museum of Wales, it becomes particularly important to examine what image of the nation the museum's collection presents to us.

2.1 The National Museum of Wales

The establishment of a National Museum of Wales in 1907 was 'originally intended to show that Wales was a fully-fledged nation with the requisite institutions: a national museum, a national library and a national university' (Mason, 2004, p. 19). What has been debated ever since is the kind of Wales that the National Museum represents (see Mason, 2004, 2007).

Among the many debates, the most prevalent concern the alleged emphasis on the rural and agrarian at the National History Museum in St Fagans near Cardiff and its lack of emphasis on the idea of struggle and conflict at the heart of Welsh urban life (Mason, 2004, p. 21). One example is that it would be possible to emphasise more strongly the painful struggles associated with the decline of traditional Welsh industry. This might include a greater presence for major historical events such the 1984 miners' strike, which had a particularly powerful impact on south Wales in a variety of ways.

We will not attempt here to discuss this line of criticism in very much depth, but what it draws attention to is that there are a number of ways of collecting, presenting and interpreting the ordinary details of Welsh life.

For Mason (2004, p. 29), the National History Museum (in particular, though similar arguments can be made about all the national museums and galleries of Wales) 'represents a meeting point for competing ideas about national identities and that this is a result of the ways in which the museum's own working definition of what counts as "Welsh" has, and will continue to, shift'.

Finally, you might note another trend that has become prevalent in museums internationally and which the National Museum of Wales has also subscribed to – that museums should encourage their visitors to be self-reflexive about their experience of history and what it is that any museum collection offers to them. On the National Museum's website, the headline 'Main message' reads:

> There is no such thing as one Welsh identity – there are many. The exhibition will explore how our sense of who we are, and where we belong, is shaped by language, beliefs, family ties and a sense of nationhood. It will show that culture and traditions are constantly evolving, and will question what the future holds for a nation like Wales in a global age.
>
> (National Museum of Wales, 2009)

You can see, then, how, to some extent at least, the National Museum has evolved from being part of an assertion that a nation exists at all to one that is trying to reflect the more contemporary notion of a nation encompassing almost endless possible identities.

Activity 9.2

Visit the website of the National Museum of Wales (or go to one of the sites in person if you can). Make a list of the most prominent visual images that have been selected to represent the museum and its role in its publicity.

This consideration of the artefacts and images that are chosen by the National Museum to represent Wales will help you reflect on the idea that representations of any nation are always selective, even if they attempt to be genuinely comprehensive.

2.2 Institutions and representation

National institutions are organisations such as museums, theatres and libraries set up with the purpose of expressing and contributing to national identities.

You have seen the role one key **national institution**, the National Museum of Wales, plays in the way that the idea of Wales is thought about both within Wales and in other countries.

There are a number of other institutions that play a similar role in representing different facets of Wales and in so doing help in the continual process of defining and redefining what Wales is and can be in the future. At this point, though, it is worth remembering that the idea of the 'imagined' nation and the quotations above suggest strongly that there is no such thing as one single national identity and that there is a constant process of national reimagining.

2.3 Arts Council of Wales

The Arts Council is hugely important in its influence on the representation of Wales, because it controls which artists receive public funding across all the art forms for which it is responsible. Arts councils in the UK have always operated on what is known as the 'arm's-length principle', which is designed to ensure that governments cannot exercise direct control over the art forms that they subsidise through tax revenues (and indirectly through the proceeds of the National Lottery). The appropriate minister (in the case of Wales, the Assembly minister responsible for culture) is responsible for appointing the board and chair, who in turn appoint the officers who run the Arts Council on a day-to-day basis.

The arm's length principle has been the subject of much debate, not only in Wales but across the UK, since the formation of Arts Councils in the UK after the Second World War (Shade, 2004, pp. 83–125). In Wales, a radical challenge to this principle came in 2006 when the minority Labour administration asked the Assembly to consider taking direct control over Wales's largest arts organisations away from the Arts Council and putting it in the hands of the minister. This resulted in a fierce public debate over the principle of control over artistic expression and, in terms of our concerns, over who has any measure of 'control' over the way that Wales is represented by its artists. Extract 9.1 addresses the issues in this debate.

Extract 9.1

Arts funding row breaks out in Wales

Brian Logan

The government in Wales has suffered an embarrassing defeat in its attempt to take control of funding for the arts. Plans to bring the country's leading arts organisations – including Welsh National Opera and the BBC National Orchestra of Wales – under direct government jurisdiction were halted on Thursday, when the opposition parties used their majority of one to force them into consultation.

The vote was the culmination of a political storm – dubbed 'Artgate' – that has seen culture minister Alun Pugh attacked for sacking the popular chairman of the Arts Council of Wales, Geraint Talfan Davies, last December, and for seeking to erode the traditional 'arms length' principle of arts funding. Pugh claimed that the governments proposals – which would have relieved the Arts Council of responsibility for the WNO [Welsh National Opera], the BBC NOW [National Orchestra of Wales], Diversions dance company, Clwyd Theatr Cymru, the Welsh National Theatre and the literature body Academi – were necessary to widen access to the arts.

The Arts Council of Wales welcomed the vote, which promises a comprehensive review of the arts quango's role. 'We hope that both the process and its outcome will ... reconcile the needs of democratic accountability and the value of the arm's length principle in a way that will have the support of the arts sector and the wider public,' it said in a statement.

The 'Artgate' row in Wales follows a recent announcement that the Scottish executive is to take direct control of its national arts companies. Both are being watched with interest in England, where a recent Department of Culture, Media and Sport review of the Arts Council admitted to tensions between ACE and the government. ACE chairman Christopher Frayling said in his 2005 annual review: 'We are monitoring developments in Wales and Scotland with some concern ... Lines must be drawn between elected politicians or civil servants and an independent funding body.'

But the DCMS insists that the Arts Council and the 'arm's length' principle are safe for the foreseeable future. A spokesperson said: 'We have no plans to change the fundamental structures of funding in England at the moment.'

Source: *The Guardian*, 7 February 2006

2.4 BBC Cymru Wales

Television programmes have been produced in Wales by the BBC since the 1950s, but in 1964 BBC Cymru Wales came into being as a production centre. At the time of writing in 2010, it is the largest production centre outside London, partly because of the volume of programmes in Welsh it produces for S4C.

The presence of a distinct BBC set-up in Wales is in itself one way that Wales is able to represent itself as a separate nation, but BBC Cymru Wales reinforces this in a number of ways. One of the most distinctive of these is through the so-called 'idents' or graphics that accompany both the announcement of the next programme and the advertising of programmes in the future. The way that the distinctive identity of BBC Wales is reinforced varies from a simple logo bearing the name 'BBC Cymru Wales' to the use of elaborate and often humorous markers of Welsh identity.

Frequently, the idents relate to sport. One reason may be that BBC Wales offers a different service to viewers in Wales through its coverage of Welsh national sporting events. Another reason may be that sport, as we saw in Chapter 1, plays a powerful role in the formation of many people's national identity (supporting a team, wearing colours and so on).

Since the 1990s BBC Cymru Wales has based a number of its best-known idents around the broadcasting of rugby or soccer internationals involving Wales. These have become, in some cases, almost as memorable as the programmes themselves and frequently involve a degree of tongue-in-cheek nationalism, sometimes at the expense of another nation or nations.

Figure 9.1
BBC One Wales ident broadcast following the Welsh international soccer team's defeat of Germany in May 2002

One example followed the defeat of the powerful German soccer team, an occurrence so rare that it even inspired the mildly transgressive use of the BBC One Wales logo. Over a picture of jubilant fans celebrating there were two logos: one read BBC ONE Wales, in red as usual; the other was in the German black and white and read BBC NIL Germany (see Figure 9.1).

On the whole, this 'branding' is done lightly and with a great deal of humour and charm, but it is worth pointing out that there are clear choices involved in this act of representation and the emphasis on sport will clearly exclude a number of people. There are those who would see, for example, that an overemphasis on sport is part of a representational past that tends to be male-orientated – as you read in Chapter 1 – although in fairness it must be said that Nicole Cooke's cycling gold medal at the 2008 Beijing summer Olympic Games was also celebrated through the creation of a special ident reading 'Nicole Gold Wales'.

Summary

- This section has examined the idea of how small or 'banal' things in our lives are some of the most important markers of our national identity.

- It has also considered some of the key organisations that play a major part in 'official' representations of Wales through, for example, the exhibits that appear in museums or the art forms that receive some form of public subsidy.

In the next section we will look at theatre and performance produced in Wales and at how key artists and companies have produced work that represents Wales in particular ways.

3   Theatre, performance and Wales

In order to examine some of the issues outlined above in a little depth we are now going to look at the first of three important areas in which we can find the idea of Wales represented in ways that are often contradictory and which are rapidly evolving.

The idea of imagined communities is perhaps of particular relevance to how theatre makers have approached the idea of national identity. Read the piece below, taken from *Staging the UK* (Harvie, 2005). As you do so, consider how far you feel convinced by the idea that national identities are 'creatively produced or staged'.

We will be considering this in a number of ways in the following section.

Extract 9.2

This book is about how performance has produced national and related identities in the United Kingdom, focusing on the period from the 1980s into the twenty-first century. It is concerned with national identities because their long-standing profile as some of the most pervasively felt and socially potent forms of identity has been both accentuated and fundamentally disturbed by radical changes to national configurations in the UK's recent history. In 1997 ... Tony Blair's New Labour government was elected proclaiming the advent of a 'New Britain'. The 1999 acts of devolution redistributed national power throughout the UK by restoring a parliament in Scotland and launching assemblies in Wales and Northern Ireland. At the end of June 1997, near-final vestiges of the UK's empire were dismantled as Hong Kong was handed over to China. Despite this enactment of the 'end of empire', ongoing 'race'-related violence within the UK has indicated the resilience of imperial power relations: the mishandled murder inquiry of black South London teenager Stephen Lawrence in 1993 led to a diagnosis of 'institutional racism' in the Metropolitan Police; 'race'-related rioting occurred in Oldham, Burnley, and Bradford in the North of England in summer 2001; and racist – as distinct from sectarian – violence was reported in Belfast in late 2003. In Benedict Anderson's still-resonant formulation from 1983: 'nation-ness is the most universally legitimate value in the political life of our time' [Anderson, p.3].

This book focuses on national identities because of their extreme topicality but also – more importantly – because they produce and distribute power, power that can be both oppressive and enabling. As the examples above indicate, national identity can be oppressive when for example, it is seen as homogeneous, superior, and/or unchanging and it acts to exchange or oppress minorities or perceived 'others' or to restrict cultural change. It can be enabling when it helps develop community identities. Often it is simultaneously, in different degrees, both oppressive and enabling.

In order to scrutinise these national identities and their configurations of power this book examines contemporary UK performance practices. A founding principle here is that national identities are neither biologically nor territorially given; rather they are creatively produced or stages. I am not arguing, wilfully, that political acts, legislation and material conditions of geography have no influence on national identities. But it is necessary in this context to distinguish between a state and a nation. A state is a political authority that asserts power, but a nation is a *sense* that people share a culture, a culture that may or may not be conterminous with the state's borders. As Benedict Anderson proposed most influentially in his book *Imagined Communities* ... a person's sense of his or her nation is largely on participation in shared cultural practices such as reading newspapers, listening to radio, watching television, and reading novels. Few people may ever read the legislation that constitutes them as citizens of a particular state, and probably none will ever traverse the state's whole topography and meet all their fellow nationals. But most people will have a sense of a shared national identity through shared cultural practices that are both everyday or 'banal' as Michael Billig puts it – eating food, dressing, talking, listening to the radio, watching television – and 'special' – celebrating holidays, participating in festivals and major sports events, and so on. Through their cultural activities people will imagine their communities. And one of the ways they will do so is through performance.

Anderson's premise has at least three very important implications for understanding the functioning of national identities and attending to their effects of power. First, if national identities are creatively imagined, that means they are dynamic. In this understanding, 'the UK' is not a stable, universally and timelessly agreed entity, rather, it and its meanings are constantly conceived in many different ways. Second, if national identities are dynamic, they can be changed, and such change might contribute to social improvement – or decline. Xenophobic jingoism, for example, may exist in any nation, but its purchase will never be comprehensive or entirely secure. It might be destabilised – or it might be reinforced. It is cultural practice that will enact both outcomes ... Third, if national identities are creatively imagined by numerous people and not just by legislators, authority is necessarily dispersed from the formal centres of state power. Instead of seeing national identity as strictly a tool of state control, a means for the state to define and manage its citizens, Anderson's premise suggests that national identity can be a tool of dispersed, democratic empowerment. By giving 'power to the people', this may have some very positive effects. But it may also mask the risk that the power is more apparent than real. Many argue this is the case in the dominant neo-liberal market economy, where a sense of proliferating consumer choice masks the possibility that there is no meaningful choice... As these examples indicate, Anderson's premise likewise has important implications for social criticism and analysis: it makes examining cultural practise a political imperative. It locates the lived, social effects of national change not just in the majority of nations political institutions – the legislation of devolution and European unification, for example – but in the various cultural activities and structures people engage in, from reading newspapers, to shopping, to making or watching theatre performance. Anderson's premise makes it necessary to examine cultural practices to explore what identities and power dynamics they produce, and not just through their narratives, but also in their forms and institutional structures.

Reference

Anderson, B. (1983) Imagined Communities: Reflections on the Origin and Spread of Nationalism, London, Verso.

Source: Harvie, 2005, pp. 1–4

We can see the justification for this chapter in Harvie's final sentence. The examination of representation is one important way in which we come to understand nations and the way that citizens feel the importance of national identity and structures of power in their daily lives.

3.1 National theatres

You looked briefly above at the way that 'institutions' play a role in how a nation is represented. Those institutions with the term 'national' in the title carry a particular burden in the implicit claims they make for representing a country, as in the case of the National Museum of Wales.

In the case of theatre there exists, in 2009, a fascinating situation in that Wales possesses two national theatres. These are entirely separate organisations, one operating in the Welsh language, the other in English. *Theatr Genedlaethol Cymru*, the Welsh-language company, was launched in 2003 and National Theatre Wales, the English-language company, in 2008. Both receive funding from the Arts Council of Wales.

The founding of a national theatre is one of the many ways that nations have sought to express their national identity, particularly at moments in history when the identity of a particular nation is under threat or open to question.

The idea of a Welsh National Theatre has been around for most of the twentieth century and there have been a number of previous attempts to establish one, some of which were at least partially successful. What is distinctive about the situation in the decade since devolution is that, first, there is an Assembly government with the power to channel money through the Arts Council to fund the theatres, and, second, the decision was made to create separate theatres in each of the nation's two principal languages.

The structure of both national theatre organisations in Wales is perhaps also significant for the role they have in the representation of Wales. Just like the National Theatre of Scotland, neither organisation has a grand public building as a base – there is no actual 'national theatre' in the physical sense (as there is in the case of the Royal National Theatre in London). Instead, the work of both organisations is designed to take place around Wales, sometimes in existing theatres, sometimes in unconventional spaces. There is a willingness to embrace the idea of 'national' as something for and by all the people of Wales, rather than a symbol based in a capital city.

Instead of national theatres with grand statements to make about the definition of Wales, then, we are perhaps seeing the birth of a kind of national institution that is more interested in what some have called a national 'conversation'. This would be a theatre of questions, of plurality and of wide participation.

3.2 Theatre places and spaces

In common with most other art forms, theatre in Wales since the 1980s has often been preoccupied with finding a distinctive 'voice' that defines it as 'Welsh'. Just before devolution in 1996 the theatre critic David Adams wrote about the search for 'a new, vibrant and distinctive theatre tradition in Wales, one which is relevant and responsive to the perceptions, experience, aspirations and concerns of a minority culture and a small nation and which is more than just a pale reflection of English theatre convention'(Adams, 1996, p. 5).

As well as emphasising the desire in Welsh theatre for traditions that define Wales, Adams touches on one of the key issues about the culture of Wales, namely the problem of defining traditions in relation to England. This tendency to see a national identity in relation to that of a powerful neighbour is part of what some have seen as Wales's **postcolonial** identity (Aaron and Williams, 2005). Though this is very much open to debate, it is an idea that sees Wales's contemporary attempts to define itself as a nation in a similar light to the struggles for national self-definition in countries that are much more traditionally seen as former 'colonies' of the British empire in Africa and Asia.

> **Postcolonial** is a wide-ranging term that refers to how societies work in the period following the gaining of independence from another, more powerful, state or empire.

These are complex arguments, which we will not go very far into here, but it is worth noting that one of the key questions for makers not only of Welsh theatre but of all Welsh art that tries to engage with ideas of the nation is how far artists in Wales examine the nation in relation to its powerful neighbour, and how far that relationship can be seen as one between 'former colony' and 'colonised'.

Activity 9.3

Consider for a moment some of the countries across the globe that are former British colonies. Think about the range of different ways that you view such countries and the current relationship that they have with Britain. (The feature film *Slumdog Millionaire* is one very high-profile example that might start you thinking in this way.)

Does the fact that the former 'empire' was 'British', not 'English', make a difference to the way that people in Wales might see themselves today?

Comparing Wales to former British colonies is a potentially important way in which we might define contemporary Wales. In the context of theatre we will briefly examine the idea that Wales is distinctive because of the actual forms that performance takes in the country.

> Wales is a performative culture and increasingly its perception is as such, as the land of song, sport and language/words – in recitation, sporting prowess, choral singing, poetry, preaching, oratory, cerdd dant, rock concerts, acting, singing, painting, creating installations, erecting public art, making theatre and in all manner of creative public assemblies.
>
> (Sherlock, 2004, p. 152)

According to this line of argument, the distinctive representation of Wales through performance is less about the kinds of things that writers or directors have to say in the theatre and more about a vision of what theatre and performance are about. In this case, less about grand buildings and plays about the state of the nation and more about a performance tradition that produces work in a whole variety of places and in spaces that are often unconventional.

3.3 Theatre voices

Despite the argument above, it is also possible to find strong examples of theatre made in Wales that has sought to engage quite directly with the idea of nationhood. One of the most prominent in the 1980s and 1990s was the company *Brith Gof*, though the company never, as Harvie (2005, p. 50) points out, made any attempt to suggest one single idea of a 'true' Welsh identity to which people should aspire.

Instead, *Brith Gof* created very large-scale works of public performance that often used Welsh history to reflect on the present identity in Wales. One of the best-known of these, *Gododdin* (1988–90), was first produced in an enormous, disused Cardiff car factory. It used the sixth-century poem *Y Gododdin*, which tells the story of an epic battle in which a small army of 'Celts' defeats a much larger Anglo-Saxon force. The mix of a poem of anti-imperial oppression and the closed car factory resulted in a powerful take on contemporary Welsh identity while at the same time bringing to life a rich cultural past.

Though Wales still has a relatively small body of work written for the theatre, there is now in print a number of collections by substantial writers who have contributed to a sense of the nation even if they are not writing plays that are overtly about national identity and redefinition. These include Ed Thomas, Ian Rowlands and Gary Owen, all of whom have had work produced and published across the world and whose work is widely acknowledged as being part of any 'national conversation' (see Thomas, 1999; Owen, 2005; Rowlands, 1998).

There are also companies and individuals as varied as Eddie Ladd, Hijinx Theatre, Volcano Theatre and Arad Goch that produce work that consistently suggests a Welsh theatrical identity that is varied, inventive and full of possibilities. While Eddie Ladd works with the aid of a grant from the National Endowment for Science, Technology and the Arts to explore the possibilities of digital media for theatre, Hijinx continues its work to provide accessible theatre for small communities, Volcano continues to enhance its international reputation for bold, physical theatre from its base in Swansea, and Arad Goch organises 'Opening Door', an international festival of theatre for young people 'from Wales and beyond'.

While not all of the work by these small companies is directly about Wales and its national identity, collectively they add up to a theatre scene in Wales that is about lively experimentation. This in turn contributes to the way that the world is able to see Wales and the possibilities that exist here. To take just one example of a show that has toured all over the world, Eddie Ladd's production of *Scarface* (2000–) is a highly original homage to the American actor Al Pacino. While the play has no obvious connection with Wales, it implicitly raises questions about identity in a solo performance by a woman that imitates a very macho role. The play is highly physical, performed in a mixture of Welsh and English, and has contributed to a sense of Welsh culture as being one of originality and possibility.

Summary

Theatre in Wales can therefore be understood to be very much engaged with the idea of an evolving sense of Wales. This engagement takes many forms, but the key ones in this context are:

- the formation of national theatres in both languages
- the search for distinctive forms of theatre in a 'postcolonial' Wales

■ the use of performance not to assert a single fixed Welsh identity, but to open up new possibilities and ways of being Welsh.

The next section looks at how cinema approaches similar questions, but in ways that are inevitably different both because of the formal differences between cinema and theatre, and also because of the ways that the two art forms are funded and consumed.

4 Cinema and Wales

For many people the way that Wales has been represented in cinema will always be linked in some way to the 1941 Hollywood adaptation of Richard Llewellyn's novel *How Green Was My Valley* (dir. John Ford), which won the Academy Award for best picture. For Kate Woodward, 'Ford's film spawned a million clichés about terraced streets and black faced miners, singing on their way home from the pit … Ford's Welsh valley, created in the San Fernando Valley in Malibu, was sanitized of all traces of dust and dirt, and Hollywoodized beyond all recognition' (Woodward, 2006, pp. 54–5).

However, during the 1990s and in the period since devolution there have been powerful attempts in both the Welsh and English languages to create a contemporary cinema culture in Wales that avoided such clichés and attempted to engage with a more diverse sense of the nation and its evolving place in the world.

4.1 Wales at the Oscars

In terms of Welsh-language cinema, it is perhaps not well known that two films made in the Welsh language were nominated for Academy Awards in the Best Foreign Language category in the 1990s. These were *Hedd Wyn* (dir. Paul Turner, 1992) and *Solomon and Gaenor* (dir. Paul Morrison, 1998). In some ways the very fact of the two films receiving the global attention that comes with 'Oscar' nomination is a significant moment for the representation of Wales internationally. It not only signalled the existence of a significant and distinct film-making culture in Wales, but also drew attention to the Welsh language as not only alive but thriving, and being used in contemporary art forms.

Both films also used language and its divisive potential as part of their subject. In *Hedd Wyn*, the central character, the Welsh poet Elis Evans (Huw Garmon), is conscripted into the British army to fight in the First World War. During his basic training, Evans's use of his native Welsh is the subject of scorn and abuse by English officers and NCOs, something which the film turns to powerful ironic effect as the young poet dies in the service of the British empire at Pilken Ridge in Belgium in 1918. *Solomon and Gaenor*'s use of language is even more complex, especially as two versions were made 'back-to-back' – one predominantly in English, one mainly in Welsh, though the complexity is further compounded by the use of Yiddish in both versions as the film is set at the times of anti-Semitic-related civil disturbance in the south Wales Valleys. The film has resonance not only for a bilingual Wales, but for a UK that struggles with the many different ethnicities and languages that make up its population.

It is possible to argue, then, that both these films made contributions to how both Wales and the Welsh language were seen internationally, though their relatively limited distribution in the UK restricted this effect.

4.2 A Welsh film revival?

For English language cinema in Wales, 1997 looked as though it would be a watershed year. It saw the release of three fairly high-profile feature films by young directors and seemed to offer the promise of a developing film culture that would steadily increase the presence of Wales on international cinema screens. *House of America* (dir. Marc Evans), *Twin Town* (dir. Kevin Allen) and *Darklands* (dir. Julian Richards) were all very different in tone and subject matter, but they all sought to 'reread' some of the traditional ways of seeing Wales exemplified by the tradition of *How Green Was My Valley*.

Of the three, *Twin Town* (Figure 9.2) reached the largest commercial audience and its brand of irreverent humour has ensured that its subsequent DVD sales remain strong. However, its view of Wales and the Welsh did not find universal approval, and its online trailer gives a sense of its approach to any traditional idea of Welsh culture:

> Rugby. Tom Jones. Male Voice Choirs. Shirley Bassey.
>
> Llanfairpwllgyngyllgogerychwyrndrobwllllantisiliogogogoch.
>
> Snowdonia. Prince of Wales. Anthony Hopkins. Daffodils. Sheep.
>
> Sheep Lovers. Coal. Slate quarries. The Blaenau Ffestiniog Dinkey-Doo Miniature Railway. Now if that's your idea of thousands of years of Welsh culture, you can't blame us for trying to liven the place up a little can you?
>
> (*Twin Town*, 1997)

It is fairly obvious, then, that the film takes an irreverent look at the traditional elements of Welsh representation, something that attracted the displeasure of a range of people, including clergymen and the Wales Tourist Board (Morris, 1998, p. 27).

To set against these criticisms, others argued that *Twin Town* marked a new cultural maturity as Wales gained the confidence to laugh more freely at the parodying of its own cultural icons in a similar vein to the representation of the Irish in the television drama series *Father Ted* (Perrins, 2000).

Figure 9.2
Poster for *Twin Town* (dir. Kevin Allen, 1997)

House of America was a much more subtle approach to a changing sense of Welsh identity. Adapted by Ed Thomas from his stage play of the same name, the film again used some of the staple clichés of the representation of Wales – family, mining community, matriarch – and subjected them to poetic scrutiny through the filter of the leading character's obsession with key aspects of American culture. Again, an older Wales is seen as passing away and a struggle to imagine a new one into being is taking place, this time a struggle that takes place against the backdrop of an all-pervasive American culture that surrounds us all.

The director of *House of America*, Marc Evans, said that 'In some ways *House of America* and *Twin Town* were not the first of a new generation of films but the last of the old' (Evans, 2002, pp. 290–1) in that they were still preoccupied with the stereotypes of an older Wales, even as they were undermining them. With this in mind, then, perhaps we can see a slighter later film, Justin Kerrigan's *Human Traffic* (1999), as the first Welsh feature film to offer a true break with the past and provide a new way to imagine being young and Welsh as we approached the millennium. This break with a traditional representational past was picked up in one of the film's early reviews:

> Just as *Trainspotting* makes a clean break with the traditional Scotland of tartanry and kailyard, of Scott and Barrie, so *Human Traffic* turns its back on the Wales of male voice choirs and the whimsical humour of *The Englishman Who Went Up a Hill But Came Down a Mountain* ... it seems more like an American picture than a British one ...
>
> (French, 1999)

Human Traffic is hardly preoccupied in any obvious way with representing national identity. It shows a group of young friends in dead-end jobs as they live for the weekends spent in the hedonistic club scene that characterised the late 1990s. The fact that it is set in Cardiff rather than London, Birmingham or Manchester seems to offer the idea that Wales is emerging from a preoccupation with an older essentialist identity and instead its young people can feel connected to a wider international culture.

In some ways the period at the end of the 1990s was a slightly false dawn in that the number of subsequent feature films to have emerged from Wales has not increased in the way that was once hoped. Nonetheless, there were important examples of films that did try to look again at life in Wales in ways that were a significant contribution to the way that the country saw itself in the context of its new political power. We will finish this section by looking at one of these because of the particular way in which this film sought to open up the question of Welsh identity.

4.3 *A Way of Life* and 'new' Welsh identities

A Way of Life is a rare example of a fictional narrative that scrutinises Welsh identity in relation to the nation's ethnic populations. Released in 2004, the film was made by Amma Asante, a woman raised in Streatham in south London by parents who were born in Ghana. Asante's connection to Wales came through her brother's marriage to a Welsh woman and their children, who, in Asante's own words, were 'half of everything you could possibly imagine' (Blandford, 2004, p. 15).

The complex ethnic and racial identities of her niece and nephew were part of Asante's motivation to make a film that is explicitly concerned with the interaction between ethnicity and national identity. Another part came from her initial sense of Wales, particularly Cardiff, as a place of greater racial harmony than the rest of the UK because of the length of its history of multiculturalism, only to be disabused of the fact as she got to know it better (Blandford, 2004).

The film's plot revolves around the murder of a man in a south Wales community by a group of teenagers, including a young single mother, Leanne (Stephanie Williams), who becomes the film's leading character. The murdered man is of Turkish origin and has lived in Wales for thirty years. The film is unflinching about the brutality of the murder and the casual racist attitudes on the part of the young people that contribute to it, but its daring is to have us also feel for the difficulty of the lives that the perpetrators lead.

This is frequently a painful film to watch and it represents those parts of south Wales still badly affected by deindustrialisation as very difficult places to grow up. On the other hand, it is a film that is brave enough to look at the origins of racism in an honest and unflinching way. That it is set in Wales, with financial support from the Lottery via the Arts Council of Wales, is arguably a positive signal of a healthy culture that is able to examine its problems from within rather then relying on outmoded myths to sustain itself.

Activity 9.4

Pause and consider how many times you have seen non-white characters on screen that are Welsh. Can you think of examples in other art forms, for example in literature?

One of the complex things about discussing the representation of any nation is the point at which the representation of, in this case, Wales meets the representation of another aspect of identity. The idea of being both black and Welsh is obviously perfectly normal, but it adds a dimension to the representation of Wales that is still somewhat neglected.

Now read this piece by Martin McLoone, who has often written about cinema in Ireland, but who here applies the same kind of thinking to all the Celtic countries. He suggests that cinema from Wales (and the other Celtic nations) is 'on the cutting edge of contemporary cultural debate about identity'. As you read Extract 9.3, consider how far you agree with this suggestion with regard to what you know about cinema from Wales.

Extract 9.3

Like *Divorcing Jack*, Kevin Allen's Swansea-set *Twin Town* (1997) elects to tackle stereotypes and cinematic clichés directly. As its already bizarre plot rushes towards a climax of melodramatic excess and bad taste, central icons and cultural markers of Welsh identity (rugby, community and male-voice choirs) are lampooned into absurdity. *Twin Town* – anarchic, populist, youth orientated – contrasts with the more meditatively inclined group of Welsh language films. At the centre of the films is the place of the Welsh language itself and indeed, the most impressive aspect of the Welsh language films in general has been the total confidence they demonstrate in the contemporary relevance of the ancient tongue.

In Endaf Emlyn's *Un Nos Ola' Lewad/One Full Moon* (1991) the relationship between the English and Welsh language is a factor in the crisis of identity that faces the films protagonist, an unnamed boy (Tudor Roberts). In the village school, the children speak English and are encouraged to associate English with access to power and influence – the Welsh speaking children are clearly seen as objects of exploitation and in the case of one young girl, of sexual exploitation as well. The boy is asked to read a passage of English by the school master and the local Anglican canon. He performs the task well enough in a halting, cautious manner but pronounces the word 'society' according to Welsh phonetics. This reduces his superiors to laughter. Society, the film suggests, just like community, culture and history, is recognised through the language that describes it.

It would be wrong though to see Welsh language cinema as an unthinking nationalist response to dominant English culture or one that collapses the complexities of identity into dubious essentialist categories. *Un Nos Ola' Lewad* is as critical of the oppressive aspects of Welshness as it is of English superiority and is especially scathing about the negative impact Welsh fundamentalist religion has had on women and the young. (In this it dovetails with a tendency in recent Irish cinema which similarly attacks the abuses of religion, especially as those were visited on the young and on women). In his next film, *Gadael Lenin/Leaving Lenin* (1994), Emlyn considerably lightens the mood. Here, he explores contemporary Welsh identity through the device of removing the Welsh characters from Wales itself to post-Soviet Russia. A group of Welsh speaking sixth formers go on an educational visit to St Petersburg, accompanied by their art teacher Eileen (Sharon Morgan) and the old style Welsh Communist husband Mostyn (Wyn Bowen Harries) the deputy headmaster Mervyn (Ifan Huw Dafydd) with whom Eileen had a weekend affair once before, who also travels hoping that as the marriage seems to be unravelling, the affair can be resuscitated. The mix-up on the train between Moscow and St Petersburg splits teachers from students and the film contrasts the two groups' adventures in parallel narratives. The dialogue is in Welsh, Russian and English and this is one aspect of the film's audacity and ambition.

Here the minority language, which has such a low profile internationally that the Academy doubted its very existence, is vying for public space with two of the great imperialist languages of the world, engaging at the same time with themes and issues of global as well as of local importance.

The foreign location adds an extra dimension to the underlying theme of Welsh identity and the film explores this to great effect through the sense of loss and disillusionment that Mostyn feels at the collapse of the Soviet Union. Perhaps the moist poignant theme of all, reflecting early 1990s concerns, is the confusion and dilemmas that face today's young people, whether the youth of St Petersburg adrift in a post-Soviet Russia or those struggling to adulthood in post-Thatcherite Wales. The film proposes a need for new beginnings – whether personal, political or artistic. The irony of the film's message is that at least Mostyn in his youth had political ideals that allowed him to imagine and work towards a new beginning.

This is a privilege, the film suggests, which today's young don't have and must work for.

In this way, the Welsh films resemble some aspects of recent Irish cinema. As the traditional belief systems wither away, religion, patriotism, political beliefs – the loss of something to believe in, especially the loss of political hope – is particularly debilitating.

This sense of loss is evident in Paul Morrison's *Solomon and Gaenor* (1998), which returns to the pre-World War One Wales of both *Hedd Wyn* (1992) and *The Englishman Who Went up a Hill But Came Down a Mountain*. This is a complex historical moment for Wales. At the beginning of the 20th century, it still carried its identity as an industrial force of nineteenth-century British expansion but was also about to assume a central role in the radical and progressive labour politics of the 20th century. Within this complex, the film plays out a Romeo and Juliet scenario – the Jewish Solomon hiding his identity behind an English facade to woo Gaenor from a fundamentalist Christian community. In the tragedy that unfolds, the film is again scathing about the impact the fundamentalist religion has on the lives of young people in particular (in this case, both orthodox Jewish as well as Protestant Christian).

But this is more than just a Welsh cry of 'a plague on both your houses'.

In identifying some aspects of the cinema from the Celtic fringes, we are identifying a cinema that has a double focus. These films are concerned to explode myths and move beyond the regimes of representation that have tended to romanticise and to marginalise the Celtic fringe. Dominant cinema portrayed the Celtic countries as regressive and primitive and if this portrayal was sometimes amiable and sometimes hostile, it was always patronising. However, a second focus of this cinema has been inwards, exploiting the rationalist responses to the representation of the centre. This has meant that the films reflect an uncertainty, an exploration that is as conscious of internal contradiction as it is of larger external realities. Above all, this is a cinema that refuses to operate on the margins. These are cultures that are no longer content to be the peripheral and exploited partners in a strict cultural division of labour. In fact this new cinema has pushed peripherality in to the centre and now operates on the cutting edge of a contemporary cultural debate about identity.

Source: McLoone, 2009, pp. 354–6

Martin McLoone's arguments apply specifically to the kind of cinema where writers and directors have a degree of freedom to experiment and present viewpoints. In the next section, covering television, we look at the representations of Wales in an industry that tends to constrain those that work in it a little further, though as we will see there also emerge important contributions to an evolving sense of Wales.

Summary

■ Contemporary film makers have tended to work explicitly against some of the older cinematic representations in Wales, typified by *How Green Was My Valley*.

■ Welsh-language cinema has played a role in representing Wales as a bilingual culture through its small successes internationally.

■ Cinema has been part of a process of representing Wales and Welsh life as part of an international urban culture.

■ Cinema has a kind of freedom to explore some of the more uncomfortable dimensions to contemporary society, such as the role of racism in Wales.

5 Television 'fictions' and Wales

In terms of the numbers of people that have access to them, it is representations of Wales on television that have by far the greatest significance and probable impact. In this section we will look specifically at the way fictional programmes are significant in the representation of Wales.

At the start of the decade it was a common complaint in Wales that the nation was seen on British television far too rarely, even in comparison to Scotland and Northern Ireland (see Blandford, 2005). There was (and in some quarters still is) a longstanding sense that Wales as a nation, and therefore as a producer of broadcast television, is treated in the centres of power with rather more suspicion and mistrust than the other nations and regions of the UK.

The case of Welsh-language drama is different because it is produced largely in Wales, for Welsh audiences, but it is fair to say that therein a different problem existed. At the end of the 1990s, S4C's representations of Wales were commonly seen as outdated and narrow (see, for example, Gramich, 1997, p. 106).

While it would be a distortion to say that the entire picture has changed over a decade, it is certainly now possible to claim that both the range and the quantity of representations of Wales in television in both languages have increased and are likely to increase further.

5.1 An S4C drama revival

Sianel Pedwar Cymru (S4C), the television channel set up in Wales in 1982 to provide a service in the Welsh language, has commissioned several drama series in the last decade that have, at the very least, opened up the range of ways in which drama represents life in which Welsh is the dominant language.

Among the most prominent drama productions on S4C that have fundamentally altered many people's perception of the channel's image are: *Fondue, Sex and Dinosaurs* (2002–3), *Caerdydd* (2004), *Con Passionate* (2005–8) and *Y Pris* (2008–9). Though they are all very different, the common thread running through these and a number of other series is the sense of newly confident and, predominantly, young Wales.

Conversely, one of S4C's most successful dramas of the period – *Con Passionate* – used a central idea that has frequently been associated with Wales in the past and has changed in significance for the representation of Wales in the present. An interview with the writer of the programme indicates this when she says 'I was eager to take an iconic image of Wales, such as a male voice choir and use it as a backdrop to say something about contemporary Wales' (Con Passionate, 2009).

Though less formally inventive than *Con Passionate, Caerdydd*'s four series have foregrounded the way that the Welsh capital has changed and become home to a class of young flat-dwellers with lifestyles associated with Europe's growing city culture. While the programme has not been to all tastes, in terms of the representation of Welsh-speaking Wales, it is a fundamental change to see a long-running drama set among the flats, bars and nightclubs of Cardiff rather than predominantly in rural Wales.

Y Pris, dubbed '*The Sopranos* by the seaside' is in some ways a familiar tale of organised crime, but the twist is that it is set in Carmarthenshire. Like the other series discussed here, its use of Welsh within a highly contemporary fictional structure contributes to an extension of the way that this dimension of contemporary Welsh life is reimagined.

What these S4C dramas have to say individually is possibly less significant than the fact that they signal the capacity of the Welsh language to be used in highly contemporary dramatic contexts. In turn, they represent Wales as a bilingual country with many different identities rather than the outmoded idea that the Welsh language is the province of the rural north and west.

If by far and away the longest-running drama on S4C remains *Pobol y Cwm* (which began in 1974), the drama of semi-rural village life made by BBC Cymru Wales for S4C, the channel can now claim with some conviction to have commissioned a range of work that suggests that Welsh is no longer confined to its former heartlands.

5.2 *Dr Who* and *Torchwood* – BBC Cymru Wales and network success

In 2004, one of BBC's flagship programmes, *Dr Who*, was revived. More significantly for our purposes, it was decided that responsibility for producing the series would be given to BBC Cymru Wales in Cardiff. This was part of the BBC's overall decision to spend more of its commissioning budget in the UK 'nations and regions'. In this section we consider the significance for the representation of Wales of two related science-fiction series, *Dr Who* and *Torchwood*, which mainly use Welsh locations.

Figure 9.3
Star of *Torchwood* John
Barrowman outside the
Torchwood hub in
Cardiff Bay

The following quotation from the BBC director-general, Mark Thompson,
in an interview in the *Western Mail* provides a useful starting point: 'We
wondered whether Wales could be portrayed as modern and forward-
looking and *Torchwood* is the answer. It's obviously Welsh and it's sexy,
modern and fantastic' (Price, 2007).

Though Thompson is talking about just one programme, his remarks have a clear significance for the whole question of the representation of Wales, particularly in the global sense. Thompson appears to start from the position that Wales is not a place that is easily associated with modernity, particularly of the kind that sells 'sexy' television programmes. For him at least, the delivery of very high-profile success through *Dr Who* and *Torchwood* in particular has changed that.

In case such casual remarks are dismissed as flimsy evidence, it is worth stating here that, at the time of writing, Cardiff is the proposed site of a BBC 'drama village' as a base for a significant amount of the BBC's network drama production. The BBC has already moved one more of its flagship series, the long-running medical drama *Casualty*, to Cardiff as well as commissioning more *Dr Who* and *Torchwood* and a number of new drama projects that are in development.

Not everybody in Wales of course is convinced. High-profile though *Dr Who* and *Torchwood* undoubtedly are, inevitably they only represent certain dimensions of Welsh life, which means that others are excluded. It could also be argued that although the programmes are made in Wales they do not represent Welsh life or disseminate any sense of Welsh identity to a wider audience.

On the other hand, as a recent study (Mills, 2008) set out to investigate, there are other ways in which the making of a high-profile programme in a particular location can contribute to an evolving sense of identity. The pleasures we experience when we see the place in which we live shown on television are explored in Brett Mills's article 'My house was on *Torchwood*: media, place and identity'. There is a sense, however small, that life where you live has been given significance and value in a world dominated by mediated images. With one or two reservations, then, we can see that recent high-profile success in television drama has increased the profile of Wales, particularly the city of Cardiff. In so doing, it has altered the range of ways in which Wales can be seen from both inside and outside the country.

5.3 *Gavin and Stacey*

Although not made by BBC Cymru Wales, the BBC comedy series *Gavin and Stacey* (2007) offers one representation of Wales and the Welsh that has reached the highest possible profile. Rob Brydon, one of the show's leading actors, said of *Gavin and Stacey*, 'What it's done is create a version of Wales that's palatable to everyone, something which I don't think anyone's managed before' (Jewell, 2009, p. 62).

Brydon's comments probably stem from what most have seen as the unusual warmth and generosity of a show within a genre that has grown increasingly cynical and dependent on aggressive satire. If that makes

Gavin and Stacey seem a little anodyne, it is worth also considering this view of perhaps the best-known of the show's Welsh characters:

> Large and masculine, sexual and feminine, Nessa's Welshness is overt and tangible, with her upper arm decorated with a tattoo of a Welsh dragon. It can be reasonably argued that Nessa is a breakthrough character in British situation comedy history – here is a woman who is unconventionally attractive, sexually voracious and clearly independent of any male influence.
>
> (Jewell, 2009, p. 63)

In some ways, the creation of Nessa (Ruth Jones) typifies *Gavin and Stacey*'s ability to subvert expectations. If conventional situation comedy has traditionally used larger women exclusively as objects of derision, then *Gavin and Stacey* places one at the controlling heart of the action. Arguably, perhaps, Nessa's Welshness is secondary to what she has to say about gender, but the fact that the overtly Welsh Ruth Jones not only plays the character but is the co-writer of the series makes a powerful contribution to changing perceptions not only of the range of possibilities for women in situation comedy, but for Welsh identity as well.

Gavin and Stacey offers a vision of Wales through the vehicle of a spectacularly successful comedy that takes many traditional features of Wales – strong local community, close family ties and so on. Indeed, the characters in *Gavin and Stacey* offer representations of Welsh life that are by turns warm, generous and outrageously subversive.

Figure 9.4

Ruth Jones, Rob Brydon and Joanna Page in a photograph for Comic Relief 2009. This event featured a cover version of 'Islands in the Stream', retitled '(Barry) Islands in the Stream', by Brydon and Jones after its appearance in *Gavin and Stacey*, further increasing the profile of the comedy hit

Summary

- Television has the power to circulate widely representations of a culture or community. It can therefore be said to have particular significance in any discussion of the representation of a small nation such as Wales.

- The ways that television portrays Wales have broadened significantly during the period since devolution.

- Welsh-language drama on S4C has been particularly noteworthy for the range of its responses to the changing face of contemporary Wales.

- The high-profile international success of key television programmes made by the BBC in Wales has probably resulted in some changes in the way that the country is seen not only by the television industry, but by the wider audience.

6 Conclusion

You have seen that the idea of representation can be especially important to a small nation such as Wales, which struggles to get its voice heard in the world. For many, Wales is invisible underneath the more general idea of the UK or 'Britain'.

The circulation of images and narratives of Wales in the arts and popular cultural forms can be a vital part of creating a sense that the devolved nation has a part to play in the world. This in turn can be part of creating a sense of national confidence that a Welsh identity has genuine significance.

This is very much in tune with thinkers who use concepts such as the 'imagined nation' to convey the idea that a national identity is not something fixed and needing to be continuously reasserted but, rather, something that evolves and is shaped.

Part of this process of re-imagining is done by artists, but also by the audiences who engage with work that has elements that can contribute to a nation's sense of itself. The process is therefore not passive but dynamic, and something in which we all participate, however unconsciously.

You have also seen that a nation's identity and culture are frequently and most eloquently expressed through the 'banal', that is, the ordinary things that make up the rituals of our existence.

In the decade since devolution, there have been significant changes to the way that Wales is represented. Some of these have been the result of artists and companies reimagining the country, sometimes inspired by the idea of a measure of political independence and what some refer to as Wales's 'postcolonial' status.

Some changes have been the result of the evolution or creation of 'national' institutions, part of whose job it actually is to represent Wales as a separate nation with a distinct identity. These include the National Museum of Wales, the BBC and the Arts Council of Wales.

The significance of some changes to the way that Wales is seen in the wider world will, however, always remain open to debate. The international success of *Dr Who* and *Torchwood* is for many a watershed in the shifting identity of Wales, which will ensure that Wales is seen as a place in which contemporary forms of creativity can flourish. For others, these programmes have little to do with the lives of most people in Wales.

Similarly, the establishment of national theatres in both languages is for many an important step in broadening the 'national conversation' and offering opportunities for artists to remain in Wales and play a part in its construction. Others see it as Wales repeating outmoded ideas about what a 'nation' is by creating outdated institutions.

What can be claimed is that there is now a much greater variety to the ways that Wales is represented to a wider world. The tired national stereotypes to which Ed Thomas referred may not be quite dead, but they now must compete with the idea that Wales is a place in which there are vibrant cityscapes as well as threatened rural communities, dancers and performance artists as well as brilliant rugby players and, above all, a sense of reimagining the nation even if the economics of 21st-century media mean that there will always be a struggle for voices to be heard.

References

Aaron, J. and Williams, C. (eds) (2005) *Postcolonial Wales*, Cardiff, University of Wales Press.

Academi (2009) www.academi.org/about-academi/ (accessed August 2009).

Adams, D. (1996) *Stage Welsh*, Llandysul, Gomer.

Anderson, B. (1983) *Imagined Communities: Reflections on the Origins and Spread of Nationalism*, London, Verso.

Arad Goch (2009) www.aradgoch.org/english.php (Accessed August 2009).

Bala, I. (2009) www.iwanbala.com/index.html (Accessed August 2009).

BBC (2009) news.bbc.co.uk/1/hi/wales/1716165.stm (Accessed August 2009).

Billig, M. (1995) *Banal Nationalism*, London, Sage.

Blandford, S. (2004) 'Being half of everything', *New Welsh Review*, no. 65, Autumn.

Blandford, S. (2005) 'BBC Drama at the margins: the contrasting fortunes of Northern Irish, Scottish and Welsh television drama in the 1990s' in Bignell, J. and Lacey, S. (eds) *Popular Television Drama: Critical Perspectives*, Manchester, Manchester University Press.

Blandford, S. (2008) 'A way of life and new British identities', *Journal of British Cinema and Television*, vol. 5, pp. 99–112.

Con Passionate (2009) www.s4c.co.uk/conpassionate/e_index.shtml (Accessed 9 December 2009).

French, P. (1999) 'Something for the weekend', *The Observer*, 6 June.

Gramich, K. (1997) 'Cymru or Wales? Explorations in a divided sensibility' in Basnett S. (ed.) *Studying British Cultures*, London, Routledge.

Harvie, J. (2005) *Staging the UK*, Manchester, Manchester University Press.

Herbert, H. (1993) 'Tutti frutti', in Brandt, G. (ed.) *British Television Drama in the 1980s*, Cambridge, Cambridge University Press.

Hijinx Theatre (2009) www.hijinx.org.uk/Hijinx.asp (Accessed August 2009).

Internet Movie Database (2009) http://us.imdb.com/title/tt0120394/ (Accessed August 2009).

Ladd, E. (2009) www.eddieladd.com/ (Accessed August 2009).

Logan, B. (2006) *The Guardian*, Tuesday 7 February, www.guardian.co.uk/uk/2006/feb/07/wales.artsfunding (Accessed 9 December 2009).

Mason, R. (2004) 'Nation building at the museum of Welsh life', *Museum and Society*, vol. 2, no. 1, pp. 18–34.

Mason, R. (2007) *Museums, Nations, Identities: Wales and its National Museums*, Cardiff, University of Wales Press.

Mason, R. (2007) 'Representing Wales' in Osmond, J. (ed.) *Myths, Memories, and Futures: the National Library and National Museum in the story of Wales*, Cardiff, University of Wales Press.

Mills, B. (2008) 'My house was on *Torchwood*: media, place and identity' *International Journal of Cultural Studies*, vol. 11, no. 4, pp. 379–99.

Morris, N. (1998) 'Projecting Wales', *Planet 126*, December–January.

National Museum of Wales (2009) www.museumwales.ac.uk/media/2/9/3/6/ Interpretation_Strategy_for_Oriel_1_02007.pdf (Accessed 19 August 2009).

Owen, G. (2005) *Plays: 1*, London, Methuen.

Petrie, D. (2000) *Screening Scotland*, London, British Film Institute.

Perrins, D. (2000) 'This town ain't big enough for the both of us' in Blandford, S. (ed.) *Wales on Screen*, Bridgend, Seren.

Price, K. (2006) 'BBC Wales praised for "sexy and modern"' programmes', *The Western Mail*, 25 November.

Roms, H. (1998) 'Edward Thomas: a profile' in Walford Davies, H. (ed.) *State of Play: 4 Playwrights of Wales*, Llandysul, Gomer.

Rowlands, (1999) *A Trilogy of Appropriation*, Cardiff, Parthian.

Shade, R. (2004) *Communication Breakdowns: Theatre, Performance, Rock Music and Some Other Welsh Assemblies*, Cardiff, University of Wales Press.

Sherlock, C. (2004) 'The performative body – text – context and the construction of tradition', *Studies in Theatre and Performance*, vol. 24, p. 3.

Thomas, E. (2002) *Selected Work '95–'98*, Cardigan, Parthian.

Thomas, J. (2005) *Popular Newspapers, the Labour Party and British Politics*, London and New York, Routledge.

Woodward, K. (2006) 'Traditions and transformations: film in Wales during the 1990s', *North American Journal of Welsh Studies*, vol. 6, no. 1 (Winter 2006).

Welsh Assembly Government (2009) www.paneldyfarnucymru.org.uk/news/ topic/culture/2007/1835515/; jsessionid=53ZJKfkQykn2DhT9hxw8l2Tyl13hyy87TJlL1j1pTYL3vk8z2TvR!- 1895006922?cr=3&lang=en (Accessed August 2009).

Further reading

To further explore the idea of Wales as a 'postcolonial' nation and the impact of that on representation, see J. Aaron and Chris Williams (eds) (2005) *Postcolonial Wales*, Cardiff, University of Wales Press.

For a detailed historical account of the role of cinema in the life of Wales, see David Berry (1994) *Wales and Cinema, The First Hundred Years*, Cardiff, University of Wales Press.

David Barlow, Philip Mitchell and Tom O'Malley (eds) (2005) *Media in Wales: Voices of a Small Nation*, Cardiff, University of Wales Press, presents an overview of the role of media in Wales.

For a discussion of the future of television in Wales, see Geraint Talfan Davies (ed.) (2009) *English is a Welsh Language, Television's Crisis in Wales*, Cardiff, Institute of Welsh Affairs.

To examine the important role of popular music in the way that Wales has been represented, see Sarah Hill (2007) *Blerwytirhwng: The Place of Welsh Pop Music*, Aldershot, Ashgate.

The *Journal of Studies in Theatre and Performance* published a special edition on Welsh theatre and performance in 2004, vol. 24.

The following is a selection of theatre plays, films and television programmes that relate to the ideas discussed in this chapter.

Films

A Way of Life (dir. Amma Asante, 2004)

Beautiful Mistake (dir. Marc Evans, 2001)

House of America (dir. Marc Evans, 1997)

Solomon and Gaenor (dir. Paul Morrison, 1998)

Twin Town (dir. Kevin Allen, 1997)

Television

Caerdydd (not currently available on DVD, but sometimes available to watch on the S4C website)

Dr Who (Series 1, Episode 11, 'Boom Town', available from BBC Worldwide)

Gavin and Stacey (Series 1 and 2 available from BBC Worldwide)

Torchwood (Series 1, Episode 1 available from BBC Worldwide)

Plays

Owen, G. (2005) *Plays: 1*, London, Methuen.

Teare, J. (ed.) *New Welsh Drama*, Volume 2, Cardiff, Parthian.

Thomas, E. (2002) *Selected Work 95–98*, Cardiff, Parthian

Chapter 10
Conclusion

Hugh Mackay

Contents

1   Introduction

This book has provided a social science account of contemporary Wales, introducing and applying key issues, theories and concepts that help us make sense of Wales today. It has been organised around the two themes of 'difference' and 'connection', and this chapter develops these two themes a little further, by introducing two important dimensions of each that have not featured hitherto in our story.

Two aspects are worth adding to our account of the key dimensions of difference, explored in Chapters 2–5 (place, work, gender, 'race' and class). One is that, at this juncture in the history of Wales, the early years of devolution, a particularly important set of transformations is under way. These have been touched on especially in Chapters 8 and 9, which examined representational processes (in two senses of the word). Wales today is on a cusp – rooted in its history (particularly that of the more recent industrial era), but transforming in all sorts of new ways as a result of the broader processes of the information society but also the specifically Welsh dimensions of contemporary change. This focuses our attention on continuity and change, or difference over time – which is introduced briefly in Section 2.1 of this chapter. The other dimension of difference raised in this concluding chapter is the policies that have been 'made in Wales'. In this era of devolution, Wales has a new way of marking out its distinctiveness, of embodying its values and priorities, in the policies that have been developed by the Welsh Assembly's administrations. Section 2.2 of this concluding chapter examines the difference in the administrative and political priorities of post-devolution Wales. What has the Welsh Assembly done for the people of Wales? How do its policies differ from those of Westminster?

Our discussion of 'connection' (Section 3 of this chapter) has involved political ideologies or processes, including the cultural. This leaves two important matters of 'connection' that beg some discussion. Section 3.1 of this chapter addresses an issue that has become central with devolution, the mass media environment in Wales. Who has a voice, and who is listening? How does the media environment, which is itself experiencing rapid transformation, fit the needs of contemporary Wales? How do new forms of interactivity allow new forms of participation and connection? And, finally, Section 3.2 examines more extended notions of connection, exploring Wales in the wider world, by looking at aspects of Wales and globalisation. Wales, like anywhere else today, is a part of a global system, and enjoys enhanced economic and cultural connections with the rest of the world. In this section, you will examine core dimensions of Wales's place in the European and global system.

2 Difference

In the first half of this book, you explored some major dimensions of difference in contemporary Wales – regarding place, work, gender, 'race' and class. Although Wales appears homogeneous on days of international rugby matches, experiences and identities are varied. It is not the case that everyone in Wales identifies with the same culture in the same way: there is a plurality of Welsh experiences and identities. This is a far cry from essentialist notions of a pure or true Welsh identity. In the 1970s, at least one nationalist writer was referring to Wales in terms of 'the spirit which flowed through men before I was born and which will speak through others when my body has turned to dust', and to the need to safeguard 'the more pure and basic Welshness which belongs to the Welsh people' (Llewelyn, 1976, cited by Jones, 1986, pp. 235–6). This sort of thinking – which, controversially, led to one nationalist movement, *Adfer* (Return, or Restore), being likened to Nazism (Jones, 1986) – has generally been replaced by notions of a plurality of Welsh experiences.

This does not, however, mean an absence of patterning or structure to how we can conceive of Welsh society. On the contrary, key empirical differences, for example of gender, 'race' and class, remain fundamental to understanding difference in Welsh society. And, as you have seen, these differences have distinctly Welsh dimensions. Senses of belonging to place remain powerful, with feelings of attachment to local communities strong despite processes of globalisation. Even nearby places are ascribed – by locals and outsiders alike – strong and important distinguishing characteristics, as we saw with Gavin Henson's views of Llanelli in Chapter 1.

2.1 Continuity and change

While such differences have powerful elements of continuity with the past, they are far from fixed, transforming over relatively short time-spans. In recent years, experiences of Wales and differences in Wales have changed enormously – with new patterns of immigration, the restructuring of the economy, the feminisation of the workforce, the declining role of the chapel, the growth of consumer culture and a myriad of other social and cultural changes. These transformations are accompanied by, or involve, new ways whereby people in Wales imagine themselves as Welsh through ongoing and active processes. It is people in their everyday lives who imagine themselves as Welsh (as we saw in

Figure 10.1

National icons: i) the Millennium Stadium; ii) the Wales Millennium Centre; and iii) the Senedd

(i)

(ii)

(iii)

Chapter 9), and in a particular way. As the historian Gwyn Alf Williams expresses it:

> The Welsh as a people have lived by making and remaking themselves in generation after generation, usually against the odds, usually within a British context. Wales is an artefact which the Welsh produce. If they want to.
>
> (Williams, 1985, p. 304)

This process of cultural construction is not 'imagined' in the straightforward sense of a process that is in our heads. More than this, it involves creating institutions and indeed buildings to represent particular versions of Wales. The National History Museum of Wales at St Fagans (discussed in Chapter 9) demonstrates this process clearly. It now includes not only a Miners' Institute complete with a library of socialist books but also an Anglican church. Thus, contest about what is the essence of a culture (farmhouses and other rural buildings, the chapel) is translated into both new names for the institution (until 1995 it was called the Welsh Folk Museum and the name was later changed to the Museum of Welsh Life) and new exhibits (which now acknowledge that industrial south Wales, too, is a part of Welsh history and life).

The national icons of the Millennium Stadium, the Wales Millennium Centre and the Senedd are the prominent examples of recent expressions in built form of (versions of) modern Wales.

Activity 10.1

Take a look at Figure 10.1 and answer the following questions. What does each of these three buildings say about Wales? How does this meaning connect with the past? You might like to consider each building's materials and their origin; the shape, style and structure of the building; its location; and what it is used for.

Some of these buildings house new institutions that are both the cause and outcome of new ways of conceiving of the nation. Thus, what Wales and Welshness mean are imagined but in some cases they become institutionalised and, even literally, cast in concrete.

At the same time, old institutions and processes become accented in new ways. For example, and as you have seen in Chapter 7, the labour tradition lives on despite declining support for the Labour Party. The meaning of the language, the significance of speaking Welsh, is another phenomenon that has changed enormously in recent years – a consequence of a political process but also of the actions and decisions of large numbers of people in their everyday lives. A couple of decades ago, most speakers of the language were concentrated in *Y Fro Gymraeg*, 'the Welsh-language region'. Policies focused on defending the language in the more rural parts of Wales, in Ceredigion and Gwynedd. Following a series of education policies (notably regarding Welsh-medium schooling, but also the Welsh national curriculum) and language policies (notably the Welsh Language Act 1993 and the 'Iaith Pawb' policy (NAW, 2003)), together with the establishment of the National Assembly and the support that it has given the language, more Welsh speakers are now found in Cardiff than in any other town or city. Here the language is a part of an urban and cosmopolitan (rather than a traditional and rural) culture. Language policies have extended in focus from the rural communities where life is lived in Welsh to include education and the organisations that deliver services to the public across the whole of Wales. In some senses, the education system has replaced the family as the institution of language transmission.

Thus you can see how the meaning and significance of a powerful marker of identity can become transformed in a very short timespan.

2.2 The policies that have been 'made in Wales'

The National Assembly allows and provides an increasingly important way in which Wales is different – from England and from the UK as a whole. Since its inception, the Assembly has used its devolved powers to develop policies, and the Richard Commission and the subsequent Government of Wales Act 2006 have extended these to primary law-making powers through legislative competence orders (LCOs). In addition to LCOs, the Assembly can make its own legislation (in the form of Assembly Measures) on devolved matters such as health, education, social services and local government. This is done in ways that can be seen as building on the dominant political traditions in Wales, nationalism and Labour (discussed in Chapters 6 and 7 respectively) and, in the process, there has been some transformation of the democratic system in Wales (as you saw in Chapter 8).

Activity 10.2

Pause and note four Assembly government policies that you know about or have heard of. Together, what do these policies tell you about the nature of policy in Wales?

Comment

To a considerable extent, what you think of Assembly government policy as a whole will depend on what you think about devolution. Nonetheless, I want to suggest that, across the breadth of policies that have been made in Wales, we can identify three main themes: (i) greater confidence in state (or public) provision and greater scepticism of market-led policies; (ii) more localism, collaboration and partnership; and (iii) making symbolic markers of difference from England. I shall discuss each of these themes and in doing so shall refer to some of the main policies that have been made in Wales.

2.2.1 *State provision and scepticism in market forces*

The first theme is an increased commitment to state provision and a greater caution about market-led policies – the 'clear red water' of Welsh Labour to which the First Minister and others have referred (discussed in Chapter 7). You can see examples of such policies in the free prescriptions; free healthy breakfasts in primary schools; free swimming at local authority leisure centres for children during the school holidays and for over-60s during school term time; and a more cautious approach to the **Private Finance Initiative (PFI)**. (Under the One Wales coalition agreement between Labour and Plaid Cymru there will be no further PFI schemes in the NHS.) Grant-maintained schools, city academies and GP fund holding are other policies that have been rejected in Wales. These demonstrate that one important dimension of Welsh policies is how they are distinctive for what has not been done in Wales – for what has been rejected. Finally, the preference for state over more market- or business-focused bodies can be seen in the 'bonfire of the quangos'. For example, the Welsh Development Agency (WDA), the Welsh Tourist Board, Education and Learning Wales (ELWA) and others were brought into the direct ambit of the Assembly Government. However, various others, now called Assembly Government Sponsored Bodies (AGSBs), have been left as before, including the Arts Council of Wales (as we saw in Chapter 9), the National Library of Wales, and National Museum Wales.

The **Private Finance Initiative (PFI)** is capital investment by private consortia to avoid immediate public expenditure, with building and in some cases operating costs repaid, typically, over thirty years, at a higher cost to the taxpayer in the longer term.

Rhodri Morgan, the First Minister until 2009, has argued that policies in Wales, reflecting the democratic inheritance, are more collaborative and less competitive; they are more concerned with social cohesion and participation; and they show a greater commitment to universal provision (as opposed to means-tested benefits) than do Westminster policies.

> The dominant values of people in Wales ... assert that public services should be designed to improve the quality of life for all and promote success, rather than a safety net for market failure – comprehensive rather than residual, proactive rather than reactive
>
> (Morgan, 2004, p.4)

By 'residual', Morgan is referring to the lowest level of safety net for those who fail in the competitive market. He describes how the collaborative model has a distinct idea of the relationship of the citizen to the service. It views users as working with providers to secure better school results or improvements in their health.

In post-devolution Wales, a consistent theme across education, health and housing policies is the participation model of service delivery, rather than reliance on consumer choice. 'Voice not choice' is the common refrain of politicians who express their mistrust of market solutions, seeing users of services as citizens rather than consumers. Less testing in schools (the abolition of compulsory SATs at Key Stages 1, 2 and 3), the abolition of school league tables and the rejection of city academies are examples of policies made in this spirit.

2.2.2   Local and collaborative

Second is an emphasis on partnership and on working with local communities, local government and other bodies. The shape of the Assembly debating chamber and the partial PR system for the election of AMs (explained in Chapter 8) are designed to emphasise consensus and to discourage the point-scoring, polarised, conflict politics of Westminster. This is helped by the small size of Wales (compared, say, with England): with only 22 local authorities and close connections between AMs and their local parties, communities and councils, working together is relatively easy.

One study of the relationship between the Assembly and local government concluded that:

> Assembly ministers are more favourably inclined towards local government than their Westminster counterparts and have adopted a less restrictive approach to local authorities.

> The advent of the Assembly has engendered some new policy networks and given a new role and energy to established networks. Potentially, these networks perform a vital role as channels of influence and communication.

> Collectively, local government, primarily through the WLGA [Welsh Local Government Association], has been able to influence the Assembly on significant issues. Individually, local authorities have at least retained similar levels of discretion to those they enjoyed pre-devolution.

> > (Laffin et al., 2002)

Devolving power to local communities, however, is not uncontested: in 2003 the five regional health authorities were abolished and replaced by 22 local health boards, matching local authorities and devolving control of services; but in 2009 these were replaced by seven unified organisations, with planning and funding overseen by an advisory board chaired by the Minister, in other words, a recentralisation of that which had been decentralised.

The 2006 Beecham Review of the delivery of public services in Wales argued that citizens need to be put at the centre of policy; this led to Local Service Boards (one per local authority area) to coordinate service provision, and advocated partnerships and collaboration. Notions of collaboration and partnership apply not only to local government and other local organisations, but also to citizens, as the former First Minister explains:

> The unifying strand which runs through these individual policies, therefore, is one that emphasises the capacity to integrate social action by Government, providing universal services wherever possible, and working out from the core of what is already available ... to draw more people into the sort of participative, socially cohesive and successful society we are trying to build. That, then, is the central rationale, the basic case: a society that has collaboration at its core, in economic relationships and in the relation between the citizen and the state. That is the vision that the Assembly Government has for our public services in Wales.
>
> (Morgan, 2004, p. 7)

2.2.3 Markers of symbolic difference from England

The third theme in Welsh Assembly policies is that some policies have been made that highlight differences from policies that apply in England and seem intended to make a symbolic statement. However, the efficacy of the outcomes of some of these might be questioned. For instance, tuition fees for Welsh students attending Welsh universities were abolished with little apparent prior consideration of how to fund the universities. The policy was followed by a review and then a change of policy, which effectively reinstated one third of the fee. Welsh universities continue to be underfunded, compared with their English counterparts. Another example is Carwyn Jones's initiative in 2007 for all new building developments in Wales to be carbon neutral by 2011. However, the power of the Assembly to achieve its policy is highly limited: first, the UK government had made a commitment to achieve this by 2016 (the first country in the world to do so); second, building regulations are not a devolved matter, so the powers of the Assembly to achieve its policies are highly limited. Another example is the policy to introduce free car parking at Welsh hospitals (being introduced from 2008–11): this will reduce income to NHS hospitals in Wales by £5.4 million per annum (the car-parking revenue in 2006–07). It also conflicts with the Assembly's own agenda on sustainable transport.

The symbolic, of course, is not necessarily immaterial or unimportant. Some of these policies that highlight difference involve putting down a marker of the nature of the 'clear red water'; others are matters that are important in Wales although they are not in England – most obviously policies on the Welsh language.

Summary

- Differences and identities in Wales are constructed, in ongoing processes that reflect both continuities and change.

- Institutions and policies are important elements of these processes.

- The WAG's policies are many and varied. They differ from policies in England in a preference for state provision over market-led policies, and more localism, collaboration and partnerships – making markers of difference from England.

3 Connection

Section 2 of this book has examined some of the main connections that have been forged across the differences in Wales – it has looked at nationalism and the Welsh language (Chapter 6), labour traditions (Chapter 7), representation in the Assembly (Chapter 8) and cultural representations (Chapter 9). We conclude by tying these various strands together by looking at the mass media and globalisation, and exploring core ways in which connections are forged across and beyond Wales.

3.1 The mass media

In this section you will investigate how the mass media are central for understanding connections between citizens themselves and between citizens and their governments in the modern world. In Wales, the Assembly needs the media to promote its policies and to engage with the people of Wales. However, just at the moment when there is a real need for a pan-Wales mass media, there is no pan-Wales newspaper and Welsh broadcasters are experiencing reduced audiences, due to the arrival of multichannel television. While the Internet allows for interactive participation, broadband access in Wales is far from universal.

In a general sense, the modern world cannot be understood without taking account of the centrality of the media. Traditional, local and face-to-face forms of communication and community have been replaced by modern nation states and more mediated communication, with citizens and their governments communicating with one another through the media. One cannot conceive of the modern state without the mass media (Thompson, 1995), with the BBC central to constructions of Britain and Britishness (Scannell and Cardiff, 1991). But as well as constructing Britishness, the BBC has played a core role in constructing modern Wales. As the historian John Davies puts it, 'contemporary Wales could be defined as an artefact produced by broadcasting' (Davies, 1994, back cover). He points particularly to the notion of 'the Welsh news' as having, for the first time, brought together south and north Wales.

Unsurprisingly, given the lukewarm response from the electorate to devolution, the Assembly has taken its job of selling itself to the people of Wales very seriously. The Presiding Office has a particular responsibility for 'promoting democratic engagement' but it is broadly acknowledged that the mass media in Wales have a crucial role in the task – not only for getting across the message of the National Assembly and the Welsh Assembly Government (WAG), but also as a forum for developing and sustaining connections between people in Wales, and between them and the Assembly Government.

As a modern institution, much of the work of the Assembly is available, instantly, online and in Welsh as well as English. Its openness is symbolised in the architecture of the Senedd and in its procedures. It has a progressive 'access to information code' and it allocates considerable resources to assisting the public in finding information about the Assembly and the policies of its government. And it has funded a series of initiatives not only to get service providers (notably local authorities) online, but also to connect communities and to make available the culture of Wales, for example via the Wales on the Web and culturenet cymru projects at the National Library of Wales.

Through such initiatives, the Assembly is grasping the potential of the Internet to facilitate some sort of **public sphere** in Wales. For the German sociologist Jürgen Habermas, the public sphere was to be found in the eighteenth-century coffee houses of European capital cities (Habermas, 1989). Although subject to wide-ranging criticisms – did it ever exist, did it include women and the working classes, what is and is not a matter of 'public concern'? (Calhoun, 1992) – Habermas's notion offers us a model for considering how citizens engage with policy makers other than at elections or referendums. The mass media, in Wales as elsewhere, are the core institution in the public sphere; and it is because of their centrality to the democratic process that nation states have regulated their media over and above their regulation of ordinary economic enterprises – for example, with restrictions on the concentration of ownership. The media have thus been seen as important for citizenship, for information and for education, as well as for entertainment.

In Section 1 of this book, you explored core dimensions of difference in Wales. Diversity relates to the breadth of content or opinions that are disseminated: a healthy democracy should allow the expression of many

Public sphere is a discursive space in which individuals and groups can rationally discuss matters of mutual interest in order to influence one another and inform politics.

views, not simply some orthodox perspective on any matter of social concern. There are two aspects to diversity in the mass media: the right to a voice, to be heard; and the right to hear a diversity of voices. The greater the diversity of the mass media, the broader the range of interests that are being served. The media should reflect the diversity of the society – the greater the diversity of the mass media, the broader the range of interests that are being served. So one can ask of Wales, as any other society, 'who has access to the mass media, who enjoys the right and authority to speak?' and, conversely, 'what voices are marginalised or excluded?'

Activity 10.3

Select one of the dimensions of difference discussed in Section 1 of this book (place, work, gender, 'race' and class) and, in relation to broadcasting or the press, consider how well you think the group is represented in this mass medium.

Comment

Diversity can be achieved with or without a plurality of media voices. Plurality is not the same as diversity. Plurality refers to the number of voices: in Wales, news is provided by *The Daily Post* (in the north) and *The Western Mail* (in the south) (both owned by Trinity Mirror), by the BBC, ITV and S4C – so there are quite a few voices, bodies, organisations or channels for the expression of opinion (in strong contrast with, say, *Pravda* in the era of the Soviet Union).

With a growing concentration of ownership of the press and the decline of ITV Wales's Welsh programming, the plurality of voices in the press and broadcasting in Wales is reducing. Across the mass media in Wales and the UK today, notions of readers, listeners and viewers as citizens have been replaced to a substantial degree by seeing them as consumers. The mass media are not serving the public sphere or the democratic system, but are seeking audience size or shareholder value. Many of the media are produced for profit, with income generated mostly from sales and advertising, with the notable exception of the public service broadcasters.

The most popular newspapers in Wales are the UK newspapers, which are produced in London and distributed throughout England and Wales (and very much less so in Scotland, which by and large has its own press). Indeed, the *Sun* is the most popular paper in Wales, as it is in England. Coverage of Wales in these English-produced newspapers is very limited. This problem is compounded by the fact that the two Welsh morning daily newspapers circulate in either the south (the *Western Mail*) or the north (the *Daily Post*) but not across Wales as a whole. With no single Welsh newspaper, there is something of an information deficit, with profound implications for democracy in Wales and for the capacity of the Assembly Government to communicate its message. However, newspaper circulations are declining quite dramatically anyway – in the case of the *Western Mail*, for example, from about 57,000 to about 32,000 between 1999 and 2009. Moreover, newspapers (qualities and tabloids alike) now focus on 'infotainment', lifestyle and celebrity reporting, so are substantially for entertainment rather than news (Franklin, 1997).

On the broadcasting front, too, there are issues that reduce the potential of the mass media to facilitate connection across the different groups in Wales and with the Assembly Government. With the arrival of multichannel television, audiences for the older, terrestrial broadcasters (BBC, ITV, S4C and Five) have declined. While BBC One Wales and ITV Wales remain by far the most-watched channels, their audiences are declining year on year. So a 'national audience' is less attainable. With choice, as consumers we can pursue our diverse interests, but we come together less as citizens watching the same television.

ITV is funded by advertising revenue, but due to declining audiences (plus the recession) has a reducing income. Consequently, Ofcom, which regulates ITV, keeps reducing the requirements for ITV Wales to broadcast quality (e.g. religious and children's) and Welsh programming – because it feels unable to enforce the regulations in the context of declining audiences and income.

The **public service broadcasters** – which in Wales means the BBC and S4C – face similar pressures. Although the BBC is financed by the licence fee, it has to achieve large audiences to justify its income to the government and the public. S4C, financed largely by the Department of Culture, Media and Sport of the UK government, although somewhat cushioned from this pressure because of its specific cultural remit to promote the Welsh language, faces the problem of declining advertising revenues and a grant linked to the Retail Price Index, which (at the time of writing) is almost static. While its peak-time audience has been increasing, its overall share of the audience and reach has been declining (S4C, 2008). Some AMs are among those who have called for it to provide an English-language Welsh broadcasting service – though responsibility for the mass media in Wales lies with Westminster and not Cardiff Bay.

Public service broadcasting, exemplified by the BBC, is generally universally available, independent of commercial and political interests and committed to diversity and impartiality.

The outcome is intense competition and a shift to the middle ground, with the public service remit of the BBC less apparent than it used to be. So just when a Welsh broadcasting system is most needed, what Wales in fact has can be seen to be in retreat.

Coinciding with the growth of multichannel television, however, is the development of broadband Internet. Low-cost, instant and global, it allows consumers to become producers, profoundly transforming the one-to-many, one-way flow that is built in to broadcasting and the press. Accommodating all previous media, the Internet's interactivity democratises access, eliminating the gatekeepers of the 'old media' – the media organisations and their journalists and producers. It allows participation and discussion (access to information and the discussion that takes place on forums and blogs) that can be seen as fulfilling some form of Habermas's public sphere.

However, broadband penetration in Wales is low – 58 per cent of households have access to broadband Internet, albeit 72 per cent in Cardiff, compared with 70 per cent in England (Ofcom, 2009, p. 56) – so we are far from the situation of radio or television, where ownership is almost universal. So while it enhances choice and diversity, the Internet is currently not a medium that provides communication across the whole population.

3.2 Globalisation

Wales is closely connected with England and its culture, economy and society, and the Welsh experience is very much a British experience, albeit less so than is the case for England and notwithstanding vital differences, notably the Welsh language. Welsh connections beyond its borders, however, are much broader and more extended than simply with England or the UK. This final section of this chapter introduces some aspects of Wales's place in the wider world.

The coal and steel on which twentieth-century Wales was founded linked Wales closely with the British empire, with coal from south Wales feeding the boilers of the British fleet around the world. So Wales has for long been connected to the global economy. Today key export markets for Wales are metals, energy, engineering, chemicals and automotive components, to the USA, Germany, Ireland, Belgium and France. Indigenous Welsh companies continue to become internationalised: for example, Graig Shipping has operations in Asia and Admiral Insurance operates in Spain, while Japanese electronic assembly plants and European aerospace factories have developed in Wales. Thus economic globalisation works in multiple directions.

It is also one reason why companies come and go. While inward investment is one dimension of globalisation of the economy, the relocation out of Wales of industry and work – whether to eastern Europe or the Far East – is another: high-volume, low-value activity goes to where labour is cheap. This leads to policies to upgrade skills in Wales: what is needed, it is argued, is to add higher value, to provide premium goods and services, and to develop a 'knowledge economy' (House of Commons, 2009).

Global connections, of course, are not confined to the economy. A series of cultural events put Wales firmly on the map – including Brecon Jazz, the National Eisteddfod, Hay Literary Festival, Faenol Festival. Some are explicitly international in their orientation – including the Llangollen International Eisteddfod, the Celtic Media Festival (held annually to bring together film and television producers from Brittany, Cornwall, Wales, Ireland and Scotland), Artes Mundi (an international visual arts initiative) and the Venice Biennale (where Wales's artists have been represented since 2003).

Sport is another powerful form of global connection, with the Millennium Stadium providing an international showcase for Wales. Rugby, of course, has the relatively local internationalism of the Six Nations but also more global matches and competitions, notably the rugby world cup. International football is played at the Millennium Stadium and the new Cardiff Swalec Stadium, the Glamorgan ground in Cardiff, and the 2010 Ryder Cup tournament was held in Newport.

In politics, too, we can identify a distinctly Welsh form of connection with the global order in the form of a commitment, in some quarters, to internationalism and world peace, which have been strands of both nationalist (Chapter 6) and labour (Chapter 7) traditions. Welsh miners

Figure 10.2
John Cale at the Venice Biennale

Figure 10.3
An anti-militarism
demonstration

were prominent in the International Brigade fighting fascism in Spain in the 1930s (Francis, 1984). There are also important strands of Welsh politics that strive for world peace (as you read in Chapter 6). David Davies, Liberal MP for Montgomery (and son of Lord Davies of Llandinam, developer of the Rhondda and of Barry Docks), was active in founding the League of Nations in 1919 and built the Temple of Peace in Cathays Park, Cardiff. Today this provides a home for various Welsh international and peace organisations, and is the reason for the memorials in Cathays Park to the Armenian genocide of 1915–1922 and to the Cardiff to Greenham Common march in 1981.

Calls for 'Wales in Europe', particularly during the Thatcher years, were a strategy for getting around (or out of) the jurisdiction of the Conservative UK government. Today, all of the major political parties support the notion, to varying degrees – in part because of the funding that comes to Wales from the EU, notably structural funds. One argument in favour of devolution was that it would give Wales a stronger voice in Europe. But the EU is also important because of the development and growth of its role as a legislative authority. The EU provides the framework for legislation at both Westminster and Cardiff Bay. Today, much economic and social legislation comes from Europe, to the extent that one can see Welsh society as shaped by decisions from Brussels as well as by Westminster, the relative significance of which is declining.

Much of the work of the Assembly involves implementing EU legislation in areas of its remit. Any legislation made by the Assembly can be made only if it complies with relevant Community law. The Assembly Government has an interest in EU programmes, on which matters it deals directly with the European Commission.

So how is Wales represented in the EU? There are five Welsh MEPs though they cannot speak in a formal capacity for Wales. And there is no representation of Wales on the key decision-making forum, the Council of Ministers, where ministers from each member state meet, though representatives could be invited to attend. The Welsh Assembly Government has an office at the EU, which is linked closely with UK representatives at the EU. And the First Minister represents the WAG on the Joint Ministerial Committee (Europe), which meets four times a year to develop UK–EU strategy. In addition, WAG ministers sometimes attend the Council of Ministers as a part of the UK delegation, with agreement of the relevant Whitehall department and to speak as representatives of the UK. Wales has four representatives (two full and two alternate) on the Committee of the Regions, an advisory body of representatives of the EU's regional and local authorities. These are nominated by the Assembly Government and have been credited with raising the profile of Wales in Europe, for example over broadband availability. And Wales is a member of a various other EU groups.

As a supra-national institution, the EU is one important example of globalisation. Not a commonly used term until the 1980s, globalisation is today used rather loosely and without definition.

Activity 10.4

Pause and note your understanding of what is meant by globalisation. You might like to consider the realms of the economy, culture and politics.

Comment

At its most general, globalisation refers to the integration of local, national or regional economies, societies and cultures. Generally, globalisation is viewed in polarised terms: for those who extol the virtues of the free market (and Internet communities), it is seen as progress; for others (the anti-globalisation movement), it is seen as the neo-liberal nightmare, an oppressive and unjust system.

Our analysis of contemporary Wales suggests something rather more nuanced. Clearly, with the Internet and other new communications technologies, we can see the strengthening of the global infrastructure. At an institutional level we have referred to the growing significance of the EU. And in considering the Welsh economy, we have referred to the relevance of global trends and processes – including the global nature of both the division of labour and the stock market. We can see greater inter-connectedness, networks are more global, and flows have increased (Castells, 1996; Held, 2000).

In cultural terms, one thing that this leads to is homogenisation – with McDonald's and Coca Cola the most obvious examples. But the interpenetration of cultures is more complex than this. As well as homogenising, globalisation leads to cultural mixing (e.g. world music) and also to the wider dissemination of diversity or difference. This is well illustrated by Wales and the Welsh language on the Internet. Far from threatening the viability of the language, the Internet allows speakers and learners from all over the world to access a wealth of relevant resources and to talk with one another. Members of the Welsh diaspora today, like members of any other diasporic community, are more connected than in the past, such that 'being away' has a very different meaning and possibilities for identification are extensive. Far from being threatened by the Internet, Welsh culture is more broadly sustained. Thus, paradoxically, globalisation strengthens localism.

Having said that, the fundamental problems facing Wales today – as anywhere else in the world – are global. We have discussed the economy, but not the environment much – yet the future of Wales depends on the world (including Wales) developing a sustainable economy and culture (Cato, 2007). It is probably this more than anything else that will shape the future of Wales.

Figure 10.4
Sustainable housing at the Brithdir Mawr intentional community

Summary

- The Welsh media are weak, with no pan-Wales newspaper, falling newspaper circulations, and declining audiences for BBC One Wales and ITV Wales, due to the arrival of the Internet and multichannel television.

- This poses a challenge for the Assembly, committed as it is to engaging the public in its work. It reduces possibilities of a public sphere. Though the Internet allows interactivity and instantaneity, it is far from universally available in Welsh households.

- Wales is not isolated; its politics, culture and economy are connected not only with England and the UK, but also with Europe and the wider world.

- Globalisation is a complex and multi-directional process, providing both threats and opportunities.

4 Conclusion

In this book you have explored core dimensions of difference in Wales, and the main forms of connection that have been forged across these differences. In this conclusion we have added some discussion of two additional aspects of difference (difference over time; and the different policies that have been made in Wales) and of connection (the mass media and globalisation), raising additional dimensions of contemporary Wales that were not explored in the substantive chapters. This extends and rounds off our discussion of difference and connection, the organising themes of this account of contemporary Wales.

References

Calhoun, C. (ed.) (1993) *Habermas and the Public Sphere*, Cambridge, MA, MIT Press.

Castells, M. (1996) *The Rise of the Network Society. The Information Age: Economy, Society and Culture*, vol. I. Oxford, Blackwell.

Cato, M.S. (2007) 'Green and pleasant land: Building strong and sustainable local economies in Wales', *Contemporary Wales*, vol. 19, pp. 96–115.

Davies, J. (1994) *Broadcasting and the BBC in Wales*, Cardiff, University of Wales Press.

Francis, H. (1984) *Miners Against Fascism: Wales and the Spanish Civil War*, London, Lawrence and Wishart.

Franklin, B. (1997) *Newszak and News Media*, London, Arnold.

Habermas, J. (1989) *The Structural Transformation of the Public Sphere: An Inquiry into a Category of Bourgeois Society*, Cambridge, MA, MIT Press (Published in German in 1962).

Held, D. (2000) *A Globalizing World? Culture, Economics, Politics*, London, Routledge.

House of Commons (2009) *Globalisation and its Impact on Wales*, Welsh Affairs Select Committee Report.

Jones, R.T. (1986) 'The shadow of the Swastika' in Hume, I. and Pryce, W.T.R. (eds) *The Welsh and their Country*, Llandysul, Gomer.

Laffin, M., Taylor, G. and Thomas, A. (2002) A New Partnership? The National Assembly for Wales and Local Government, York, Joseph Rowntree Foundation, www.jrf.org.uk/publications/national-assembly-wales-and-local-government (Accessed 13 November 2009).

Llewelyn, E. (1976) Adfer a'r Fro Gymraeg, Cyhoeddiadau Modern Cymreig.

Morgan, R. (2004) 'Collaboration not competition', *Agenda*, Autumn, Cardiff, Institute of Welsh Affairs, pp. 4–7.

NAW (2003) *Iaith Pawb – a national Action Plan for a Bilingual Wales*, Cardiff, NAW.

Ofcom (2009) Communications Market Report 2009. London, Ofcom.

Scannell, P. and Cardiff, D. (1991) *A Social History of British Broadcasting, Volume One, 1922–1939*, Oxford, Blackwell.

Sianel Pedwar Cymru (S4C) (2008) Annual Report, Cardiff, S4C.

Thompson, J. (1995) *The Media and Modernity*, Cambridge, Polity.

Williams, G.A. (1985) *When Was Wales*, Harmondsworth, Penguin.

Further reading

Social sciences research on the economy, culture, politics and society of contemporary Wales is published mostly in the journal *Contemporary Wales*. A breadth of emerging issues is discussed in *Agenda,* the journal of the Institute of Welsh Affairs (the IWA), which also publishes research reports, discussion papers and Assembly monitoring reports; while the Bevan Foundation, 'the social justice think tank for Wales' publishes its *Review* as well as policy papers, books and pamphlets.

Policy is a fast-changing area, in which useful sources include the work of Robert Hazell at the Devolution Monitoring Programme at the Constitution Unit, University College London; Richard Wyn Jones at the Wales Governance Centre,

Cardiff University; and Roger Scully at the Institute of Welsh Politics, Aberystwyth University.

For more on the mass media in Wales, see Barlow, D.M., Mitchell, P. and O'Malley, T. (2005) *The Media in Wales. Voices of a Small Nation,* Cardiff, University of Wales Press.

Acknowledgments

Grateful acknowledgement is made to the following sources:

Cover: Copyright © Wojtek Gurak;

Figures: Figure 1.1: Sports Council Wales (2009) 'Adult participation in sport', *Sportsupdate*, No 61, August 2009. Copyright © Sports Council for Wales; Figure 1.2 (i): Copyright © Torsten Blackwood/AFP/Getty Images; Figure 1.2 (ii): Copyright © David Rogers/Getty Images; Figure 1.2 (iii): Copyright © Marr Cardy/Getty Images; Figure 1.3: Copyright © David Davies/PA Archive/Press Association Images.

Figure 2.2: Copyright © David Lyons/Alamy; Figure 2.3: Copyright © The Photolibrary Wales/Alamy.

Figure 3.1: Copyright © Jason Bye/Rex Features; Figure 3.2: Copyright © Getty Images; Figure 3.3: Copyright © Cezza/Alamy; Figure 3.4: Copyright © Jeff Morgan industry and work/Alamy; Figure 3.5: Welsh Assembly Government (2008) Statistical Bulletin, Welsh Assembly Government.

Figure 4.1: Copyright © Bert Hardy/Getty Images; Figure 4.2: Copyright © Fox Photos/Getty Images; Figure 4.3: Copyright © Paul Box/reportdigital.co.uk; Figure 4.4: Copyright © The Photolibrary Wales/Alamy; Figure 4.5: Copyright © Keith Morris/Alamy.

Figure 5.1: Institute for Social and Economic Research (2008) British Household Panel Survey; Figure 5.2: Ronald Grant Archive; Figure 5.4: Copyright © Dave Ellison/Alamy; Figure 5.5: Copyright © Keith Morris/Alamy.

Figure 6.4: Copyright © Barn; Figure 6.5: Courtesy of the Welsh Language Society.

Figure 8.1: By permission of Llyfrgell Genedlaethol Cymru/The National Library of Wales; Figure 8.3: Copyright © Jeff Morgan politics and government/Alamy; Figure 8.4: Courtesy of The All Wales Convention; Figure 8.5: Friends of the Earth Cymru; Figure 8.6: Copyright © Roger Scully.

Figure 9.1: Copyright © BBC Cymru Wales; Figure 9.2: Ronald Grant Archive; Figure 9.3: Copyright © BBC; Figure 9.4: Copyright © Doug Peters/Empics Entertainment/Press Association Images.

Figure 10.1 (iii): Copyright © Huw John/Rex Features; Figure 10.2: Courtesy of Wales at the Biennale of Art; Figure 10.3: Copyright © Roger Rees; Figure 10.4: Copyright © Jeff Morgan alternative technology/Alamy.

Text: Extract 6.3: Webb, H. (1995) *Harri Webb Collected Poems*, Gomer Press. By permission of Meic Stephens; Figure 6.4 (text): Street-Porter, J. (2001) 'If you want lessons in racism, look no further than North Wales', *The Independent*, 21 January 2001. Copyright © The Independent.

Extract 9.1: Logan, B (2006) 'Arts funding row breaks out in Wales', *The Guardian*, 7 February 2006. Copyright © Guardian News & Media Ltd 2006; Extract 9.2: From *Staging in the UK*, by Jen Harvie, 2005, Manchester University Press, Manchester, UK; Extract 9.3: McLoone, M (2009) 'Internal de-colonisation? British cinema in the Celtic fringe', in Murphy, R (ed) *The British Cinema Book* (third edition), Palgrave.

Index